Prisons Ov

Deportation and Colonizatio
Prisons of T

Arthur Griffiths

Alpha Editions

This edition published in 2024

ISBN 9789362517562

Design and Setting By
Alpha Editions
www.alphaedis.com
Email - info@alphaedis.com

As per information held with us this book is in Public Domain.
This book is a reproduction of an important historical work.
Alpha Editions uses the best technology to reproduce historical work
in the same manner it was first published to preserve its original nature.
Any marks or number seen are left intentionally to preserve.

Contents

INTRODUCTION	- 1 -
CHAPTER I THE FIRST FLEET	- 3 -
CHAPTER II THE GROWTH OF NEW SOUTH WALES	- 17 -
CHAPTER III CONVICT LIFE	- 30 -
CHAPTER IV A CONVICT COMMUNITY	- 44 -
CHAPTER V THE PROBATION SYSTEM	- 55 -
CHAPTER VI CONVICT SHIPS	- 66 -
CHAPTER VII THE EXILES OF CRIME	- 81 -
CHAPTER VIII THE COLLAPSE OF DEPORTATION	- 101 -
CHAPTER IX GIBRALTAR	- 113 -
CHAPTER X THE BRITISH SYSTEM OF PENAL SERVITUDE	- 122 -
CHAPTER XI FRENCH PENAL COLONIES	- 137 -
CHAPTER XII PENAL METHODS IN THE UNITED STATES	- 152 -
FOOTNOTE:	- 161 -
CHAPTER XIII BRITISH PRISONS OF TO-DAY	- 162 -

INTRODUCTION

It will hardly be denied after an impartial consideration of all the facts I shall herein set forth, that the British prison system can challenge comparison with any in the world. It may be no more perfect than other human institutions, but its administrators have laboured long and steadfastly to approximate perfection. Many countries have already paid it the compliment of imitation. In most of the British colonies, the prison system so nearly resembles the system of the mother country, that I have not given their institutions any separate and distinct description.

No doubt different methods are employed in the great Empire of India; but they also are the outcome of experience, and follow lines most suited to the climate and character of the people for whom they are intended. Cellular imprisonment would be impossible in India. Association is inevitable in the Indian prison system. Again, it is the failure to find suitable European subordinate officers that has brought about the employment of the best-behaved prisoners in the discipline of their comrades: a system, as I have been at some pains to point out, quite abhorrent to modern ideas of prison management. As for the retention of transportation by the Indian government, when so clearly condemned at home, it is defensible on the grounds that the penalty of crossing the sea, the "Black Water," possesses peculiar terrors to the Oriental mind; and the Andaman Islands are, moreover, within such easy distance as to ensure their effective supervision and control.

Nearer home, we may see Austria adopting an English method,—the "movable" or temporary prison, by the use of which such works as changing the courses of rivers have been rendered possible and the prison edifices of Lepoglava, Aszod and Kolosvar erected, in imitation of Chattenden, Borstal and Wormwood Scrubs. France has also constructed in the outskirts of Paris a new prison for the department of the Seine, and she may yet find that the British progressive system is more effective for controlling habitual crime than transportation to New Caledonia. In a country where every individual is ticketed and labelled from birth, where police methods are quite despotic, and the law claims the right, in the interests of the larger number, to override the liberty of the subject, the professional criminal might be held at a tremendous disadvantage. It is true that the same result might be expected from the Belgian plan of prolonged cellular confinement; but, as I shall point out, this system is more costly, and can only be enforced with greater or less, but always possible, risks to health and reason.

But prisons are only one part, and perhaps not the most important part of a penal system. It is obviously right that they should be humanely and judiciously administered, but they exist only to give effect to the fiats of the law, which, for the protection of society, is entrusted with power to punish and prevent crime. How far these two great aims are effected, what should be the quality and quantity of the punishment inflicted, what the amount, if any, of the prevention secured, are moot points which are engaging more and more attention. Although great inequalities in sentences exist in Great Britain, as in every country, dependent as each must be upon the ever varying dispositions of the courts and those who preside over them, the general tendency is towards leniency. Imprisonment is imposed less and less frequently and the terms are growing shorter. The strongest advocates of this growing leniency claim for it that it has helped to diminish crime, and it is certainly contemporaneous with the marked reduction in offences in the last few years. In other words, crime has been least when punishment was least severe. Whether this diminution is not more directly traceable to other causes, and notably to the better care of juveniles and better measures to rescue and reform adult criminals, it is impossible as yet to determine. But it is beyond question that imprisonment, almost the only form of punishment now known to the law, is just as effective as the older and severer measures, if not more so. An ever increasing number of judges adhere to the axiom laid down by Mr. C. H. Hopwood, Q. C., one of the most distinguished of their number, "never to send a man to gaol if you can keep him out of it." The wisest of modern laws dealing with the prevention and punishment of crime is based upon it as a principle. Such acts as the British "First Offender's Act" and "Summary Jurisdiction Act" have done more to keep down the English prison population than all other measures combined.

The whole subject is one of the greatest importance and interest, and I have endeavoured to treat it adequately in the following pages.

CHAPTER I THE FIRST FLEET

> First idea of riddance of bad characters—James I removes certain dissolute persons—Sale of criminals as indentured servants to American Colonies and West Indies—Prices and profits—American Revolution closes this outlet—Discoveries by Captain Cook leads to the adoption of Botany Bay as the future receptacle—First fleet sails March, 1787—Settlement made at Port Jackson, christened Sydney—Landing of convicts—Early labours—Famine and drought—Efforts to make community self-supporting—Assisted emigration a failure—General demoralisation of society—Arrival of convict ships and growth of numbers—Unsatisfactory condition of Colony.

News of the discoveries, by Captain Cook, of vast lands in the South Seas reached England just as the scheme of Penitentiary Houses had been projected by John Howard, the great philanthropist, to remedy and reform the abuses of gaol administration. Why embark on a vast expenditure to build new prisons when the entire criminal population might be removed to a distance to work out their regeneration under another and a brighter sky? The idea was singularly attractive and won instantly in the public mind. The whole country would be rid of its worst elements, the dregs and failures of society, who would be given a new opportunity in a new land to lead a new life and by honest labours become the prosperous members of a new community established by virtue. The banishment of wrong-doers had long appealed to rulers as a simple and effective means of punishment, combined with riddance.

The first actual record of transportation is in the reign of James I, when prisoners were conveyed to the youthful Colony of Virginia, where Cromwell had sent his political captives beyond the Atlantic to work for the settlers as indentured servants or assigned slaves. Early in the eighteenth century the penalty was regularly introduced into the British criminal code. An act in that year commented upon the inefficiency of the punishments in use and pointed out that in many of his Majesty's colonies and plantations in America there was a great want of servants, who, by their labour and industry, would be the means of improving and making the said colonies more useful to the nation. Persons sentenced nominally to death were henceforth to be handed over to the contractors who engaged to transport them across the seas. These contractors became vested with a right in the labour of convicts for terms of seven and fourteen years, and this property was sold at public auction when the exiles arrived at the plantations. The competition was keen and the bids ran high at a date prior to the prevalence of negro slavery. To meet the demand the pernicious practice of kidnapping came into vogue and flourished for half a century, when it was put down by law. The price paid according to the mercantile returns ranged at about £20 per head, although it appears from a contemporary record that for two guineas a felon might purchase his freedom from the captain of the ship. The condition of these "transports" was wretched, and contractors often complained that their cargoes of human beings were so damaged on the voyages, and the subsequent mortality was so great, that serious misgivings arose as to whether it was worth while to enter upon the traffic.

Suddenly the successful revolt of the American Colonies closed them as a receptacle for the criminal sewages of Great Britain. Another outlet must be found, and for a time convicts sentenced or liable to transportation were kept at hard labour in the hulks in harbours and arsenals at home. Then Captain Cook found Botany Bay in the antipodes, and for a long time after their inauguration public opinion ran high in favour of penal establishments beyond the seas. "There was general confidence," says Merivale, "in the favourite theory that the best mode of punishing offenders was that which removed them from the scene of offence and temptation, cut them off by a great gulf of space from all their former connections, and gave them the opportunity of redeeming past crimes by becoming useful members of society." Through whatever mire and discomfort it may have waded, beyond doubt Australia has risen to a rank and importance which entitles it to remember unabashed the origin from which the colony sprang. It has long since outgrown the taint of its original impurity. Another writer asserts that "on the whole, as a real system of punishment it (transportation) has failed; as a real system of reform it has failed, as perhaps would every other plan, but as a means of making men outwardly honest, of converting vagabonds most useless in one country, into active citizens in another, and thus giving birth to a new and splendid country, a grand centre of civilisation, it has succeeded to a degree perhaps unparalleled in history." All this is of course indubitable. But in the process of manufacture, Great Britain in fifty years expended eight millions of hard cash, and remained as full of criminals as ever.

The early history of New South Wales as told in the pages of Collins reads like a romance. Captain Arthur Phillip, R. N., the first governor, started from Portsmouth in the month of March, 1787, with nine transports and two men-of-war—the "first fleet" of Australian annals. Unlike the *Mayflower*, bearing its Pilgrim Fathers, men of austere piety and worth, to the shores of New England, this first fleet carried convicts, criminals only, and their guards. Some vessels were laden deeply with stores, others with agricultural implements. Before the fleet was out of the English channel a plot was discovered among some of these desperate characters to seize the ship they were on board, and escape from the fleet. Nearing the Cape of Good Hope a second similar conspiracy came to light, and all through the voyage offences, such as thefts, assaults, abscondings, attempts to pass counterfeit coin, were numerous, and needed exemplary punishment. After a dreary eight months at sea, broken only by short stays at Teneriffe, Rio, and the Cape of Good Hope, the fleet reached Botany Bay in January, 1788. Never had name been more evidently misapplied. The teeming luxuriant vegetation was all a myth, and on closer inspection the "Botanists' Bay" proved to be mere barren swamps and sterile sands. The anchorage though extensive was exposed, and in easterly gales torn by a tremendous surf. Before debarking, therefore, Captain Phillip determined to seek along the coast some site more suitable for the new settlement. Starting with a select party in a small boat for Broken Bay, he passed *en route* an opening marked upon the chart as Port Jackson, named thus from the look-out man in Cook's ship, who had made it out from the masthead. This is known now as one of the finest and most secure harbours in the world. Here in a cove, where there was deep water for ships of the heaviest burden close in shore, the foundations of the new town were to be laid. It was christened Sydney, after the Secretary of State for the Colonies; and thither a party of convict artificers, guarded by marines, was at once removed to clear land for the intended settlement. When this was accomplished, the remainder of the colonists, 1,030 souls in all, were put on shore.

There was plenty of work to be done, and but few hands to do it. Enlarged clearings were needed; barracks, storehouses, hospitals, dwellings for the superior and other officers, huts for the convicts. Although at the time when the "first fleet" sailed, many thousands of convicts awaiting deportation crowded the various gaols of England, no attempt had been made to select for the new colony those who, from their previous condition and training, would have been most useful to the young community. Of the six hundred male convicts actually embarked, hardly any were skilled as artisans and mechanics. Nay more, though it was meant that the colony should be if possible self-supporting, and that every effort should be made to raise crops and other produce without delay, few, if any, of either the convicts or their keepers had had the least experience in agricultural pursuits. Yet with ordinary care the whole number might have been made up of persons specially qualified, accustomed to work either at trades or in the fields. Nor were there among the sailors of the men-of-war many that could be turned to useful account on shore.

Again, it had been forgotten that if the convicts were to be compelled to work, overseers were indispensable; for laziness is ingrained in the criminal class, and more than change of sky is needed to bring about any lasting change in character and habits. To these retarding causes was soon added wide-spread sickness, the result of long confinement on ship-board, and an unvarying diet of salt provisions. Scurvy, which during the voyage all had escaped, broke out now in epidemic form. Indigenous anti-scorbutics there were next to none, and the disease grew soon to alarming proportions. Many convicts died, and others in great numbers sank under an almost entire prostration of life and energy. On the voyage out there had been forty deaths; now within five months of disembarkation there had been twenty-eight more, while sixty-six were in hospital, and two hundred others were declared by the medical officers to be unfit for duty or work of any kind.

Another difficulty of paramount importance soon stared the whole settlement in the face. So far "the king's store" found all in food, but the supply was not inexhaustible, and might in the long run, by a concurrence of adverse circumstances, be almost emptied, as indeed happened at no remote date. Famine was therefore both possible and probable, unless in the interval the colony were made capable of catering for its own needs. To accomplish this most desirable end it was necessary to bring ground at once into cultivation, breed stock, and raise crops for home consumption. The first farm was established at Paramatta, fourteen miles from Sydney, and at the same time a detachment under Lieut. King, R. N., of the *Sirius*, was sent to colonise Norfolk Island, a place highly commended by Captain Cook for its genial climate and fertile soil. "Here," says Laing, "notwithstanding the various discouragements arising from droughts and blighting winds, the depredations of birds, rats, grubs, and thieves to which the settlement was at first exposed, a large extent of ground was gradually cleared and cultivated, and the prospect of raising subsistence for a considerable proportion appeared in every respect more favourable than at Port Jackson."

At the headquarters settlement in these earlier years prospects were poor enough. The land being less fertile needed more skill, and this was altogether absent. The convicts knew nothing of farming—how could they?—and there was no one to teach them. One or two instructors expressly sent out were found quite useless. The only person in the colony competent to manage convicts, or give them a practical knowledge of agriculture, was the governor's valet, and he died in 1791. To add to these troubles a lengthened drought afflicted the country during the first year of the settlement, under which the soil, ungenerous before, grew absolutely barren and unproductive. A man less resolute and able than Captain Phillip might well have recoiled at the task before him. The dangers ahead threatened the very existence of his colony. Hostile natives surrounded him. Within the limits of his settlement he had to face imminent starvation, and to cope with the innate lawlessness of a population for the most part idle, ignorant, and vicious. For it soon became plain that to look for the growth of a virtuous community, except at some remote period, from the strange elements gathered together in New South Wales, was but a visionary's dream.

England's social sewage was not to be shot down in Botany Bay, to be deodorised or made pure just because the authorities willed it. It was vain to count upon the reformation of these people in the present, or to build up hopes of it in the future. We have seen how their natural propensities displayed themselves on the voyage out. These, directly the convicts were landed, developed with rapid growth, so that crimes and offences of a serious nature soon became extremely rife. On the day the governor's commission was read, the governor addressed the convicts, exhorting them to behave with propriety, promising to reward the good while he punished heavily all evil-doers. Next morning nine of the people absconded. Within a week it was found necessary to try three others for thefts, all of whom were flogged. Before the month passed, four more were arraigned charged with a plot to rob the public stores, for which one suffered death, and the others were banished from the settlement. Yet at that time there was no possible excuse for such a crime. When goaded by hunger and privation in the coming years of scarcity, it was at least intelligible that desperate men should be found ready to dare all risks to win one plenteous meal, though even then each convict shared to the same extent as the governor himself. Each man's weekly allowance consisted of 7 lbs. biscuit, 3 lbs. peas, and 6 ozs. butter; 7 lbs. salt beef, or 4 lbs. salt pork. But in the first year the rations were ample, and inherent depravity could alone have tempted these convicts to rob the common store.

About this time another convict offender was pardoned on condition that he become the public executioner. Both "cat" and gallows were now kept busy, yet without effect. "Exemplary punishments," says Collins, "seemed about this period to be growing more necessary. Stock was often killed, huts and tents broken open, and provisions constantly stolen about the latter part of the week; for among the convicts there were many who knew not how to husband their provisions through the seven days they were intended to serve them, but were known to have consumed the whole at the end of the third or fourth day. One of this description made his week's allowance of flour (8 lbs.) into 18 cakes, which he devoured at one meal. He was soon after taken speechless and senseless, and died the following day at the hospital, a loathsome, putrid object." Here again was felt the want of overseers and superintendents of a class superior to that of the convicts, through whom discipline and interior economy might be maintained and regulated. Naturally those selected felt a tenderness for the shortcomings of their fellows, and it was more than difficult to detect or bring home offences to the guilty. A common crime was absence. Many, undeterred by fear of starvation, or savage natives, went off to the woods. One remained there nineteen days, returning to the settlement at night to lay his hands on food. In some cases the absentees were murdered by natives, and their bodies found sometimes with their heads pounded to jelly, but always mutilated, speared or cut in pieces. There were other crimes quite new, as were the punishments meted out to them. One impostor pretended to have discovered a gold mine; but it was proved that he had fabricated the gold dust he produced from a guinea and a brass buckle, and he was condemned to be flogged and to wear a canvas dress decorated with the letter R, "to distinguish him more particularly from others as a rogue." This same offender being afterwards caught housebreaking, suffered death, but not before he had betrayed his accomplices—two women who had received the stolen property. One of these was also executed, while of the other a public example was made. In the presence of the assembled convicts the executioner shaved her head, and clothed her in a canvas frock, on which were painted the capitals R. S. G.—receiver of stolen goods. "This was done," says Collins, "with the hope that shame might operate, at least with the female part of the prisoners, to the prevention of crime; but a great number of both sexes had been too long acquainted with each other in scenes of disgrace for this kind of punishment to work much reformation among them."

Thieving continued on all sides, and the hangman was always busy. Repeated depredations brought one man to the halter, while another, for stabbing a woman, received seven hundred lashes. Scarcely any of the convicts could be relied upon, yet many, in the scarcity of honest freemen, were appointed to posts of responsibility and trust. Generally they abused the confidence reposed in them. The case is mentioned of one Bryant, a seafaring west-country man, who was employed to fish for the settlement. Every encouragement was held out to this man to secure his honesty: a hut was built for him and his family, and he was allowed to retain for his own use a portion of every taking. Nevertheless he was detected in a long continued practice of purloining quantities of fish which he sold for his own gain. But he was too useful to be deprived of his employment, and he was still retained as official fisherman, only under a stricter supervision. Even this he eluded, managing a year or two later to make good his escape from the colony, together with his wife, two children, and seven other convicts. Having for some time laid by a store of provisions, and obtaining from a Dutch ship, in the port of Sydney, a compass, quadrant, and chart, together with information to help him in reaching Timor and Batavia, he stole one of the government boats and made off. Bryant and two of his convict companions being well trained in the management of a boat, and having luck upon their side, in due course reached the ports for which they steered. Others were less fortunate in their attempts to escape; like those who tried to walk to China northward through the Australian continent. Nor did much success wait upon the scheme laid by the convicts at Norfolk Island to overpower their guards, seize the person of the governor, and decamp. Although too wild and preposterous a plot to raise serious alarm, the very existence of this serves to prove the treacherous, untrustworthy character of these felon exiles. Some years later, indeed, in the reign of Governor King, an outbreak somewhat similar, but planned with secrecy and judgment, came actually to a head, and for the moment assumed rather serious proportions. In this, several hundred convicts combined "to strike for their liberty." They had pikes, pistols, and several stands of arms. The insurrection broke out suddenly. Two large bodies marched upon Paramatta, but were closely followed by an officer, Major Johnson, with forty men of the New South Wales Corps, who brought them to an action at Vinegar Hill, and in fifteen minutes dispersed them with great loss.

It is abundantly evident from these and other instances, that the convict population could only be ruled by an iron hand. But I think Governor Phillip would have forgiven them much if they had but been more industrious. Everything hung upon their labour. The colony must continue to be dependent on the mother country for the commonest necessaries of life, until by the work of these felon hands sufficient food was raised to supply subsistence, whenever the public store should grow empty or come altogether to an end. Yet the convicts by no means exerted themselves to the utmost; they foolishly conceived that they had no interest in the success of their labours. Task work had been adopted as the most convenient method of employing them; a certain quantity of ground was allotted to be cleared by a certain number of persons in a given time.

The surplus gained was conceded to them to bring in materials and build huts for themselves. But few cared to take advantage of the privilege, preferring to be idle, or to straggle through the woods, or to visit surreptitiously the French warships lying in Botany Bay. Indeed, the sum total of their efforts was to do just enough to avoid immediate punishment for idleness. Moreover, as time passed, the numbers available for work dwindled down, till at the end of the first year, in January, 1789, that is to say, only two hundred and fifty were employed in the cultivation of land. Many were engaged at the wharves and storehouses, but by far the greater portion were utterly incapacitated by age or infirmity for field labour of any description.

The evil days that were in store did not long delay their coming. Throughout the latter part of 1789, and the early months of 1790, the colony saw itself reduced to terrible straits for food. Relief was daily expected from England, but daily unaccountably delayed. Emptier and more empty grew the King's store. In the month of February, 1790, there remained therein not more than four months' provisions for all hands, and this at half rations. To prepare for the worst, the allowance issued was diminished from time to time, till in April, that year, it consisted only of 2 lbs. of pork, 2 lbs. of rice, and 2½ lbs. of flour per head, for seven days. More than ever in the general scarcity were robberies prevalent. Capital punishment became more and more frequent, without exercising any appreciable effect. Garden thefts were the most common. As severe floggings of hundreds of lashes were ineffectual to check this crime, a new penalty was tried, and these garden robbers were chained together in threes, and compelled to work thus ironed. "Any man," said, years and years afterwards, one of these first fleet convicts who had reached affluence and comfort at last—"any man would have committed murder for a month's provisions; I would have committed three for a week's. I was chained seven weeks on my back for being out getting greens and wild herbs." No doubt in those days of dire privation and famine the sufferings of all were grievous; but the statements of these people must be accepted with the utmost caution, even when divested of half their horrors. The same old convict said that he had often dined off pounded grass, or made soup from a native dog. Another old convict declared he had seen six men executed for stealing twenty-one pounds of flour. "For nine months," says a third, "I was on five ounces of flour a day, which when weighed barely came to four. The men were weak," he goes on, "dreadfully weak, for want of food. One man, named 'Gibraltar,' was hanged for stealing a loaf out of the governor's kitchen. He got down the chimney, stole the loaf, had a trial, and was hanged next day at sunrise."

Food, food, all for food! In its imperious needs hunger drove the unprincipled to brave every danger, and the foolish to excess not less terrible. Collins tells another story of a woman who devoured her whole week's allowance in one night, making up a strange compound of cabbage and flour, of which she ate heartily during the day, "but not being satisfied, she rose again in the night and finished the mess," and died. Throughout these trying times, Governor Phillip maintained a firm front. It is told of him, that seeing a dog run by he ordered it to be killed at once,—as a mouth that was useless, it could not in these days be entitled to food. Then, to ease the mother settlement, a large number of persons were drafted to

Norfolk Island, where, thanks to the presence of numbers of wild birds, supplies were more plentiful. In transit, H. M. S. *Sirius*—the only ship left in the colony—was wrecked in full view of the settlement.

Relief came at length, but in driblets. At the time of greatest need, more mouths arrived instead of more barrels of pork and flour. In February, as I have said, there were but four months' provisions in the stores; yet on the third day of June, two hundred and twenty-two women arrived—"a cargo," says the chronicler, "unnecessary and unprofitable;" while H. M. S. *Guardian*, which came as convoy and carried all the stores, was lost at sea. Another store ship, the *Justinian*, happily turned up about the 20th of June.

Later in this month, eleven sail, composing the "second fleet," came into port. In this second fleet the arrangements made were about as good as in slave ships from the Guinea Coast. The mortality on the voyage out had been absolutely frightful. One thousand six hundred and ninety-five male convicts and sixty-eight females were the numbers embarked, and of these one hundred and ninety-four males and four females had died at sea; while such was the state of debility in which the survivors landed in the colony, that one hundred and sixteen of their number died in the Colonial Hospital before the 5th of December, 1791. It seemed that the masters of transports were paid head-money for each convict embarked,—a lump sum of £17 9s. 6d. each. The more, therefore, that died, and the sooner, the less food was consumed, and the greater the consequent profit. Even to the living, the rations were so much reduced below the allowance stipulated by the governor, that many convicts were actually starved to death. In most of the ships very few were allowed on deck at the same time. Crowded thus continually in a fœtid atmosphere below, many peculiar diseases were rapidly engendered among them. Numbers died in irons; and what added to the horror of such a circumstance was that their deaths were concealed, for the purpose of sharing their allowance of provisions, until chance and the offensiveness of a corpse directed the surgeon, or some one who had authority in the ship, to the spot where it lay. In one of the ships a malignant fever had prevailed during the latter part of the voyage, to which the captain, with his first and second officers, had succumbed; while in another, the usual plot to take the ship was discovered, and had to be checked with severe repressive measures, which increased the tribulation of these hapless wretches.

Colonel Collins, in his "Account of New South Wales," gives but a sorry picture of the condition in which these ill-fated exiles of the second fleet arrived at New South Wales. "By noon," he says, "the following day the two hundred sick had been landed from the different transports. The west side afforded a scene truly distressing and miserable: upwards of thirty tents were pitched in front of the hospital, the portable one not yet being put up, all of which, as well as the hospital and the adjoining huts, were filled with people, many of whom were labouring under the complicated diseases of scurvy and dysentery, and others in the last stages of either of those terrible disorders, or yielding to the attacks of an infectious fever. The appearance of those who did not require medical assistance was lean and emaciated. Several of these people died in the boats as they were rowing on shore, or on the wharf as they were lifted out of the boats; both the living and the dead exhibiting more horrid spectacles than had ever been witnessed in this country. All this was to be attributed to confinement of the worst species, confinement in a small space and in irons—not put on singly, but many of them chained together."

The years immediately subsequent witnessed a repetition of what had already occurred. The colony found itself again and again brought to the lowest ebb; and then, when in the last stage, starvation stared it in the face, there came more convicts and more salt meat. All through, the health of the inhabitants continued indifferent, in spite of the natural salubrity of the climate. This was partly due to the voyage out; also to the diet, insufficient and always salt; and not a little to the gloomy outlook for all concerned in this far-off miserable settlement. Yet, through all vicissitudes, the governors who in turn assumed the reins bore up bravely, and governed with admirable energy and pluck. They were all—at least for the first twenty years—captains of the Royal Navy, trained in a rough school, but eminently practical men. Their policy was much the same. They had to bring land into cultivation, develop the resources of the colony, coerce the ill-conditioned, and lend a helping hand to any that gave earnest of a reform in character.

It will be seen that so far the colony of New South Wales consisted entirely of two classes, the convicts and their masters. In other words, it was a slave settlement—officials on the one hand as taskmasters; on the other, criminals as bondsmen who had forfeited their independence, and were bound to labour without wages for the State. The work to be done in these early days was essentially of a public character. It was for the common good that food should be raised, storehouses erected; the whole body of the population benefited, too, by the hospitals, while the building of barracks to house the guardians of order was also an advantage to all. But such preliminary and pioneer works once fairly started, the next step towards a healthy and vigorous life for the colony was the establishment therein of a respectable middle class—a body of virtuous and industrious settlers to stand between the supreme power and the serfs it ruled. People of this kind were wanted to give strength and stability to the settlement, to set an example of decorum, and by their enterprising industry to assist in the development of the country. But they must come from England; they were not to be looked for "among discharged soldiers, shipwrecked seamen, and quandam convicts." Governor Phillip at once admitted this, and from the first strongly urged the home government to encourage free emigration by every means. The distance from England was, however, too great to entice many across the seas, and the passage out would have swallowed up half the capital of most intending settlers. Several free families were therefore sent out in 1796 at the public expense, receiving each of them a grant of land on arrival and free rations for the first ensuing eighteen months.

But this assisted emigration was carried out in a very half-hearted, incomplete fashion, so much so that for a long time—till years after the peace of 1815—says Heath in his "Paper on Secondary Punishments," "a large proportion of the free settlers are described as of a low character, not very superior to that of the convicts." Their numbers were very small, being recruited indeed from the three sources above mentioned—the soldiers, the sailors, and the convicts themselves. Naturally, as time passed and sentences lapsed, the last mentioned supplied a very numerous class. Every effort was made to give them a fair start on the new road they were expected to follow. They received grants of land, varying from ten to sixty acres, with additional slices for children or wife. Pigs, seed-corn, implements, rations and clothing were served out to each from the King's store; and, thus provided for, straightforward industry would soon have earned for them an honest competence. But in comparatively few instances did these convict settlers thrive. They formed a body of small proprietors of the worst class, ruining their land by bad farming, and making those who were still convicts far worse by the example they set of dissoluteness and dissipation.

Society now, and for years to come, presented a curious spectacle. Its most conspicuous features were its drunkenness and its immorality. The whole community might be divided into those who sold spirits and those who drank them. Everything went in drink. The crops were no sooner gathered than they went for spirits. Any hope of raising the general tone of society was out of the question so long as this unbounded intemperance prevailed. Besides this, there was neither marrying nor giving in marriage. In Governor Bligh's time two-thirds of the births were illegitimate. Bands of robbers, the first bushrangers, infested the country, levying blackmail, and, entering the homes of the defenceless settlers in open day, committed the most fearful atrocities.

This general recklessness and immorality was fostered by the monopoly of sale possessed by the officers of the New South Wales Corps. These gentlemen, who came out in 1792 as officers of this local regiment, were for very many years a thorn in the side of the constituted authorities. Bound together by *esprit de corps* and unity of interest, they were constantly at war with the governor, and generally successful. Everything was made subservient to them. They had become by degrees engaged in commercial operations, and in time they alone had permission to purchase all cargoes of merchandise that came into port. These goods they retailed at an enormous profit, so that the small farmers were nearly ruined by the prices they had to pay for such necessaries as they required. "Hence," as Laing says, "they (these small farmers) lost all hope of bettering their circumstances by honest industry, and were led into unbounded dissipation." The figure cut by officers who wore the king's uniform in thus descending to traffic and peddle is not over-dignified. Nor were they always over-scrupulous in their dealings. As my narrative is concerned rather with the convict element and the vicissitudes of transportation than with the general history of the colony, it would be beyond my scope to enlarge upon the well-known "rebellion," in which this New South Wales Corps played the prominent part. In a few words, this amounted to the forcible ejectment from office of the King's representative, Governor Bligh, by those who were themselves the guardians of the King's peace. It would be tedious to argue here the two sides of the question; but, even allowing that both sides were to blame, it seems clear that the rebellious troops were most in the wrong. Eventually this New South Wales Corps ceased to exist as such, and becoming a numbered regiment, the 102nd of the line, was removed from the colony.

Meanwhile the convicts continued to pour in. Between 1795 and 1801, 2,833 arrived; 2,398 from 1801 to 1811. In the years between the comings of the first and second fleets, attempts had been made to improve the arrangements for sending them out. As soon as the hulks at home were full, and convicts began to accumulate, vessels were chartered for New South Wales. Each carried 200 with a guard of 30 soldiers. The men selected for transportation were always under fifty, and were taken from those sentenced for life or fourteen years. When these were found insufficient to provide the necessary draft, the numbers were made up from the seven-year men, and of these the most unruly were chosen, or those convicted of the more atrocious crimes. The females were sent indiscriminately, the only provision being that they must be under fifty years of age. Lists accompanied them out in all cases. These lists were deficient in all useful information—without particulars of crimes, trades, or previous characters; points on which information had to be obtained from the convicts themselves. The transport ships were supposed to be well found in all respects: clothes, medicines, and provisions for the voyage and for nine months afterwards were put on board at the public expense. The owner supplied a surgeon, and the admiralty laid down precise instructions for his guidance. The master, too, was bound over to be careful of his living cargo. On arrival his log-book was submitted for inspection, and the governor of New South Wales was empowered to reward him a special gratuity on the one hand, or on the other to mulct and prosecute him, according to his behaviour on the voyage out.

On arrival at Sydney the convicts were either disposed of as servants to settlers, or retained in government hands. We have here the system of assignment, though as yet quite in embryo. While settlers of any wealth were few, there was little demand for convict labourers, except as simple servants; although in the case of some of the leading officials, who had already considerable grants of land under cultivation, as many as forty were, even in these early days, assigned to the same master.

The great mass of the convicts were therefore retained by the government. They were fed, clothed, and lodged by government, and organised in gangs. Each gang was under an overseer—an old convict—who was certain to err either on the side of culpable leniency towards his charges, or of brutal cruelty. Stories are told of an overseer who killed three men in a fortnight from overwork at the sawmill. "We used to be taken in large parties," says the same old hand that I mentioned before, "to raise a tree. When the body of the tree was raised, old ---- (the overseer) would call some of the men away, then more. The men were bent double, they could not bear the weight—they fell, and on them the tree, killing one or two on the spot. 'Take them away: put them in the ground.' There was no more about it." Another overseer was described as "the biggest villain that ever lived. He delighted in torment, and used to walk up and down rubbing his hands when the blood ran. When he walked abroad the flogger walked behind him. He died a miserable death: maggots ate him up. Not a man could be found to bury him." A third overseer was sent to bury a man who, though weak and almost insensible, was not dead. "For God's sake," cried the poor wretch, "don't cover me up. I'm not dead." "You will be before night," replied the overseer. "Cover him up" (with an oath), "or we shall have to come back again to do the work a second time." On the other hand, it was known that overseers connived at irregularities of every description. The men were allowed to work as little as they pleased; many left their parties altogether to rob, and returned at nightfall to share their plunder with the overseers. Naturally the work accomplished for the public service did not amount to much. The hours of labour were from 6 A. M. to 3 P. M., after which the rest of the day belonged to the convict to be spent in amusement or labour profitable to himself. Even in these days the punishment of transportation fell most unequally on different men. While the commoner classes of offenders were consigned to the gangs or drafted off to be the slaves of the low-bred settler, persons who had held a higher station in life, or who had been transported for what came to be called "genteel crimes," forgery, that is to say, embezzlement, and the like, were granted tickets-of-leave at once, which exempted them from all compulsory labour and allowed them to provide for themselves. To them the only hardship entailed by their crimes was the enforced exile.

So far we have had to deal only with the difficulties encountered by the young colony and the steps taken to combat them. It is too soon to speak of the consequences that were entailed by forming a new settlement from the dregs of society. I will only state in general terms what was the actual state of affairs. A governor at the head of all with full powers nominally, but not nearly autocratic; next to him, as the aristocracy, a band of officials not always obedient, sometimes openly insubordinate, consistent only in pushing forward their own fortunes. Between these and the general body of the colonists a great gulf; the nearest to the aristocracy being the settlers—passing through several gradations—from the better class, few in number, to the pensioner or convict newly set free; at the very bottom, the slave or serf population—the convicts still in bondage.

This was the first stage in the colony's existence. With the breaking up of the power of the New South Wales Corps and the appointment of Governor Macquarie a new era opened; and to this I devote the next chapter.

CHAPTER II THE GROWTH OF NEW SOUTH WALES

> Large amount of convict labour available for employment—Free settlers too few to utilise it—Applied chiefly to public works—Premature erection of public edifices—Convicts given good wages and plentiful drink—Many grow rich—Governor Macquarie favours convicts unduly—Hostility shown him—Strong antagonism between classes—Great impetus to free emigration—Convict labour in demand—System of assignment revived—Discipline maintained by the "cat"—Efforts toward fair administration.

The peculiar condition of the colony now was the presence therein of a supply of convict labour, growing larger also from day to day as vessels with their cargoes arrived, for which there was no natural demand. When General Macquarie assumed the government the influx of male convicts had been so great in the five years preceding 1809, that the free settlers were unable to find employment for more than an eighth of the total number, though the labour was to be had for the asking, and cost nothing but the price of raising the food the convicts consumed. In point of fact, the free settlers were still too few and their operations too limited. Seven-eighths of the whole supply remaining on hand, it became necessary for the governor to devise artificial outlets. He was anxious, as he tells Earl Bathurst, "to employ this large surplus of men in some useful manner, so that their labour might in some degree cover the expense of their feeding and clothing." The measures by which he endeavoured to compass this shall now be described.

There is a stage in the youthful life of every colony when the possession of an abundant and cheap supply of labour is of vital importance to its progress. Settlers in these early days were neither numerous enough nor wealthy enough to undertake for themselves the work of reclaiming land, of establishing harbours and internal communications on a scale sufficiently wide to insure the due development of the young country. At such an epoch a plentiful supply of convict labour pouring in at the cost of the home government is certain to be highly valuable. Merivale points out how some such timely assistance to British Columbia in more recent years would have given an enormous impetus to the development of those provinces. It would be premature to discuss, at this period of my narrative, the question whether the advantages gained would outweigh the positive evils of a recurrence to transportation on any grand scale. Some of these evils might disappear if the system were carried out with all the safeguards and precautions that our lengthened experience would supply. But the main objection—the excessive costliness of the scheme—would remain.

This stage New South Wales had now reached, and the governor, finding himself amply supplied with the labour so urgently needed, bent all his energies to bringing forward the latent resources of the colony. His reign began at a period of great scarcity. Repeated inundations on the Hawkesbury had entailed disastrous losses on the whole community. He decided, therefore, to form new towns at points beyond the reach of the floods, and to open up to them, and throughout the province, those means of communication which are so essential to the progress of a new country. Upon the construction of these roads he concentrated all his energies and all the means at his disposal. Not much skilled labour was needed, yet the work was punitive and was also beneficial to the whole community. No better employment could have been devised for the convicts. Under his directions, towns before disconnected were joined by means of excellent highways, while other good roads were driven through wild regions hitherto unsettled if not altogether unexplored. The greatest exploit of that period was the construction of the road across the Blue Mountains to Bathurst, the whole length of which was 276 miles; and there were, besides, good wooden bridges at all necessary points. Beyond doubt, to these facilities of intercommunication is to be attributed the early advance of the colony in wealth and prosperity.

But Governor Macquarie's other undertakings, though well intentioned, were not equally well designed either for the improvement of the colony or the amelioration of its people. No doubt his was a difficult task, his course hard to steer. He had means almost unlimited, a glut of labour, and behind him were the open purse-strings of the mother-country. How was he to make the most of his advantages? This labour, of which his hands were full, came from a mass of convicts, each one of whom already represented a considerable charge on the imperial funds. It had been expensive to transport him; now he was costly to keep. Could he not be made in some measure to recoup the treasury for the outlay he occasioned? It was obvious that he should, if possible, contribute to his own support. Yet Governor Macquarie, in spite of his promises, aimed at nothing of the kind. His chief object—next after making roads—was to embellish the principal towns of the colony with important public works—works for the most part unnecessary, and hardly in keeping with the status of the young settlement. Roads were urgently needed; but not guildhalls, vast hospitals, spacious quays, churches, schools, houses and public offices. In these earlier years, buildings of more modest dimensions might well have sufficed for all needs. But under the Macquarie regime Sydney sprang from a mere shanty town into a magnificent city. It was almost entirely reconstructed on a new plan, the lines of which are retained to this day. The convict huts gave place to prisoners' barracks, the mean dwellings of the settlers to streets of imposing houses. The whole external aspect of Sydney and Parramatta was changed. In all, the new public buildings numbered more than 250, and the list of them fills ten closely printed pages of a parliamentary report.

Yet all this expenditure was not only wasteful and at the time unnecessary, but its direct tendency was to demoralise the population. The labourers required for works of such importance were of course collected together upon the scene of operations. In other words, crowds of convict artisans were congregated in the towns, and countenanced each other in vice. Many of the works were carried out by contract, the contractors employing convict hands, bond or free, still serving or emancipated; and in both cases they paid wages half in cash, and half in property, which consisted of groceries and ardent spirits. This was the "truck system," neither more nor less, which the contractors made still more profitable to themselves by establishing public-houses close to their works, at which the cash half of the wages soon returned to them in exchange for the drink supplied. Naturally vice and immorality grew apace. The condition of the towns was awful, and the low pleasures in which they abounded attracted to them many people who might otherwise have been contented to live quietly upon their grants of land. But the choice between congenial society with plenty of drink, and the far-off clearing with honest labour for its only joy, was soon made in favour of the former, and every one who could, flocked into the towns. The governor had indeed tried hard to form an agricultural population. With this object he had conceded larger grants than his predecessors, in the hopes that emancipated convicts would settle upon them and reform. It was thought that "the hope of possessing property, and of improving their condition and that of their families, afforded the strongest stimulus to their industry, and the best security for their good conduct." But these advantages were remote, and gave way at once before the present certainty of being able to barter away the land they got for nothing or in exchange for ten or fifteen gallons of rum. If this plan of manufacturing industrious small proprietors out of the recently emancipated convicts was meant to answer, the grant of land should have been made conditional on actual residence thereon, and accompanied by tangible results gained by actual labour done, which must be shown before the acres were finally conveyed. Now it was proved that many of Governor Macquarie's grantees never took possession of their land at all: the order for thirty acres was changed at once for the much coveted means of dissipation. Hence, though towns grew fast in beauty and importance, the forest lands or wild tracts in the interior remained unsettled; and the crowds of ex-criminals who might, by judicious treatment, have turned into virtuous farmers, rapidly degenerated into a mass of drunken dissipated idlers.

These were indeed fine times for the convicts. There was labour for all, remunerative, and not too severe; liquor was cheap, and above all the governor was their friend. It would be, however, more than unfair to charge General Macquarie with any but the best motives in his tenderness for the convict class. He conceived that the unfortunate people who composed it were the especial objects of his solicitude. To promote their reform, and to bring them to that prosperity which should make this reform something more than mere idle profession—these, as he thought, were among the first of his duties as the governor of a penal colony. In his prosecution of such views he did not halt half way. The manner in which he favoured and encouraged the emancipists came to be a by-word. It was said in the colony that the surest claim on Governor Macquarie's confidence and favour was that of having once worn the badge of a convicted felon. Very early in his reign he made it clear that this would be his policy. The year after his arrival he advanced one ex-convict to the dignity of a justice of the peace; another was made his private medical adviser; and both, with many others, were admitted to his table at Government House. Nor were the recipients of these favours always the most deserving among their fellows for the honours showered upon them. It was taken for granted that the possession of considerable wealth was proof positive of respectability regained; yet in the case of Governor Macquarie's emancipist magistrate, it was notorious that he had become rich by methods of which honest men would hardly be proud. Transported as a lad for rick burning, after serving his time in the colony he had been a shop-keeper, a constable, and last a publican; in which line, by means of liberal credit, he had soon amassed a fortune. His case was only one of many in which ex-convicts had grown rich, chiefly by preying on their still more unfortunate comrades, taking mortgages on grants as payment for long arrears of accounts for groceries and drink, and by and by seizing all the land. But no more emancipists were made magistrates after 1824.

Then, in many instances, members of the convict class were by far the shrewdest and best educated in the whole community. Settlers of the better class were few in number, so the sharp rogues had it all their own way. They had capital moreover. Several brought money with them to the colony, the fruit of their villainies, or their wives followed them with considerable sums acquired in similar fashion. For these men, especially if they had held fairly good positions at home, transportation was almost a farce. It merely meant removal at the public expense to a land, remote certainly, but in which they were little less comfortable than at home, and where they moreover had exceptional facilities for making money fast; and they had it all to themselves. Governor Macquarie discouraged free emigration. He did not want to see settlers. He looked upon them as out of place, nay more, as a positive encumbrance to the colony. New South Wales was a settlement, he said, made by convicts for convicts—"meant for their reformation; and free people had no right to come to it." So he continued to pat his favourites on the back: gave them land, and more land, as many assigned servants—their former partners possibly in many a guilty scheme—as they wished; and last but not least, provided a market for the very crops he had assisted them (by convict labour) to raise. It was not strange, then, that with a yearly influx of thousands of new hands, and the rapid upward advance of all who were ordinarily steady and industrious, the emancipists should come as a class to gain strength far in excess of their deserts, and sufficient from their numbers to swamp all other classes in the community.

There were frequent heartburnings in New South Wales during the reign of Governor Macquarie on account of his overstrained partiality. The discontent was heightened by his plainly spoken desire to force his own views down the throats of those nearest him in the social scale: not satisfied with openly countenancing them himself, he insisted that the officers of regiments receive emancipists as guests at mess. Bigge says on this point: "The influence of the governor's example should be limited to those occasions alone when his notice of the emancipated convicts cannot give offence to the feelings of others, or to persons whose objections to associate with them are known. The introduction of them on public occasions should, in my opinion, be discontinued. And when it is known that they have been so far noticed by the governor of New South Wales as to be admitted to his private table and society, the benefit of the governor's example may be expected to operate; and it will also be exempt from the fatal suspicion of any exercise of his authority." Again, when Mr. Bent, judge of the Supreme Court, refused to allow certain attorneys, ex-convicts but now free, to practise as solicitors, the governor complained to the home government that this judge was "interfering unwarrantably with a salutary principle which he (the governor) had been endeavouring to establish for the reformation of the convicts." Now at this very time an act was in force which deprived all persons convicted of perjury or forgery from ever again practising in the courts at home, and Judge Bent in refusing to administer the oaths to these emancipist attorneys was but carrying out the law; yet on the governor's representation he was removed from the bench.

There were other cases not less plainly marked. As a natural consequence, the antagonism was deepened between the two classes which were so widely distinct—the virtuous Pharisees, that is to say, and the thriving publicans. The former despised all who had come out "at their country's expense;" and the latter hated the settlers, as people of a lower class not seldom hate social superiors to whose "platform" they are forbidden to hope to rise. Eventually, as we shall see, after a long protracted warfare and varying successes, the free population gained the day; but not till the lapse of years had strengthened their numbers out of all proportion to their antagonists, and given them the preponderance they at first lacked.

The struggles between these two classes fill up the whole of the annals of the next years of the colony. All said, however, it cannot be denied that under the administration of General Macquarie the colony prospered. The population was nearly trebled between 1809 and 1821, and there was a corresponding increase in trade and in the public revenue. Just before this governor left the colony it contained 38,788 souls; there were 102,929 horned cattle, 290,158 sheep, 33,000 hogs, and 4,500 horses; and 32,267 acres had been brought under cultivation. The moral tone of the community, too, was slightly raised; marriage had been encouraged in place of an indifferent and disreputable mode of life which till then had been largely prevalent. "In externals, at least," says Laing, "the colony itself assumed quite a different aspect under his energetic and vigorous management from what it had previously worn."

Speaking of his own administration and his efforts to elevate the convict population in the scale of society, Governor Macquarie said for himself, as against his detractors, "Even my work of charity, as it appeared to me sound policy, in endeavouring to restore emancipated and reformed convicts to a level with their fellow-subjects—a work which, considered in a religious or a political point of view, I shall ever value as the most meritorious part of my administration—has not escaped their animadversions."

And yet, however praiseworthy his efforts, they were misdirected; and beyond doubt, in his desire to discourage the influx of free people, he committed a fatal error. It was his wish, of course, to further the development of the colony; but he could not do this half so satisfactorily by the establishment of penal agricultural settlements, as could substantial emigrants working with capital behind them for their own profit. Moreover, these agricultural settlements started by Governor Macquarie cost a great deal of money. Again, the free classes of the community would not have found themselves for a long time outnumbered had not immigration been systematically discouraged. The formation of an independent respectable society, armed with weight and influence, was, as I have said, much needed in the colony. In this respect General Macquarie had departed from the policy of his predecessors. Captain Philip was eager enough, as we have seen, to attract settlers, and had his recommendations been persistently followed the colony would have found itself the sooner able to raise grain enough for its own consumption.

Sir Thomas Brisbane, on the other hand, who came after Governor Macquarie, recognised the full importance of the principle, and his reign is memorable as marking the period when settlers in any considerable numbers first flocked to the colony. But it was no longer the humbler classes who came. None of these did the governor want, but persons who were well-to-do, who could take up larger grants and find plenty of employment for the rapidly increasing convict population. Sir Thomas Brisbane held out every inducement to attract such persons. At this period, thanks to the unceasing arrival of new drafts, the number of felon exiles on charge continued to form a serious item in the colonial expenditure. To get quit of all or any the governor was only too glad to offer almost any terms. The grants of land were raised from 500 to 2,000 acres, which any one of moderate respectability might secure, provided only he would promise to employ twenty convicts; rations also were to be given from the King's store for self and servants for the first six months, and a loan of cattle from the government herds. The newcomers therefore were mostly gentlemen farmers, younger sons of land-owners, or commercial men who had saved something from a general crash in business. Most of these people were sufficiently alive to their own advantage to realise the opportunity now held out to them. Land for nothing, food and stock till the first difficulties of settlement were overcome—these were baits that many were ready enough to swallow. Labour was also gratuitously provided by the same kind hands that gave the land.

For some years this more than parental encouragement continued, till at length the influx of settlers came to be thoroughly felt. The labour that was so lately a drug, was now so eagerly sought that the demand grew greater than the supply. The governor was unable to comply with all the requisitions for servants made by the land grantees. This at once brought about the abandonment of the agricultural penal settlements established by General Macquarie. Their success had always been doubtful: although land to a considerable extent had been cleared, timber felled, buildings erected, and farming attempted, no great results had ever been obtained. Indeed now when the land which had thus been occupied was again resumed, it was found to have been little benefited. One by one they were broken up. They were costly and unproductive. On the other hand, the settlers, old and newly arrived, were clamorous for the hands thus wastefully employed. "So steadily," says Laing, "did the demand for convict labour increase on the part of the free settlers that, during the government of Lieutenant-General Darling, there were at one time applications for no fewer than 2,000 labourers lying unsatisfied in the office of the principal superintendent of convicts."

We have now really arrived at the second stage in the history of transportation. Although from the first origin of the settlement convict servants were readily provided for any master who might ask for them, the applications, as I have said, were few and far between, amounting in 1809 to an eighth only of the total numbers available, and requiring, as late as 1821, to be accompanied by the bait of distinct and tangible bribes. But now had dawned the days of "assignment" proper, the days of wholesale slavery, where private persons relieved the state of the charge of its criminals, and pretended to act, for the time being, as gaolers, taskmasters, and chaplains, in return for the labour supplied at so cheap a rate. How far the persons thus called upon to exercise such peculiar functions were entitled to the confidence reposed in them was never in question till the last few years. Emancipists got their convicts too, and of course among the settlers many were quite unsuited for so serious a charge.

The failure of assignment as a method of penal discipline will be seen later on, when its great inherent evils had had time to display themselves. At first the chief fault was over-leniency—so much so that General Darling came out as governor charged with orders to subject the convicts to more rigorous treatment. Dr. Laing, in his "History of New South Wales," is of opinion that, about this date, much unnecessary severity was noticeable in the carrying out of the sentence of transportation. He states that convicts were now treated by the subordinate agents, who saw that severity was the order of the day, "with a reckless indifference to their feelings as men which their situation as criminals could never have warranted."

Nevertheless it must be confessed that the condition of convicts could not be irksome when soldiers envied it, and committed crimes on purpose to become felons too. This was proved in the case of certain soldiers who had turned thieves in Sydney simply that they might be sentenced to transportation. They were caught, convicted, and sentenced to seven years at Moreton Bay or Norfolk Island. Had their story ended here the bare record of it might suffice, but it so happened that very serious consequences ensued, and these I cannot refrain from recounting. As it came out quite clearly upon their trial what had been the object and design of their theft, Governor Darling resolved that they should be treated with extra rigour, "it being an intolerable and dangerous idea that the situation of a soldier was worse than that of a convict or transported felon." The seven years at a penal settlement was therefore commuted to seven years hard labour in chains on the roads of the colony. The intention of this change was doubtless that their old comrades should sometimes see them as they were marched to and fro; but besides this, it was ordered that at the end of their sentence they should return to their regiments. Therefore, after the proceedings of the trial had been promulgated, the prisoners were publicly stripped of their uniforms, iron collars with spikes projecting were placed around their necks, from which iron chains hung and were fastened to basils on their legs. Thus arrayed they were drummed out of their regiment (the 57th) to the tune of the Rogues' March. Under the horrors of this punishment one man, Sudds, immediately sank, and died the following day. The survivor then made a statement to the effect that Sudds complained bitterly of his chains. The projections on the collar prevented the prisoners from stretching at full length when lying on their backs. They could not lie at full length without contracting their legs, nor could they stand upright. The collar was too tight for Sudds' neck, and the basils too tight for the other's legs.

In reporting this whole case to the Secretary of State, Governor Darling says, "However much the event is to be regretted, it cannot be imputed to severity; none was practised or intended.... With respect to the chains which are designated instruments of torture, it will be sufficient to state that they weigh only 13 lbs. 12 ozs.; and though made with a view of producing an effect on those who were to witness the ceremony, the extreme lightness of their construction prevented them from being injurious in any respect to the individual." On the other hand, Laing says the irons usually made for the road gangs in the colony did not weigh more than from 6 to 9 lbs.; while those brought out for convicts on board prison ships from England weighed only from $3\frac{1}{2}$ to 4 lbs.

Following all this came vituperative attacks in the press. Papers inspired by the government defended General Darling, and the fight was long and bitter. One result was the passing of several acts known as "Gagging Acts," intended to check the virulent abuse perpetually aimed at the government, but they failed to have the desired effect. Governor Darling grew more and more unpopular, and on leaving the colony he was threatened with impeachment. A Parliamentary commission did, eventually, inquire into his administration, and completely exonerated him from all charges.

Speaking of the trial and sentence of these soldiers, Laing observes,—"It would be unjust to consider Sir Ralph Darling's sentence by the light of public opinion in England. He was governor of a colony in which more than half the community were slaves and criminals; he had to arrest and punish the progress of a dangerous crime; but he fell into the error of exercising by *ex post facto* decree, as the representative of the sovereign, powers which no sovereign has exercised since the time of Henry VIII, and violated one of the cardinal principles of the British Constitution by rejudging and aggravating the punishment of men who had been already judged. At the present day it is only as an historical landmark that attention can be called to this transaction, which can never be repeated in British dominions." It is more than probable that, as a military officer of rank, he was doubly disposed to reprobate the offence recorded. All his soldierly instincts were doubtless hurt to the quick by the notion that the private men of an honourable profession preferred an ignominious sentence to service with the colours of their corps. From this came his uncompromising attitude, and the seemingly unjustifiable violence of his measures.

But except in this one instance, Sir Ralph Darling proved himself an efficient administrator. His sympathies were certainly with the "exclusionists" as against the "emancipists;" and therefore, by the latter and their organs, he was persistently misrepresented and abused. But he was distinctly useful in his generation. A most industrious public officer, he spared himself neither time nor trouble. Every matter, however unimportant, received his closest personal consideration. He may have made mistakes, but never through omission or neglect; besides which, he introduced order and regularity in the working of the state machine. Method followed disorganisation; ease and freedom, where before had been friction and clogging interference between its several parts. One of his earliest acts had been to regulate the system of granting land, which under the previous administration had fallen into some confusion. It was he who established a Land Board, and who ruled that grants were to be made to people only according to their means of improving the acres they got, and not as heretofore, simply in answer to mere application.

In these and other useful labours the lead he gave was consistently followed by his immediate successor, Sir Richard Bourke, who came to the colony in December, 1831. Although by the extension of the colony the personal character of the governor was no longer of such paramount importance as in earlier days, the arrival of an efficient administrator was a distinct benefit to the whole settlement. Sir Richard Bourke was unquestionably a man of character and vigour. The measures he introduced were all salutary. Not only did he encourage free immigration, but he made fresh laws for the distribution and coercion of the convict population. His regulations for assignment—to which I shall refer directly—were wisely planned; and the reforms he introduced in the constitution of the courts of justice were as sensible as they were necessary. He had found that the decisions of local magistrates in the cases of the misconduct of convict servants were extremely unequal: some were ludicrously lenient, others out of all proportion severe. He thought it advisable to establish some uniform system by which magistrates should be guided in the infliction of summary punishments; and he passed, therefore, an act known henceforth as the "Fifty Lashes Act." This substituted fifty lashes for the first offence cognisable in a summary way, in lieu of one hundred and fifty; and made the powers of a single magistrate somewhat less than those of a bench of two or more. At the same time it was ruled that a "cat" of uniform pattern should be used in every district. "Each bench had before superintended, or left to its inferior officers, the construction of its own scourges, which varied according to accident or caprice; nor could it ever be ascertained by the mere number of lashes ordered what degree of pain the culprit was likely to have suffered." This restriction of their power was not palatable to all the magistrates, and petitions were presented to His Excellency, protesting against his new act. They urged that now their authority was utterly derided. "Such a feeling," says Sir Richard, commenting on their petition, "is not to be considered extraordinary, as it requires much judgment and moderation to overcome the instinctive love of power.... The magistrates who felt the diminution of their power as a grievance may perhaps have been excited to expressions of complaint by the annoyance to which, in their character of settlers, they are exposed from the misconduct of their assigned servants. They do not perhaps consider that the natural dislike to compulsory labour, which is part of human nature, and has existed and ever will exist under every form or mode of government, must offer great difficulties to those who seek to carry on their business by such means. Severity carried beyond a certain point, especially towards men of violent and turbulent feelings, will only tend to inflame this indisposition to labour with more dangerous acts of desperation and revenge."

However, to give the petitioners no just cause for complaint, he instituted a formal inquiry into "those circumstances connected with the discipline of the prison population which formed the subject of the petitions." Reports were called for from the police of the several districts. From them it was clearly apparent that fifty lashes with the new cat were quite enough for any one, provided they were properly administered. "The sufficiency of the law and of the instrument of corporal punishment, in all cases where proper superintendence is exercised, being thus established on unexceptionable evidence," His Excellency considered it would be inexpedient, nay, dangerous, to add to the severity of either, "merely because, in some instances, the wholesome vigour of the existing law has been impeded by a negligent or corrupt execution. In reading the reports which have been presented, the governor could not fail to observe that where punishments have been duly inflicted, the power of the magistrates has been anything but derided. While perusing these painful details, His Excellency has indeed had abundant reason to lament that the use of the whip should of necessity form so prominent a part of convict discipline in New South Wales; but believing it to be unavoidable, the governor must rely on the activity and discretion of the magistracy for insuring its wholesome and sufficient application."

The clear-sighted policy adopted by Sir Richard Bourke in carrying out the last mentioned reform was no less observable in his treatment of the question of assignment. The system by which servants were assigned to settlers was undoubtedly not altogether free from abuses. It was alleged that successive governments worked it quite as a source of patronage to themselves. Governor Darling had however established an assignment board, which to some extent equalised the distribution of the convicts among the settlers. But it remained for Sir Richard Bourke to put the whole question on a thoroughly satisfactory footing. The rules he promulgated did not make their appearance till he had been four years in the colony; after he had gained experience, that is to say, and time to consider the subject in all its practical bearings. Excellent though they were, they were rather late in the field. From the date of their appearance to that of the final suspension of transportation there were but five years to run. The pains taken by Sir Richard Bourke are evident from his despatch to the Secretary of State for the Colonies, dated June, 1835. He observes, "My chief object in this measure has been to substitute for the invidious distinction hitherto more or less vested in the officers entrusted with the duty of assigning convicts to private service, strict rules of qualification, intelligible alike to the dispenser and receiver of penal labour, and from which no deviation shall be permitted. It is not until after much delay, and after maturely weighing the suggestions of the various parties, that I have ventured to deal with this important and difficult subject."

The main principle of the new regulations was that servants were to be assigned solely in proportion to the land the masters occupied. A carefully prepared scale was drawn up fixing this proportion, which, speaking roughly, was at the rate of one servant per 160 acres of ordinary land, and one per 20 acres under plow or hoe culture. At the same time it was ruled that, as all mechanics were more valuable than mere labourers, each of the former should be equal to two and sometimes three of the latter. Thus one blacksmith, bricklayer, carpenter, or cooper, counted as three labourers; while a plasterer, a tailor, shoemaker, or wool-sorter, counted only as two. An entirely new process of application for these servants was also laid down. A special sessions was to be held in every district in September, for the purpose of receiving and reporting on all such applications. It was the duty of the magistrates in sessions to "inquire into the correctness of the facts stated in each, requiring such evidence thereof as to them shall seem proper; and they shall in no case recommend the claim of any applicant unless perfectly satisfied of the truth of the statement on which the application is founded."

Over and above this they were also required to look into the moral qualifications of the assignee. They were not to recommend any person "who is not free, of good character, capable of maintaining the servants applied for, and to whose care and management they may not be safely entrusted." Had this regulation been enforced at an earlier date the system of "assignment" might have been worked with greater success. The applications having been duly passed at sessions were then forwarded to the assignment board at Sydney. Throughout, the greatest care was taken to prevent underhand dealing: when eventually the time for actual assignment arrived, it was done by drawing lots, or rather numbers from a box in the office of the assignment board, and it was impossible for the officials to show favour or affection even had they been so inclined. The whole spirit of these regulations was thoroughly equitable and straightforward. The only object was to be fair to every one. Thus the land qualification was not insisted upon in the case of tradesmen who wanted assistance in their own calling; and respectable householders were also allowed to obtain indoor servants, though without an acre of land in the colony. With these rules were included others requiring masters to remove their servants without delay, and establishing certain pains and penalties against contravention of the new law.

These arrangements were indeed admirable, all of them, but they should have been earlier enforced. Not that Sir Richard Bourke was to blame for this. The change he instituted should have been made by his predecessors. But he was probably superior as an administrator to most who had gone before. At least he was clear-sighted enough to perceive that New South Wales had already outgrown the conditions of a mere penal settlement. He was of opinion that convict labour was no longer required, and that the abolition of transportation would be really a benefit to the colonial community. He was in this ahead of his time, but within a year or two of the close of his reign the same views began to be widely entertained both in Great Britain and her colonies. In fact, the period was now approaching when the idea of the possible abandonment of transportation was to take a tangible and substantial form.

CHAPTER III CONVICT LIFE

> Various conditions described—Arrival and treatment of newcomers—Hyde Park barracks for males—Parramatta factory for females—Behaviour of assignees to their convict servants—Treatment at out-stations—Labour—How enforced—Demeanour of convicts—Disciplinary methods—The lash the chief penalty.

British transportation divides itself naturally into three periods. The first comprises the early history of the penal colonies; the second treats of the days when "assignment" flourished, then fell into disrepute; the third saw the substitution of the "probation" system, its collapse; and finally, the abandonment of transportation beyond the seas. Transportation was really continued for some years after the collapse of the probation system in Van Diemen's Land, but only to the extent of sending a few hundreds annually to Western Australia, and in keeping up the convict establishments at Bermuda and Gibraltar. Having sketched this early history in the two preceding chapters, I propose to draw now a picture of convict life, and the state of the colonies generally during the second of these periods. I shall, in this, confine myself chiefly to New South Wales, the details of management and the results having been much the same in Van Diemen's Land, or Tasmania as it is now called. But I shall refer more especially to that island in a later page.

To the voyage out and the internal management of convict ships I intend to devote a special chapter. Let us imagine that the anchor is dropped in Sydney harbour, and that the surgeon superintendent has gone on shore to make his bow to His Excellency the Governor of New South Wales and its dependencies. There is already plenty of excitement in the town. The ship had been signalled in the offing, and there are numbers of good people on the look out for useful hands from among its cargo. The days when convict labour was a drug in the market are past and gone; the rush for "assigned" servants is now so great that requisitions far in excess of the number available crowd the office of the assignment board. All sorts of tricks have been put in practice to get early information as to the qualifications of those on board: although the indent bearing the names of the new convicts goes first to the governor and then to the assignment officers, the cunning old stagers—not a few of them themselves emancipists—have found out privately from the surgeon or the master of the vessel whether there are upon the list any men likely to be useful to them. Thus a watchmaker seeks to obtain a watchmaker; an engraver, an engraver; printers, compositors;

merchants want clerks, as doctors do assistants, or as the genteel folk—"ancients" they love to style themselves—do cooks, butlers, and ladies'-maids. Many got convicts assigned to them who were distinctly unfit and unworthy of the charge. Cases were indeed known of settlers, outwardly honest men, whose only object in asking for servants was to get assistants in thieving, cattle stealing, and other nefarious transactions. All who lived inland came off second best in the general rush: unless they had some friend on the spot to watch their interests they had to take their chance later on. But these too are in want of skilled labourers: one requires a carpenter to complete a new shed or roof to his house; another a blacksmith for the farm forge; and all would be glad of men with any agricultural training or skill. If the newly-arrived ship carries female convicts, there is similar anxiety. At one time governesses were frequently got from among these outcasts; but the practice of confiding the education of innocent children to such teachers appeared so monstrous that it was soon altogether discontinued. But nursemaids and other household servants were in eager request, and it must be confessed that the moral condition of the colony was such that many of the better looking female convicts were obtained without disguise for distinctly immoral purposes.

One and all were compelled to lodge their applications for assigned servants with the assignment board, where practically the decision rested. This board was governed latterly by the clear and explicit rules laid down by Sir Richard Bourke, to which I have referred in the last chapter, but before these regulations were framed many malcontents among the settlers were ready to declare that assignment all depended upon favour and affection. "If you had no friend on the board," says one, "you might get a chimney-sweep when you wanted a cabinetmaker." In the same way complaints were made that the members of this board, and other officials in high place, were given as many assigned servants as they asked for. Thus the Chief Justice of the colony had forty, the Colonial Secretary fifty or sixty, the Brigade Major eight or ten. The principal landowners, too, were liberally supplied. One, a salt manufacturer, had sixty or seventy; another, with a farm of forty thousand acres, employed a couple of hundred servants. Laing declares that the assignment of useful hands depended often on petty services rendered to government, and that many of the settlers succeeded in getting on the weak side of the governor and his advisers.

But to return to the ship, which meanwhile lay out in the stream. No one was allowed to communicate with her, except the Colonial Secretary or his assistant. One of these officials having gone on board to muster all hands, inspect them, and investigate any complaints, as soon as these preliminaries were concluded the disembarkation took place at the dockyard. Male convicts were at once marched to the Hyde Park barracks, where they paraded for the inspection of His Excellency the governor. Then the assignees, having been first informed of the numbers they were to receive, waited in person or sent for them, paying on receipt one pound per head for bedding and the convict clothes. Assignees failing to appear, or to remove the lots assigned to them, forfeited the grant. With the women the system was much the same. They were first mustered, then they landed, decked out in their finest feathers. There was no attempt to enforce a plain uniformity of attire; each woman wore silks and satins if she had them, with gay bonnets, bright ribbons, and showy parasols. Persons who had applied for female servants were present at the dockyard to receive them. After that all who remained on government charge—and their numbers were large, for female convicts were not in great demand—passed on next to the great central depot or factory at Parramatta.

As the Hyde Park barracks and the Parramatta factory were to a certain extent depot prisons for males and females respectively, a word about both will not be out of place here.

Until later years the men's barracks had been very negligently supervised. There was no attempt to enforce discipline within the walls. The convicts were not even kept under lock and key. Half at least were absent as a general rule all night, which they spent in prowling about, stealing anything they could lay hands upon. The officers at the barracks were tampered with, and winked for substantial reasons at the nightly evasions of the prisoners in their charge. Even in the day time, and inside the walls, drunkenness was very rife, and with it perpetual pilfering from one another, and much general misconduct. Naturally in this universal slackness of control the lower officials fattened and grew rich at the public expense. Gross peculation and embezzlement were continually practised. The storekeeper was known to have abstracted supplies from government stock; and others on small salaries were found to have amassed considerable fortunes, building themselves fine villas in the best part of the town, and living on the fat of the land. Having thus full scope for license and depravity, it will be conceded that there was no attempt at punishment and restraint in this the first halting-place of the transport in the land of exile.

The condition of the Parramatta factory, the depot for females, was even more disgraceful. The building, not unlike an English workhouse, was large and stood amidst spacious courtyards and gardens. The accommodation provided was of the best. There was plenty of food and comfortable raiment. The women were not confined always within the walls, they had money in plenty, and there was little or no work to be done, even by those in the lower stages or classes. A few were made to wheel sand or gravel for gardening purposes, but the barrows used were of light construction, and the women laughed openly and made a joke of the labour imposed. The administration of the establishment was entrusted for years to a matron, whose character, to say the least of it, hardly entitled her to so responsible a charge. It was alleged that she misappropriated the labour of the convicts, keeping back the best prisoners to employ them for the benefit of herself and her daughters. It was openly said, also, that these daughters were not a bit better than they should have been. There was some attempt at classification among the female convicts according to conduct and character, but the lowest of these classes was filled with women who had been returned from service or who were sentenced to remain at Parramatta till further orders. This was just what they wished. All the women much preferred to be at the factory. It was far better, they said, than at service. If any servant misbehaved, and was taken by her master before a magistrate, she said at once, "Send me back to the factory. Send me back." These scenes in court supply curious evidence of the condition of affairs. The women constantly made use of the most desperate and disgusting language. One, after threatening her master, suddenly spat in his face. Another, when sentenced to ten days on bread and water, was so insolent that the punishment was increased to thirty. "Oh! thank you," she said coolly; "couldn't you make it thirty-one?"—knowing perfectly well that thirty days was the limit of the magistrate's power. No wonder that, with such material to choose from, decent people refused to receive convict maid-servants into their families. As a rule their characters were so bad, they gave so much annoyance, and disturbed to such an extent the peace and quiet of households, that the settlers would rather be without their assistance altogether. "They make execrable servants," says a Mr. Mudie, speaking from long experience. In many years he had only met one or two who were well behaved. Some were exceedingly savage, and thought nothing of doing serious mischief to any one. The most flagrant case of this was the assault on Captain Waldron, a retired officer and settler. Having reason to find fault with a woman for not cleaning his veranda, he threatened to send her back to the factory. "If you send her, you must send me too," cried another woman coming forward directly. High words followed; after which the two women threw themselves without warning on their master, got him down, and mauled him so seriously that he died of the injuries he received. Other servants, convicts also, were within earshot, but not one stirred a finger to help their master.

Not a pleasant picture this of the actual consequences of female transportation. Perhaps all the women were not originally bad, but the voyage out was a terrible ordeal to those who had still some faint glimmering left of the distinctions between right and wrong. Another observer remarks that the character and condition of these women was "as bad as it was possible for human beings to be; they were shockingly dissolute and depraved, steeped to the very core in profligacy and vice." But I will now leave them and return to the men, who formed the bulk of the convict population.

Let us take first the case of those assigned to settlers in the interior. The assignee, as I have said, attended and carried off his quota to dispose of them on his station, or otherwise, according to his discretion. To get the men home—often a long way off—was no easy matter. Sometimes the convict was given money and told to find his own way, and again the master assumed charge, and they marched in company. Then it happened, either that those left to themselves made straight for the nearest public-house, or that those under escort gave their masters the slip and traveled in the same direction. The next the assignee heard of his new servants was a demand made upon him to take them "out of pawn." Joining with old pals, these new chums, fresh from the restraint of the convict ship, had soon launched out into drunkenness or worse. As often as not, the master found them in the lock-up, with half their clothing gone, and charged with felony. Having cost money already, they now cost more; and the process might be repeated over and over again. Nevertheless, sooner or later, all or a part of the new labourers reached their destination. Here their position was quite that of slaves. The Transportation Act gave the governor of the colony a property in the services of every convict, and this property he made over to the assignee. The authority with which the settler became thereupon vested was not exactly absolute, but it was more than an ordinary master has over his apprentice. Nevertheless, the Australian master was bound to maintain and to protect his convict servant. He could not flog him, nor was he supposed to ill-treat him; besides, the law gave the convict the right of appeal and complaint against ill-usage. Maintenance was likewise provided by law. The regulation rations consisted weekly of seven pounds of fresh meat—beef or mutton—and eight pounds of flour, with salt, also soap and other necessaries; but this minimum allowance was often largely increased. The meat issue rose to eight or nine pounds; the flour to fourteen pounds; tea and sugar were added, and occasionally rum and tobacco. In spite of the danger of supplying such men with spirits, rum was openly given—as at time of sheep shearing, and so forth, when it was supposed to be needed medicinally. The occasion of a harvest-home was often the excuse for a general jollification. Many masters found that it was to their interest to feed their convict servants well. This was bribing them to do good work, and not a few people had more confidence in the efficacy of such treatment than in purely strict and coercive measures. Mr. Mudie, again, when before the Parliamentary Committee of 1837, confessed to having provided one servant with a flute, just to keep him in good humour. A good master was anxious to make his servants forget, if possible, that they were convicts. Really profitable labour, they argued, could only be got out of them by making them comfortable. Here at once was a departure from the very first principles of penal discipline. It was hardly intended that the felons who were transported as a punishment beyond the seas should be pampered and made much of, simply to put money into the pockets of private individuals. As a matter of fact the average actual condition of the convict servant, as far as food and lodging were concerned, was far superior to that of the honest field labourer at home, and under a good master, as we have seen, he was much better off than a soldier. He might be under some personal restraint, and there was a chance of being flogged if he misbehaved, but he had a great many comforts. He was allowed to marry, could never starve, and if industrious, might look forward in no remote period of time to rise to a position of ease, if not of actual affluence.

At all the large stations the daily routine of life was somewhat as follows: The big bell on the farm rang out an hour before sunrise, a second bell half an hour later, and a third when the sun appeared. It was the night watchman's business to ring the bells. At the last summons all hands turned out. The mechanics went to their various works, the bullock drivers to their carts, the herdsmen to their cattle and pigs. As a general rule the heaviest labour to be performed was kept for the newest comers, so as to break them in. It was their business to clear the land, fell timber, and burn it. At eight came the breakfast bell, and with it an hour's rest. Dinner was at one, after which work was continued until sunset. At 8 or 9 P. M., according to the season, a night bell recalled every one, and after that no convict was supposed to leave his hut. On the surface, then, no great amount of rest appeared to be allowed, except at actual meal times or after sundown; but the whole character of the work performed was desultory and far from satisfactory. A convict servant's value was estimated by people of experience at something much less than that of a free labourer; so much so that there were settlers who declared they would rather pay wages, as they lost rather than saved by this gratuitous labour. The convicts worked unwillingly almost always; sometimes they executed their tasks as badly as they could, on purpose to do injury. What leisure they had was not very profitably employed. One convict in twenty might read, and some few spent their time in plaiting straw hats for sale; but the greater number preferred to be altogether idle, unless they could get a pack of cards—forbidden fruit at every station, and yet generally attainable—in which case they were prepared to gamble and quarrel all the night through. There was little or no supervision over them in their huts. It was quite impossible to keep them inside. No kind of muster was feasible or even safe. The overseers were really afraid to visit the men's huts much after dark, fearing to be attacked or openly maltreated. It would have been far better if a strong stockade, with high palisading, had been in all cases substituted for the huts. The latter were open always, so that after the last bell at night, any—and they were not a few—who chose crept out and spent the whole of the dark hours on the prowl. Of course the convicts were incorrigible thieves, and the whole country side was laid under contributions by them while thus nightly at large. Sunday was another day which gave these idle hands abundant opportunities for mischief. Of course there was no regular work done on the farm on that day; but there was no attempt, either, to enforce religious observances in lieu thereof. The want of provision for public worship was at this time largely felt throughout the colony, and seldom were churches at hand for the convicts to attend, even if such attendance had been insisted upon. Some few superintendents of farms took their convicts to church, if there was one in the neighbourhood, but cases of this were few and far between. Even if there was a church, all who could do so, sneaked out of the way on pretence of going to bathe, and so escaped the service.

Thus far I have described only the pleasant side of a convict's life up the country. On the whole it was far from irksome. Nevertheless, as a set-off against the home comforts and the comparative idleness, there was the total want of freedom of action, coupled with strictly enforced submissiveness of demeanour. A convict was expected to be even cringingly subservient in manner. For insolent words, nay, looks, as betraying an insubordinate and insurgent spirit, he might be incontinently scourged. In this way he was subject to the capricious temper, not only of his master, but of the whole of the master's family. Then the local magistrates had great powers. Singly a magistrate could sentence any man to be flogged for drunkenness, disobedience, neglect of work, or absconding; with others assembled in petty sessions, they had power, however, to inflict heavier punishments for graver offences. In "Byrne's Travels" I find mention made of several convicts who had received in the aggregate many thousand lashes. The same writer asserts that he once had an assigned servant upon whom 2,275 had been inflicted. This man was said to have grown so callous that he was heard to declare he would rather suffer a thousand lashes than the shortest term of imprisonment. Life could not be very enjoyable to men liable to such treatment. And this code was for the convicts and for them alone. Another law applied to the masters, in whom, indeed, was vested a tremendous power for good or evil. Some, as I have before remarked, were quite unfit persons to have the charge of felon servants, being themselves little better than convicts, and prepared at any time to consort with them and make them their intimate friends. Others of the better classes often delegated their authority to overseers, being either non-resident on their farms, or not caring to exercise personal control. In many cases these overseers were ex-convicts, and although it might be considered advisable that the master should not make himself too cheap, and that a middleman should be employed to come into direct communion with the convict himself, still every precaution should have been taken to prevent any abuse of power. In point of fact every well-ordered establishment should have been uniformly under the eye of its resident owner.

But in reality the lot of the convict in assignment was left altogether to chance. According to his luck in masters, he might be very miserable, or as happy as the day was long: one master might be lenient, giving good food and exacting but little labour in return; another, a perfect fiend. It was quite a lottery into which sort of hands the convict fell, for until 1835 there was little or no inquiry into the character of applicants for servants, and except in the most flagrant cases requisitions were never refused.

This, indeed, comprised one of the chief objections to the system of assignment. It was altogether too much a matter of haphazard. No system of penal discipline ought to be left thus to chance; yet as we have seen, there was no supervision and little attempt to enforce hard labour or any stringent code of discipline. This neglect fostered evil courses, and tended to increase the temptations to crime. Nor was the style of labour provided that which was always most suited to the persons for whom it was intended. In some few cases it was proper enough. Men employed as shepherds were perforce compelled to drop into regular habits from being obliged to go out and return with their herds at fixed hours, and they lived much alone. But these were only a small proportion of the whole number, and the balance working in association had many opportunities for developing vicious qualities by this corrupting intercourse. Especially was this the case with the mounted herdsmen, who were free to gallop about the country, collecting together in large numbers at the squatters' huts to drink and gamble and plot schemes of depredation.

These squatters, who about this period—1825-35—sprang up in rank growth round about the principal stations, did much to give annoyance, and to increase the difficulties of the settlers. They were mostly emancipists or ticket-of-leave men, who occupied crown pastures without paying for them, or spent their energies in stealing horses and cattle. Sometimes they established themselves at the corners of the settlers' own grants of land, getting as near to estates as they could without detection. Their principal object in life seemed to make themselves useful to the convicts employed near them, for whom they kept "sly grog-shops," where they sold or bartered liquor for stolen goods. This ready market for stolen property was a source of great loss to the settlers. One calculated that it cost him £200 or £300 a year. Pigs, sheep, harness in bags, flour on its way to market—all these were purloined in large quantities, and passed at once to the receivers, who gave rum in exchange, and sometimes tea, sugar, and tobacco. The squatters were fined if caught at these illicit practices, but to recover money from them was like getting blood out of a stone. Another favourite *modus operandi* was to knock up a sort of shanty close by some halting-place on the main line of road, where there was water handy and the drays could be made snug for the night. The draymen naturally flocked to the grog-shop, and naturally also obtained the sinews of war by making free with their masters' property.

In the foregoing pages I have dwelt chiefly on assignment to the country districts. But every convict did not of course go to the interior. Many were assigned in the towns. Now, whatever evils may have surrounded the system as carried out inland, the practice of town assignment was infinitely worse in every respect. In the first place, it led to the congregation of large numbers in places where there were many more temptations to profligacy and crime. And just as these were increased, so were the supervision and control that would check them diminished till they sank to almost nothing at all. Country convicts, as we have seen, were not much hampered by rules; but those in towns were free to do just as they pleased. It was impossible for the masters to enforce any regulations. In the hours of work, such as they were, the convicts might perhaps be kept out of harm's way more or less, according to the character and style of their employment; but labour over, they had great license and were practically free men. Household servants were as well off as servants at home in England: they frequented theatres and places of amusement, and the badge of their disgrace was kept altogether in the background. Masters were not compelled by law to enforce any particular discipline; nor would the most strict among them dare to exercise much surveillance over their servants. Such conduct would have been rare and singular, and it would have drawn down upon them the animosity, or worse, of the whole convict class. Such was the state of affairs that this body really possessed some power, and could not openly be affronted.

Convicts were required in the towns, as in the country, to be within doors by 8 P. M.; but unhappily this rule was quite a dead letter. The Sydney police was miserably inefficient. Recruited from the convict ranks, they were known on all occasions to favour openly their old associates. If they gave information they were called "noses," which they disliked; or worse, they were hooted, sometimes attacked and half killed. They were known, too, to take bribes, and to be generally most neglectful of their duties. It was not to be expected, therefore, that from them would come any zealous supervision of the convicts still in assignment, even to the extent of sending all such to their homes after 8 P. M., or of preventing the commission of petty offences. But as a matter of fact, the police were never certain whether half the men they met were convicts in assigned service or people actually free. Sydney was by this time so large, and the convicts so numerous, that it was next to impossible for a constable to know every one he met, by sight. None of the assigned servants in towns wore any distinctive dress. Those in government hands wore gray, and the chain-gangs a parti-coloured suit of yellow and brown cloth, but the assigned servants appeared in their masters' liveries, or clothed just as it pleased them. Recognition was not likely to be easy or frequent. Even in our own day, with admirable police machinery, the thorough supervision of criminals at large is not always obtained. In Sydney, seventy years ago, it was lamentably below the mark. Often enough men who had arrived in recent ships, having been assigned in due course, were soon lost sight of, to reappear presently under another name, as men quite free. They had proved themselves so useful that their masters wished to give them sole charge of a business, which, if still convicts, they could not assume. In this way it was discovered that an assigned convict servant had charge of a tan-yard close under the eyes of the police, but here it was proved that the police had connived at a grave neglect of duty.

It followed, too, from the nature of their previous vocations, that the convicts assigned in towns were the sharpest and most intelligent of their class. They were therefore the more prone to dissipation, and the more difficult to restrain within bounds. Knowing their value, they presumed on it, and felt that they were too useful to be sent off as rough farm hands into the interior. Here was another blot in the system of assignment, and generally on the whole principle of transportation. The punishment fell quite unequally on offenders. The biggest villains and the most hardened offenders fell naturally into the lightest "billets;" while the half-educated country bumpkin, whose crime may have been caused by ignorance or neglect, was made a hewer of wood and drawer of water. Prominent among those of the first class were specials, or gentlemen convicts, as they were styled; men sentenced for "genteel" crimes, forgery only, or embezzlement, but whose delicate fingers had never handled the cracksman's jimmy, or tampered with foil or blow. These genteel criminals were forever, through all the days of transportation, a thorn in the side of the administration, and they were always treated with far more consideration than they deserved. Some of these were well-known men, like one who had been a captain in the royal navy, and whose proclivities were so ineradicable that he suffered a second sentence at Norfolk Island for forgery, his favourite crime. From among this class the lawyers selected their clerks, and the auctioneers their assistants. If unusually well-educated they became teachers in schools, and were admitted as such even into the public seminaries of Sydney. A flagrant instance of the consequences of this injudicious practice is quoted by Laing—a clergyman's son, who had a convict tutor, coming himself, under the influence of such a man's teaching, to be also a convict sentenced to transportation for life.

There was another very improper proceeding which for a long time held among the convicts of this superior or more wealthy class. Their wives followed them out to the antipodes, bringing with them often the bulk of their ill-gotten gains. Having thus ample funds, they established themselves well on arrival, and applied for a grant of convicts like the rest of their neighbours. Naturally they took care to secure that their own husbands should be among the number. There was one man who had received a very heavy sentence for the robbery of a custom house, who should have gone direct to Norfolk Island. Through some bribery he was landed at Sydney, and was made overseer at once of a gang working in the street. Within a day or two he absconded. His wife had joined him with the proceeds of the robbery, and they went off together. Mr. Macarthur gives another case of a farrier who was assigned to him. This convict's wife followed him, and asked permission to live with him on Mr. Macarthur's farm. When this was refused the man managed to get returned to Sydney, and was there reassigned to his wife. To something of this kind some of the largest shops in Sydney owed their origin.

Among the many lighter and more remunerative kinds of employment into which the convict of the special class readily fell, was employment on the public press. As time passed there had grown up a strong antagonism between bond and free, and both sides had their newspapers. The organs which were emancipist in tone were not of the highest class, but they were often conducted with considerable ability. Their staff was of course recruited from the convict ships as they arrived, where compositors, leader writers, and even sub-editors were occasionally to be found. The most notorious instance of this description, was the case of W., who was originally assigned as a servant to the proprietor of the *Sydney Gazette*. This paper, which was then published only three times a week, was an able and influential journal, and its editor and owner was a certain O'S., who had himself been assigned to a former proprietor, and by him employed as a reporter. To him came W., and these two, according to Dr. Laing, bent all their energies to compass "the abolition of all the moral distinctions that the law of God has established in society; to persuade the public that the free emigrant was no better than the convict, that the whole community was equally corrupt, and those of the convict class were no worse than the best in the colony, their situation being the result of misfortune, as they pretended, and not of misconduct."

W. was a Scotchman, who had been outlawed for some misdemeanour in the office of a solicitor by whom he had been employed in Edinburgh; he then went to London, and was taken into a large mercantile house, Morrison's; from which, for embezzlement, he was transported for fourteen years. He was sent out in Governor Darling's time, and was sent to Wellington Valley, then a penal settlement for educated convicts. He stayed there but a short time, thanks to his interest with the superintendent, and returning to Sydney obtained a ticket-of-leave, being afterwards employed as a clerk in the corporation office, under the archdeacon of the colony. On the dissolution of the corporation he was no longer required there, but he found great demand for his services from editors of newspapers, having two sub-editorships offered to him at the same time. He went to the *Sydney Gazette*, and thenceforward had it under his entire control, the ostensible editor being a person of dissipated habits, who let him do as he pleased. This W. was a man of considerable talent. From that time forth he proved a source of prodigious demoralisation from the sentiments he disseminated, and the use he made of the powerful engine he had under his control, in endeavouring to exasperate the prison part of the population against the free emigrants. He was tried at length on a charge of having bribed a compositor to steal a printed slip from another newspaper office in the colony. The printed slip was a proof of a letter that had been sent for publication to the editor of the paper, and which contained libellous matter, reflecting on the character of a certain emancipist. The letter was not very carefully examined by the editor until it had been set up in type, but on discovering the nature of its contents he considered that he ought not to publish it. Though actually printed, it never appeared in the paper. W. came to know that such a paper was in type, and he bribed a convict compositor in the office to which the letter had been sent to purloin a copy, or one of the proofs of the letter. He then sent the letter in an envelope through the post to the person libelled, in order that there might be proof of its publication. The person to whom the letter referred thereupon brought an action against the editor of the paper to which it had been sent, and endeavoured to establish the fact of publication from the circumstance of his having received the letter through the public post; but the action failed. On inquiry, W.'s complicity in the matter was discovered, and he was tried for being a party to the theft. Of this he was acquitted, as the property found was not of value sufficient to constitute grand larceny; but the judge considered that he should not be allowed to remain at Sydney, and the governor sent him to Port Macquarie, a station for gentlemen convicts. Though now two hundred and fifty miles from Sydney, he still continued to contribute articles to the *Sydney Gazette*; and soon afterwards the widow of the late proprietor of the paper, into whose good graces he had insinuated himself, went down to Port Macquarie and married him. He then got into trouble by stirring up a feud between the harbour master and a police magistrate. In the investigation which followed, both these officials were dismissed and W.'s ticket-of-leave was cancelled. He was sentenced to be classed again with the convicts in government hands, and on hearing this he absconded. Nothing more was heard of him.

I think it will be evident from what I have said that the actual condition of men who were in assigned service was not very disagreeable if they were skilful hands and useful to their masters. This much established, they found their lives were cast in pleasant places. They did not want for money: they were allowed openly a portion of their earnings, and these gains were often largely increased by illegal methods. Besides this, many masters gave their servants funds to provide for themselves. They even went so far as to allow their men to marry—saddling themselves with the responsibility of having perhaps to keep both convict and his family. These convict marriages, when permitted, took place generally in the convict class, though cases were known of free women who had married assigned servants, and *vice versa*. Among the latter, Byrne, in his "Travels," speaks of a certain old lady, the mother of very respectable people, who had married when a convict, and who did not, to the day of her death, quite abandon the habits of her former condition. Her husband had been an officer of high rank, and her sons rose to wealth and prosperity in the colony; but no considerations for the feelings of those belonging to her were sufficient to wean her from her evil propensities. She was so passionately addicted to drink, that it was in vain her children sought to keep her with them: she always escaped, taking with her all on which she could lay hands, and returned to her favorite associates—the brick-makers in the suburbs of Sydney.

But such marriages as these were the exception. As a general rule the assigned servant, whether in town or country, paid a visit to Parramatta factory, and made his case known to the matron by whom it was governed. "Turn out the women of such and such a class," forthwith cries Mrs. G., and the marriageable ladies come trooping down, to be ranked up in a row like soldiers, or like cattle at a fair. Benedict walks down and inspects, then throws his handkerchief, and if the bride be willing, the two retire to a corner to talk a little together. If the conversation is not quite satisfactory to "Smith, *Aboukir*," or "Jones, *Lady Dacre*,"[1] he makes a second selection; and so on, perhaps, with three or four. Cases were known of fastidious men who had run through several hundreds, and had declared in the end that there was not a single woman to suit. Others were less particular. Men up country have been known to leave the choice to their masters, upon the latter's next visit to Sydney. There was of course no security against bigamy: often both parties to the colonial marriage had wife or husband alive at home, and just as inevitably the conduct of these factory brides was most questionable after the new knot was tied.

FOOTNOTE:

[1] A convict in Australia was always known by his name and the name of the ship in which he had come out.

CHAPTER IV A CONVICT COMMUNITY

> Convicts in public hands—How employed—Road parties—Chain gangs and the penal settlements—Life and labour in each—Classes of convicts—The emancipists—Many acquire great wealth—Irritation among the free settlers—Growing party pledged to abolish transportation—Deplorable state of the Colony—Crime prevalent—Drunkenness the besetting sin—Judge Burton's charge: "Transportation must cease"—Arguments against it.

In the latter part of the preceding chapter I have dealt with convicts in assignment. These of course did not comprise the whole number in the colony. Putting on one side the ticket-of-leave men,—who were still really convicts, though for the moment and during good behaviour masters of themselves,—and not including emancipists, who though, to all intents and purposes, men free as air, still carried a class-brand which generations only could efface—there were, in addition to the servants assigned to private individuals, a large body of convicts retained in the hands of the government of the colony. A certain proportion of these were men so chosen on arrival for satisfying certain demands, and therefore kept back from ordinary assignment because the government officials, so to speak, assigned them to themselves. There were public works to be carried out, and the government was clearly as much entitled to share in the supply of convict labour as the settler. It was said that the condition of these convicts in government employ was always worse than those in private hands. About one fourth of the whole available number were thus appropriated for the colonial works. But over and above these, the government held the entire number of refuse convicts in the colonies. Every man who did not get on with his master; every man who committed himself, and was sentenced to undergo any correction greater than flogging or less than capital punishment, came back to government, and was by it disposed of in one of three ways: First, the road parties; second, the chain-gangs; and third, the penal settlements.

The road parties were employed either in Sydney itself and other towns, or along the many miles of roads wherever their services were required. Those at Sydney were lodged in the Hyde Park barracks, whence they issued forth daily to their work, under the charge of overseers, at the rate of one to every thirty men. These overseers were themselves convicts; chosen for the post as being active, intelligent, and perhaps outwardly more respectable than their fellows. Naturally the control of such overseers was not very vigilant. They were paid no wages, and had no remuneration but certain increased indulgences, such as an allowance of tobacco and other minor luxuries. Hence they connived at the absence of any men who were disposed to forage in the town and run the risk of capture. If caught thieving, or as missing, the culprits were to take the consequences; but if all went well, they shared whatever they stole during the day with their complaisant overseer. Parties in the country were under similar management, but they were dispersed over such a very wide area that efficient supervision was even more difficult. The surveyor-general of the colony was the responsible head of the whole department; but under him the parties were actually worked by these overseers. The convicts were free to come and go almost as they pleased. Their dwellings were simple huts of bark, which presented no obstacles to egress after hours at night. In the day time they were equally unrestrained. They did odd jobs, if they pleased, for the neighbouring settlers, though under Sir Richard Bourke's assignment rules, which were promulgated in 1835, any settler who gave employment to convicts from the road parties thereupon forfeited all his assigned servants. Any artisan might earn money as blacksmith, carpenter, or cooper. Many others were engaged in the straw hat trade, a very favourite occupation for all the convicts. Great numbers, less industriously disposed, spent their time in stealing. A large proportion of the robberies which were so prevalent in the colony were to be traced to the men of these parties on the roads. They were highwaymen, neither more nor less; and every settler far and near suffered from their depredations. Sometimes they went off in gangs, and, encamping by the side of the road, laid every passing team under contribution. Increased facilities were given for the commission of these crimes through the carelessness of the settlers themselves, when they were permitted to employ men from the road parties on Sundays or during leisure hours. Wages in cash were paid in return, and the door was thus open to drunkenness and the evils that follow in its train. Worse than this, at harvest time, when the road parties were eagerly drawn upon for the additional hands so urgently required, the settlers were in the habit of giving the men they had thus employed passes to rejoin the stations from which they had come. Of course the convicts did not hurry home, and of course, also, they did no little mischief while on their way.

The work that was done by these parties was certainly irksome in character. Breaking stones under a broiling sun is not an agreeable pastime. But the amount of labour performed was ludicrously small, and has been described by an eyewitness as a disgrace to those in charge. On the whole, therefore, the convicts of this class had no great cause of complaint. They had plenty of congenial society, even outside their own gangs, for they were not prevented from associating with the assigned servants around; their food was ample; and they had abundant opportunities for self-aggrandisement in the manner most agreeable to themselves. It was not strange, then, that idle, worthless servants in assignment greatly preferred service in the parties on the road.

Nevertheless, there were not wanting among the free residents intelligent persons who saw how the labour of these road parties might have been made really productive of great benefit to the colony. There was still plenty of work to be done in developing colonial resources: over and above the construction and repair of roads, they could have been usefully employed in the clearance of township lands, the widening and deepening of river beds, in quarrying, fortifying, and building piers. But to have accomplished these results, a system more complete than any that was even dreamed of then must have been indispensable. Success only could have come from regular effective supervision by a thoroughly trustworthy staff, and by carefully constructed prison accommodation, such as was provided later in carrying out public works by convict labour in Western Australia.

In the chain-gangs there actually was greater restraint, and some semblance of rigorous discipline. The convicts were relegated to this system of punishment as a general rule for colonial crimes, though at times new arrivals of a desperate character were also drafted into them at once. In these gangs the convicts were kept in close custody, and condemned to work which was really hard. There were some few chain-gangs in Sydney, living on board a hulk, employed at the magazines on the island, and in improving the streets; but as a general rule they were to be found chiefly at out stations, or in the interior. They were guarded always by a detachment of troops, and when most efficiently organised were governed by a military officer, who was also a magistrate. Under him there was also a superintendent in charge of each stockade or barrack, with a staff of constables in the proportion of one to seventy-five convicts. The duties of the constables were analogous to those of warders in permanent prisons at home. The stockades were substantial buildings, in appearance somewhat similar to American log houses, but of greater strength, sufficient to preclude all possibility of escape. These stockades accommodated one hundred or more men each. They were of simple construction: the walls formed of timber, split into strong slabs, which rested in grooves at top and bottom; the roof was of timber also, covered with bark. In most cases the materials were found close to the spot, timber being everywhere plentiful; but it was possible to take down the stockade and remove the pieces to another locality if required. The prisoners were not badly fed, on flour, maize meal, and beef. Their clothing was two suits a year. They had medical attendance, and regular divine worship. Their beds were of plank, but there was no lack of bedding. The great hardships were the unremitting labour—

at not less than ten hours daily, and in chains—leg-irons weighing six or seven pounds, which were never for a moment removed. So important were these irons considered, that it was the stockade superintendent's business to examine closely every prisoner's chains daily before the stockade was emptied for labour. In this way chiefly escapes were prevented, as the convict found himself rather too heavily handicapped to run, carrying with him several extra pounds of metal.

One other unpleasant feature at the stockades was the official "scourger," as he was called—a convict specially appointed to execute corporal punishment. He was not himself an "iron-gang" man, but came from assigned service together with the convicts' cooks and wardsmen required for the interior economy of the stockade. What with work unremitting, weighty chains that were never removed, isolation from the dissipation of the towns, the convict in the iron-gang was on no bed of roses. Nor could he, under the later régime, escape as easily as he had done heretofore. Sentries with loaded muskets guarded every exit, and they gave him only one chance to halt when summoned, before they fired. After two years' trial Sir Richard Bourke reported that his new system was eminently successful. By its assistance he was at length enabled to dispense altogether with the road parties without irons, which I have already described as being so fruitful of evil to the community at large. Another evil to which I have not referred, and which was attributable to the slackness of control over these road parties and chain-gangs, was the existence of a class of desperadoes sufficiently well known to every reader—I mean the notorious "bushrangers" of the Australian colonies. Certain numbers of these were recruited from among the assigned servants, who absconded when they and their masters could not agree, but by far the greater proportion was furnished by the government gangs, escapes from which were for a long time frequent and generally successful. Whenever a man of courage and ability got away, he collected around him a band of brigands like himself; and then, for periods varying in length according to the nature of the pursuit, these villains subjected the whole neighbourhood to their depredations. They attacked chiefly the outlying huts and houses, but seldom large establishments. One case was known where some sixty men of a chain-gang had plotted to break out simultaneously and make for the bush. Thence they were to march on Macarthur's station, bent on pillage. Nothing came of this plot, because precautions were taken to meet it. But at other times bloody affrays were common enough between the bushrangers and the mounted police. Indeed, it was well known that unless a gang of these highwaymen was entirely exterminated there was no peace for the district in which they were at large. If one survivor escaped he soon became the nucleus of a new gang. What between attacks on dwelling-houses, and the daily stoppage on the highways of carts and wagons, the country generally was most insecure. People went about in fear of their lives.

The penal settlements contained, as a matter of course, the dregs of convictism. These settlements were the superlative degree of infamy. The convicts in the road parties and chain-gangs were bad enough, Heaven knows, but they were angels of light compared to those in the penal settlements. Offenders were not indeed transferred to these terrible receptacles till all other treatment had failed. When there, "it seemed," to quote Judge Burton's words, "that the heart of a man was taken from him, and that he was given the heart of a beast." It will not beseem me to go fully into all the details of these cesspools of iniquity, but I shall have to refer at some length further on to Norfolk Island, the worst of them all. The settlements used as penal by New South Wales were Moreton Bay and Norfolk Island; whereas Van Diemen's Land used Tasman's Peninsula. This place was cut off altogether from the settled districts, having only one communication—at Forestiers Peninsula—with the main island. On this neck of land, between Pirates' Bay and Norfolk Bay, stood an officer's guard; and besides his sentries, a chain of fierce dogs kept watch and ward from shore to shore. These dogs had been trained to give tongue at the slightest noise day or night. So successful was the guard they kept, that only two prisoners ever escaped from Port Arthur. One was recaptured, the other died in the woods. This station on Tasman's Peninsula had the great advantage that it was not, like Norfolk Island, distant several days' sail. Being but six hours from headquarters at Hobart, it was brought directly under the supervision of the governor and other officials.

I have now described the condition and style of life of all convicts, still such; of all, I mean, who were not yet nominally or actually free. The whole of these were comprised in the numbers at assigned service, in the road parties, chain-gangs, or penal settlements.

Next above them, on a sort of debatable land, free for the time being, but liable to degradation anew, stood the convict on ticket-of-leave. This expression and the practice to which it applies has been adopted into home legislation and language, but the term itself was a colonial invention. The first tickets were granted by Governor Phillip with the intention of instituting some stage intermediate between complete freedom and actual restraint. As time passed new orders varied the details; but the meaning of the term remained practically the same. The holder of a ticket-of-leave was a convicted felon, who had permission to be at large before the whole term of his sentence had actually expired.

At the top of the convict ladder were the emancipists, whose term of transportation was at an end, who were free to return to the land from whence they came, and begin life afresh, but who were never actually whitewashed in the colonies, or permitted to rise in the social scale to an equality with the free settler who had never broken the laws. We have seen how successive governors sought to bring the emancipists forward, and the heartburnings it occasioned. Their efforts were doubtless supported by the wealth and importance of many of the emancipist class; but it was on this account that the antagonism exhibited by the free population was the more unvarying and bitter. Many of the respectable inhabitants had been outstripped in the race for fortune by men who had arrived in the colony bearing the felon's brand; and the free settlers felt that in fighting against the pretensions of these ex-convicts they were fighting for very life. The position of the latter was so strong, that with the slightest success they would have swamped the former altogether. No doubt the injudicious tone of the emancipist press, and the flagrant conduct of many of the principal emancipists, drove the free settlers into opposition more strenuous than was absolutely required. A man who had been a convict was not necessarily to be taken by the hand and made much of from pure sentimental philanthropy. But neither, on the other hand, should he have been kept perpetually at a distance, and treated as an outcast forever. It was because the emancipists formed a body so powerful that their opponents were more or less afraid of them, and stood really at bay, fighting with their backs to the wall. Not a little of this bitter hostility has survived to the present day. Even now, in the towns where transportation had effect, the convict element stands in a class apart; there are caste distinctions stronger than any in the mother country, of which the barriers are rarely, if ever, overpassed.

But beyond question, many of the emancipists throve. The pictures drawn of their wealth and prosperity may be a little exaggerated, but in their main outlines they were undoubtedly true. There was one who made a fortune of £45,000 in a year. Several others had incomes of £20,000. One or two of the largest shops in Sydney were owned by them. They had public-houses, and farms, and ships, and newspapers, and all the outward signs of material wealth. They spared no pains or cost to get gorgeous furniture and costly plate. They had grand carriages and good horses, and were fond of lavish and ostentatious expenditure. But with all this, low tastes prevailed. No one bought pictures or works of art: the only literature they valued was the "Newgate Calendar," and they preferred a prize-fight any day to an opera or a decent play. It was said, indeed, that the principal wealth of the colony was for a long time held in the hands of those emancipists. Honest people less successful in the race for money declared that these others made fortunes because they were quite unscrupulous. No doubt the accusation held. One case was proved in which a certain shop undersold all others, simply because its owner, an ex-convict, was a receiver of stolen goods, which he naturally was able to retail at remarkably cheap rates. A number made their fortunes by dealing only with their fellow-convicts, whom a sort of freemasonry attracted always to convict shops. The practice, at one time prevalent, and to which I have already referred, of giving small grants of land to ticket-of-leave men, was another opening to convict shopkeepers and general dealers. These farmers came into Sydney to sell their produce. As there were no markets, certain individuals bought all that came, paying for the same in "property,"—in drink, that is to say, and other articles of consumption. The countrymen got drunk always, and stayed a day or two on the same spot: at last the landlord would ask if they knew how much they owed, and name the amount as £50. When they expressed surprise, he would tell them they had been too drunk to know what they were doing. Of course the victim was unable to pay, and had to sign a power of attorney, or paper binding himself to give up all his produce until the debt was cancelled. This fraud was repeated again and again, till all the man's property was pledged. Then he was sold up. One man had been known to drink away his farm of 100 acres in a single night. It was by carrying on this line of action that the emancipist already mentioned as worth £20,000 a year became a large landed proprietor. But he was also a thrifty, careful man, from the time he had come out when almost a boy with one of the first fleets. He was a sober man, moreover; and when spirits were issued to the convicts employed in building at Parramatta, he saved his and sold it to his fellows. Then, putting by all the time he was a prisoner every shilling he could make, he was able when free to set up a public-house, and buy a horse and gig which he let for hire. One day when his trap was wanted he drove it himself, and had as "fare" an ex-convict woman who owned a little property—some two or three hundred pounds. This woman he married, and thus little by little increased his possessions.

On the whole it was not strange that there should be fierce warfare between the better classes and the emancipists as a body. Beyond doubt, the emancipists formed a very corrupting element in general society. They looked with leniency on men who had committed serious crimes, and welcomed those whom honest people naturally shunned. One of the sorest points of contention was the admission of these emancipists to serve on juries in criminal and other trials. It was not alone that they leaned to the side of the accused, and could not, even in cases clearly proved, be persuaded to convict; but respectable people objected to be herded with them in the same panel. The question was warmly argued. Petitions were presented for and against; and this of itself showed the extent to which the convict element arrogated power to itself. One petition praying for the abolition of the practice was signed by the clergy, landowners, merchants, and gentry generally; while the counter petition was prepared and signed mostly by men on ticket-of-leave. Irritated, undoubtedly, by the general state of affairs, a party among the free settlers grew up, and daily gained strength, which was pledged to the abolition of transportation.

Truly the state of New South Wales was at that time terrible. Crime was extraordinarily prevalent. Morals were loose and drunkenness was the besetting sin of the colony. It affected all classes. Drunken people were to be seen in all directions, men and women fighting in the streets, and riotous conduct everywhere. At the Rocks—the Seven Dials of Sydney—scenes of debauchery were repeated and always disgraceful. In the upper classes, at the hotel bars, the same tastes prevailed; and the gentry fuddled themselves with wine, just as the lower orders did with rum. This *penchant* for drink was curiously contagious. Free emigrants who came out with sober habits were soon as bad as the old hands. Of course among the convict class the drunkenness knew no bounds. The favourite drink was rum—not fine old Jamaica, but East Indian, fiery and hot—which was handed round undiluted in a bucket at all regular "sprees." Often assigned servants were found downstairs hopelessly drunk while host and guests waited upstairs for dinner, the roasts being in the fire and the meat boiled to rags. Even good servants, fairly honest and capable, could not resist the bottle. The hardest drinkers were the "old hands," or convicts who had finished their terms and had become free. These fellows worked hard for a year or two till they had put by some £40 or £50, then posted off to Sydney to squander the whole in one big debauch. They stood treat to all,—rum flowed like water,—and if the money did not go fast enough they called for champagne. "It is, in truth, impossible to conceive," continues the same writer, "the lengths to which drunkenness proceeds and the crime it leads to, not only to obtain the means of gratification, but as a consequence on indulgence." To purvey to the universal thirst there were dram-shops and publics by hundreds everywhere. Licenses were seldom, if ever, refused, even to persons of unknown character. For them it was quite sufficient to get the good word of the chief constable—himself an old convict. He was not above a bribe, and his recommendation always carried the day. "In no city of the world," says Byrne, "are there the same proportion of public-houses, paying high rent, and doing an excellent business.... From high to low—the merchant, mechanic, and labourer, all alike are a thirsty community. The bar-rooms of the hotels and inns are as much crowded as the taps of the dram-shops. Drink, drink, drink, seems to be the universal motto, and the quantity that is consumed is incredible; from early morning to night it is the same—Bacchus being constantly sacrificed to."

Of the extraordinary prevalence of crime there could be little doubt. One eminent judge spoke of the colony as composed of two classes; one whose main business was the commission of crime and the other, the punishment of it. The whole colony, he said, seemed to be in motion towards the courts of justice. Beyond question the criminal statistics were rather startling. The number of convictions for highway robbery in New South Wales alone was equal to the whole number of convictions for all offences in England. Murders and criminal assaults were as common out there as petty larcenies at home. The ratio was one offender to every twenty-two of population; while in England about the same period it varied from one in seven hundred and forty to one in a thousand. It is but fair, however, to state that nearly the whole mass of crime proceeded from the convicts, or those who had been such. Among the reputable portion of the population the proportion was no greater in New South Wales than elsewhere. Sydney was a perfect den of thieves; and these, being indeed selected from the whole felonry of England, were quite masters of their business, and stood at the head of the profession. The report of the police magistrate of Sydney, printed in October, 1835, gives an awful picture of the state of the town. Of the whole population of twenty thousand a large proportion were prisoners, past or present, "whose passions are violent, and who have not been accustomed to control them, yet for the most part have no lawful means of gratifying them. It includes a great number of incorrigible characters, who, on obtaining their freedom, will not apply themselves to any honest mode of earning their living, but endeavour to support themselves in idleness and debauchery by plunder."

"There is more immorality in Sydney," he continues, "than in any other English town of the same population in His Majesty's dominions." It contained two hundred and nineteen public-houses, and there were besides sly grog-shops innumerable. "There is no town which affords so much facility for eluding the vigilance of the police. The unoccupied bush near and within the town itself will afford shelter to the offender and hide him from pursuit; he may steal or hire a boat, and in a few minutes place an arm of the sea between him and his pursuers.... The drunkenness, idleness, and carelessness of a great portion of the inhabitants afford innumerable opportunities and temptations day and night to live by plunder." Sir Francis Forbes, the Chief Justice of the colony, endorses the foregoing statements. "That this is a true description," he says, "of the actual state of Sydney cannot be denied."

Another powerful voice was raised by Judge Burton, whose charge to the grand jury of Sydney in November, 1835, attracted universal attention. Not alone were crimes constantly detected and punished, but others, often the most flagrant, stalked undiscovered through the land. And numerous executions exercised no effect in deterring from crime. The example of repeated capital punishments caused no alarm. There was no attempt by the masters to raise the moral tone of their convicts; no religious worship on Sundays, as we have seen; and instead of it, drunkenness and debauchery.

Masters, indeed, exercised hardly any control over their men. To this Judge Burton traced nearly all the crime. Many of the most daring robberies were to be attributed to this, and this alone. Convict servants, as many as five and six together, went about openly to plunder, masked, and armed with muskets—a weapon not capable of much concealment. Even in broad daylight, and in the open highway, harmless folk had been stopped by these miscreants and robbed.

In a word, Judge Burton intimated clearly that transportation must cease. The colonies could never rise to their proper position; they could not obtain those free institutions for which even then they were agitating; in a word, the whole moral aspect of the colony suffered so terribly by the present system, that the time must come when it must be abandoned altogether.

The reader who has followed me through this and the preceding chapter will probably admit that the method of transportation, as it had been administered, was indeed a failure. Looking at the actual tangible results, as they appeared at that date, at an early period of the colonial history, and before years of subsequent prosperity and cleanly life had purged the colony of its one constant infectious bane, they were most unsatisfactory. Hardly any one could be said to have profited in all these years but the convicts for whom transportation had been instituted. But it had been instituted as a punishment, not as a boon; and although we cannot actually quarrel with a system which had the undoubted effect of turning large numbers of criminals into wealthy and therefore, to a certain extent, honest men, we may fairly condemn it on principle. Transportation to the antipodes was about the kindest thing we could do for the criminal class. It was, indeed, removing them to a distance from their old haunts and ways of life, but they went to a land flowing with milk and honey. After the earlier years the vague terrors of that unknown country had disappeared. Hardly a family of thieves but had one or more relatives at the other end of "the pond." Those without relatives had numerous friends and pals who had gone before. Besides which there was this distinct anomaly, that convicts were now sent for their crimes to a land which was held out as a land of promise to the free emigrant. "It not unfrequently happens, that whilst a judge is expatiating on the miseries of exile, at the same time, and perhaps in the same place, some active agent of emigration may be found magnifying the advantages of the new country; lauding the fertility of its soil, and the beauties of its climate; telling of the high wages to be there obtained, the enormous fortunes that have been made; and offering to eager and willing listeners, as a boon and special favour, the means of conveyance to that very place to which the convict in the dock has been sentenced for his crimes."

But all the arguments against transportation are now as clear as noonday. It failed to reform, except in a curiously liberal, unintentional fashion; it was no punishment; it was terribly costly; and as it was carried out was, at least for a time, distinctly injurious to the best interests of the colonies in which it took effect. Archbishop Whateley summed up the situation in forcible language in his "Thoughts on Secondary Punishment."

"In any of the leading requisites of any system of secondary punishment transportation was defective. Thus, it was neither formidable—in other words, the apprehension of it did not operate as much as possible to deter men from crime, and thus prevent the necessity of its actual infliction—nor was it corrective, or at least not corrupting—tending to produce in the criminal himself, if his life be spared, and in others, either a moral improvement, or at least as little as possible of moral debasement. Nor, lastly, was it cheap, so as to make the punishment of the criminal either absolutely profitable to the community, or at least not excessively costly. In all these requisites transportation had been found deficient, but chiefly in the most important, viz. in the power of exercising a salutary terror in offenders."

CHAPTER V THE PROBATION SYSTEM

Reform in system of secondary punishment—Convicts still to be sent to the antipodes but after passing through various stages of improvement—Van Diemen's Land, or Tasmania, chosen as sole future receptacle of convicts who are to pass through probationary treatment—Real imprisonment—Removal to Government gangs—Conditionally at large—Ticket-of-leave—Absolute pardon—Development of Norfolk Island—Its degeneration—Domination of the "Ring"—Port Arthur—Convicts in excess of the resources of the colony—Ominous prospect.

We now arrive at a new stage in the history of penal legislation. The time had come when transportation was to be distinctly discountenanced and its approaching abolition openly discussed. Many concurrent causes contributed to this. Sir William Molesworth's committee, in 1837, had spoken against transportation in the plainest terms. It was condemned because it was unequal yet without terrors to offenders. It was extravagantly expensive, and most corrupting to convict, colonist, and all concerned. Last, but not least, the protest of the colonists themselves, now for the first time formulated and put forward with all the insistence that accompanies the display of a virtuous determination, could not be entirely ignored. Important changes therefore were inevitable, nor could they be much longer delayed.

In point of fact, in the matter of secondary punishments it was a return to the position of fifty years before. At one and the same moment the three latest devised outlets through which the graver criminals had been disposed of were practically closed: the antipodes, by agitation and the strident voice of public opinion; the hulks, by the faultiness of their internal management; and the great reforming penitentiary, by the absolute barrenness of results. If deportation beyond the seas were to come to an end, then the convicts must remain in the mother country. But where? Not in the hulks; that was out of the question. Sir William Molesworth had recommended more penitentiaries, as the Nabob ordered more curricles. But the country grudged another half million: there had been little or no return for that spent years before on Millbank. Then it was suggested that large prisons should be constructed on the principle of Pentonville, for ordinary offenders, while the more desperate characters were to be drafted to Lundy Island and other rocks that might hold them. A third scheme was to construct convict barracks in the neighbourhood of the dockyards, to replace the hulks; but this, which contained in itself the germ of the present British prison system, was far too radical a change to be tolerated at that time or for many years to come. All action being thus impeded and beset with difficulty, the British Government steered a middle course. It was thought that by grafting certain important so-called improvements upon the old system it might be retained. Doubtless, judged by later experience, the plan appears shifty and incomplete; but in theory and as seen at the time it was excellent. It was deduced by sound logical arguments from given premises, and had those premises remained unchanged the system might perhaps have existed longer without collapse. But reasoning on paper is not the same as in real life: one small accident will upset the profoundest calculations. The plan of "probation" which I am about to describe was admirably devised; but it failed because the conditions of the colonies varied, and because small obstacles, that were at the time of conception overlooked or ignored, grew in course of time sufficiently powerful to upset the whole scheme as originally devised.

Beyond question the task was not a light one. The Government did not shirk its duty, but it was fully alive to the difficulties that lay in the way. Speaking some years later, a member of that administration thus deprecates adverse criticism. "We could hardly hope," says Earl Grey, "to succeed at once in devising a system of secondary punishments effectual for its purpose and free from objections, thereby solving a problem which has for many years engaged the attention of legislators and statesmen of most civilised countries, and has hitherto proved most difficult for them all." But they met the question manfully, and this is what they devised.

Transportation was to continue in force, but it was to be governed by certain checks and safeguards which had been altogether absent before, through all the long years that convicts had been sent out to the antipodes. And now the whole stream was to be directed on Van Diemen's Land alone. This Van Diemen's Land, which was thenceforth to be only a colonial prison, had been settled some years later than Botany Bay, by a party under Colonel Collins from the parent settlement. It had struggled for life amid the same vicissitudes of famine and privation as New South Wales, and similarly some years had elapsed before its home products were sufficient for its own support. Up to the year 1821 it was solely a penal settlement for the transportation of convicts from Sydney; but after that date a few free settlers planted themselves in it, and by-and-by ships landed their living cargoes at Hobart Town direct from England, just as they did at Sydney in New South Wales. The system of assignment was practised precisely as in the senior settlement, with this difference, that the discipline was more perfect, and the machine worked with greater ease. Two thirds of the whole number there were thus in assigned service, the balance being employed as in New South Wales in chain-gangs, at penal settlements, or on the roads.

Colonel Arthur, who was for many years governor of the colony, and who was well known as a strenuous supporter of transportation, claimed, and with some show of right, that the management and treatment of convicts had been attended with a greater measure of success in Van Diemen's Land than elsewhere. This may have had some weight with the government; for the existence of a good system of administration was essential to the execution of the new project: but it is probable that Van Diemen's Land was chosen as the sole future receptacle of convicts because as yet it had had no thought of refusing to receive them. New South Wales had rebelled, but Van Diemen's Land was still obedient; and no time was lost in turning its willingness to good account.

Although for years it had been more or less a penal settlement, as now constituted it became essentially a colonial prison. Vast masses of convicts were to be congregated in its chief towns; its out-stations were to be overrun with convicts in various stages of emancipation; free convicts were to be the pioneers and settlers of its back lands: in a word, the whole colony was to be permeated, inundated, swamped with the criminal class. That I am using no figure of speech, and to give some idea of the amount of evil with which the small colony had now to deal, I will mention here that in four years no less than sixteen thousand convicts were sent out to Van Diemen's Land, and that the average annual number of transported convicts in the colony was nearly thirty thousand.

The new method came into force on the 20th May, 1840. It was christened the "Probation" system, because the progressive improvement of the convicts was intended to depend on their progress through certain periods of "probation." Every convict was to be subjected to certain punishments and restrictions peculiar to the stage in which he found himself; but these rigours were to diminish, step by step, till he had passed by many gradations from actual imprisonment to the delights of unshackled, unconditional freedom. The plan of procedure is fully detailed in a despatch addressed by Lord Stanley, on the 15th of November, 1842, to Sir John Franklin, then lieutenant-governor of Van Diemen's Land. All convicts, with certain exceptions, were to be subjected to the new process. By it, as I have said, the convict was compelled to pass through certain stages, five in number; and his progress was to be regulated altogether by his good conduct in each stage. The rules were the same for boys and females, but their stations were, of course, different.

Stated briefly these five stages were: 1. Detention at a purely penal station in a state of real imprisonment; 2. Removal to gangs working in various parts of the colony for government, but still under restraint; 3. The first step towards freedom, in which the convict was granted a pass to be at large under certain conditions, and to seek work for himself; 4. The second step to freedom, when the convict gained his ticket-of-leave, and was free to come and go much as he pleased; 5. Absolute pardon.

Only the worst criminals entered the first stage, and for them (*a*) Norfolk Island and (*b*) Tasman's Peninsula were set apart. These were the colonial convicts, and men who had been sentenced at home to "life," or fifteen years for heinous offences. The term at Norfolk Island was to be not less than two years, and not more than four; but misconduct consigned an offender to an indefinite term within his sentence.

(*a*) First as to Norfolk Island.

Situated in semi-tropical latitudes, richly gifted by nature, picturesque, fertile, of fairly equable climate, this small spot seemed to contain within itself all the elements of a terrestrial paradise. It was finely timbered, chiefly with the graceful tree known as the Norfolk Island pine; limes, lemons, and guavas were indigenous; all manner of fruits—oranges, grapes, figs, loquats, bananas, peaches, pomegranates, pineapples, and melons—grew there in rare profusion. Flowers, wild or cultivated, throve everywhere. On all sides the eye rested on long fields of oats, or barley, or Indian maize. And yet the social condition of the island, as compared with its external aspect, was as the inner diseased core of an apple to its smooth and rosy skin. From the earliest days of the Australian colonies this bountifully gifted island had been made the sink of all the lees and dregs of mankind. Occupied in the first instance on account of its fertile aspect, it was soon afterwards abandoned for no sound or substantial reasons. By and by it was again re-occupied, but then only as a penal settlement. And as such it served New South Wales during all the years that transportation was in full swing. It was a prison, and nothing more; convicts and their keepers were its only population. The former at times varied in numbers: one year there were five hundred, another seven; but their lot and condition was always much the same. The worst wore chains. All worked, but not enough to hurt themselves; and the well-conducted were allowed, as their time dragged along, certain immunities from labour and a modicum of tobacco. Occasionally the gaol-gangs, the most depraved of this gathering of wickedness, broke loose, and attacked their guards with brutal desperation. Numbers were always shot down then and there, and of the balance, when overpowered, a fair proportion were forthwith hanged. Stated broadly, life in Norfolk Island was so bitter to the convict that many for choice sought death.

Thus was Norfolk Island constituted, and such the condition of its residents, when the home government, in working out its new penal scheme, resolved to increase the numbers on the island, by drafting to it the most flagrant offenders from home. We have come by this time to accept it as an axiom in prison affairs, that it is unwise to concentrate in one spot the pith and essence of rascality; preferring rather to subdivide and distribute the most dangerous elements at several points. But the statesmen who were then legislating on penal matters ignored this principle; they forgot that they were about to recruit the old gangs at Norfolk Island by the very men most predisposed to become as bad as those they found there. If the administration had been really anxious to perpetuate the leaven of wickedness already existent in the penal settlement, they could not have devised a plan more likely to attain that result.

Under the new rules Norfolk Island was intended to contain—and thereafter usually did contain—some 2,000 convicts. Of these about two-thirds came from England direct. The rest were sentenced in the colonies. There were three stations: the headquarters settlement or "King's Town," Longridge, and Cascades. The first, situated on the south side of the island and facing the sea, was the most important. Here was the principal landing-place; but a coral reef prevented the near approach of shipping, and the anchorage outside it was insecure. Hence all loading and unloading was done by boats; and this, in itself a tedious operation, was rendered more difficult and dangerous by the heavy surf that rolled perpetually across the bar. But except those that came on the public service no vessels visited the island. There was another landing-place at Cascade station, on the north side of the island, which was used when the state of the bar at King's Town rendered it absolutely impracticable for boats. At King's Town the bulk of the convicts were retained. Here were their barracks, in which some 800 convicts slept; here the lumber-yard, where the same numbers messed; here too the hospitals, and the gaols for the retention of those again about to be tried for fresh offences in the island. The barracks, built of substantial limestone and surrounded by a high wall, stood some eighty yards from the beach; the lumber-yard close at hand was simply a high enclosure, two sides of which were roofed in and provided with rough chairs and tables, the whole area within no more than half an acre. Next to the lumber-yard, through which was the only entrance, stood the slaughter-houses and cooks' houses, all filthy in the extreme. There was no supervision over the issue of rations: meat was sold openly at a penny per pound, and the convicts went to and fro from this and the bakehouse just as they pleased. The gaol was close to the landing-place, and right in front of its chief entrance stood the gallows—so placed that to pass the doorway one came almost in contact with the gruesome engine of death. The hospital accommodation for the whole settlement was here at "King's Town," and it amounted to twenty beds, with a detached convalescent ward, cold and cheerless; and this for a population of 2,000, in an island where epidemic dysentery of a malignant type, especially during the summer, was by no means uncommon. In matters of supply the settlement was equal to its own requirements, except after seasons unusually bad. There was an abundance of water in the neighbouring creeks, and, although this was rendered impure by flowing past gardens and stock-yards, it was easily filtered: and there were springs too in abundance. Stock was raised and grain grown chiefly at Longridge, a mile and a half from headquarters. The soil was fertile but light, and required good management.

The day's work began at the several settlements at daylight, when all the men were roused by a bell. Any, and they were not few, who felt idle and indisposed to work, remained behind in bed. But presently—let us stand and look on—six or seven hundred men have collected in the barrack yard, and are to be seen walking leisurely about, waiting for the chaplain to say morning prayers, or if he failed to appear—and this was not unusual—waiting for the commencement of muster. Should the chaplain show himself, some ten or twenty prisoners go with him to the chapel which is close at hand; the rest remain outside, and no effort is made by the overseers to compel their attendance. The overseers are indeed powerless then, as at other times, and exercise no authority whatever.

Prayers over, muster follows; but the performance is as unlike the strict parade it should be as anything it is possible to conceive. There is no attempt at formation by classes, messes, or wards; no silence, no order. The convicts lounge to and fro, hands in pockets, and talking to one another while their names are read out by convict clerks from the superintendent's office—the assistant superintendent, whose duty this would be, being generally unable to read or write. As each convict hears his name he answers or not, as it suits him, and then saunters over to join the working gang for which he has been detailed. As soon as the muster is concluded the men disperse, leaving the yard in groups or one by one, and proceed to breakfast. Here the whole force breakfast on hominy—or paste made from maize meal—seated under cover or in the open areas, preserving no appearance of order, talking and laughing just as they please among themselves. Breakfast over, some go to work, but a great many do not. They have their bread to bake; and this each man does for himself, spending half the day in sifting meal, kneading dough, and loitering leisurely to the bakehouse and back. The only men told off to regular labour are the two gangs who work the crank-mill, and the labour there was so regulated that half usually were idle half the day; while those at work were riotous and disorderly, shrieking, yelling, hooting and assailing every passer-by, whether subordinate official, magistrate, or the commandant himself, with the vilest personal abuse. The great mass of the convicts were engaged in quarrying or in agricultural pursuits. They were superintended by convict sub-overseers, and not by free persons; and the work done was naturally not large, more particularly as these convict overseers went in daily terror of their lives. Indeed, at the time of which I am writing—after the introduction of "probation," that is to say, and probably before it too—there was practically little or no discipline whatever maintained among the convicts. But for the bayonets and bullets of the military guard by which they were more or less awed—though even against them they rose at times, to their own disadvantage—they would have become the real masters of the island; and if they were thus restrained by fear from overt rebellion, they did not hesitate to display as much sullen disobedience and active insubordination as they dared without bringing on themselves retaliatory and coercive measures.

Flagrant outrages, like the seizure of boats which carried stores, were not uncommon, on which occasions the men of the military escort were usually thrown overboard. But perhaps the following occurrence, which took place before the eyes of Mr. R. P. Stewart, a special commissioner sent from Hobart Town, will prove most forcibly the anarchy that prevailed. I cannot do better than use his own words.

"On the first of my morning visits to the lumber-yard," says he, "accompanied by the superintendent of English convicts, I observed, on our entry, a man very deliberately smoking, standing among a crowd round the fire, inside the cook-house." An officer advanced to make the man give up his pipe; but he was received with a look of the most ineffable disdain, and the smoker, getting up with his hands in his pockets, moved to a part of the mess known as the "Ring," where all the worst characters collected. On this an order was issued to have the man taken to gaol; but no one stepped forward to execute it, until at length the acting chief constable, "who had been standing in the rear, advanced with admirable coolness and determination to the spot. The whole yard was now like a disturbed hive, and the superintendent expressed his conviction that there would be a riot, as the men would never suffer the culprit to be taken into custody. However, after a short time had elapsed, the culprit was seen emerging from the dense crowd by which he had been surrounded, with hands in pocket, attended by, rather than in custody of, the chief constable of the island. He (the convict) deliberately advanced to the superintendent, who was standing by my side, and in the most insolent manner said, 'What have you ordered me to gaol for?' The superintendent very coolly expostulated with him and advised him to go quietly, when he deliberately struck him two blows in the face, and using some very opprobrious expressions, fiercely rushed upon and nearly threw him upon the ground." He was seized by a constable, who asked if he should shoot him. But both convict and constable were borne away to another part of the shed by a dense crowd. The men got out their knives, and matters looked desperate, when the acting chief constable again went forward and persuaded the offender to give himself up. Had it not been for the presence of Mr. Stewart, an officer accredited from His Excellency the governor of Van Diemen's Land, a very serious disturbance might have been expected. As it was, the most foul and abusive language was used by the convicts to all the officials present.

This "Ring" which has just been mentioned was in itself a power on the island. All the worst men were leagued together in it, and exercised a species of terrorism over the rest. This was especially noticeable on the arrival and debarkation of a batch of new convicts from England, when every effort for their protection made by the proper authorities proved always ineffectual. If the new hands were lodged under lock and key, the men of the Ring contrived generally to break into the ward and rifle them of all they possessed. If they were marched under an escort of constables to bathe, the old stagers attacked them en route, or while they were in the water plundered them of their clothes. Thus banded together and utterly reckless, the more depraved exercised a power almost absolute over their fellows, so that of these even the well disposed were compelled to submit, in mortal terror of the deadly threats of this vicious, tyrannical confederacy. A convict whose conduct was good could not be protected from violence if there was even a suspicion, with or without reason, that he had borne witness against any member of the Ring, or was otherwise distasteful to it. Speaking in general terms of Norfolk Island, Mr. Stewart states that he was satisfied, from his inquiry, that a confirmed insubordinate spirit existed among the convicts, "constantly exhibiting itself in threats of personal violence towards subordinate officers, towards the constabulary if they resolutely do their duty, and towards their fellow-prisoners if they should be suspected of giving information or assistance to their officers; which threats are rendered more serious and alarming from the general practice of carrying knives, and from their having been fulfilled in instances of stabbing, of assaulting by beating to a cruel, nearly mortal extent, and of personal injury in attempted disfiguration by biting off the nose, and in other overt acts of such a character as to produce a most serious effect in deterring all holding subordinate authority from the vigorous and prompt performance of their duty."

I have lingered thus long over Norfolk Island because it was the starting-point and centre of the new scheme of penal legislation. In actual truth the picture I have drawn is painted with colours far less sombre than the subject deserves. I have shown how, beyond the absolute isolation and exile, the punishment was not severe, the work light, food plentiful, and discipline a mere farce. I have shown how the most criminal were banded together to defy authority and exercise a species of awful tyranny over the timid and weak; I have shown how these malefactors who were supposed to be expiating their crimes swaggered about, armed, and with knives in their hands, insulting their keepers with vile abuse, lording it over their weaker fellows, using violence whenever the spirit moved them to murder a constable, beat a comrade to death, or make a mouthful of his nose. I have said that when matters went too far firearms and the halter were called into play, and for a time worked a certain cure; but from this, the relapse was worse than the original disease. On other points I have not touched, because I do not care to sully my pages with reference to other atrocities perpetrated in that loathsome den—atrocities the existence of which was not and never could be denied, and for which those who inaugurated the system can hardly be held blameless. Regarding these, it must suffice that I refer to them thus vaguely and pass on.

(b) But Norfolk Island was not the only penal settlement: that at Port Arthur, on Tasman's Peninsula, was also included by the new scheme as one of the first-stage depots. Being within easy reach of Hobart Town, and not like Norfolk Island, hundreds of miles away, Port Arthur was under the more searching supervision of the supreme authority. The peninsula was separated from the mainland by a narrow isthmus, across which, as I have said, sentries and fierce dogs forever kept watch and ward, and escape thence was next to impossible. At the southern extreme of the peninsula lay Port Arthur, having an excellent harbour, of difficult entrance but wide within, and with plenty of deep water. To Port Arthur were sent all convicts in the classes little less criminal than those of Norfolk Island, their number being some 1,200, their work chiefly what is called in the Western Hemisphere "lumbering," or procuring wood for the sawyers and shipbuilders, who were also convicts. Every now and then a ship of decent tonnage was launched, and much coal and timber were also exported. There was a trade-wheel and a corn-mill, and the settlement was to a certain extent self-supporting. The convicts were lodged in hut barracks, in association with each other, but not in great numbers. On the whole, the establishment at Port Arthur was as well managed and the discipline as good as could be expected with such insufficient prison buildings. The conduct of the convicts was generally good, and punishments few and far between.

And now for the second stage, and the system of "Probation."

Norfolk Island and Port Arthur, the purely penal settlements, I have described. At one or other of them, subject to such restraints as they found there, the nature of which I have already detailed, the convict of the worst class remained till he earned by good conduct his removal to the second stage, or that of the probation gang. To this second stage those convicts whose crimes were less serious had been inducted on first arrival from England. They might therefore be supposed to avoid a certain amount of contamination. But if they escaped the island, they could not escape from those who had been at it; and around these seemingly purified spirits hung something of the reeking atmosphere of the foul den through which they had passed. In this way the contagion spread; for wherever there were convicts there were those who had been at Norfolk Island, and their influence, if not the most dominant, was always more or less felt. But even without the presence of this pernicious virus wherewith the whole mass might be permeated, the probation gangs as constituted were bad enough to originate wickedness of their own. Having, therefore, errors inherent, without counting the super-added vice that came from the first-stage men, they served admirably to perpetuate the grand mistake of the whole new scheme. Soon after the development of this new order of things there grew to be sixteen of these stations. Four of them were on Tasman's Peninsula, and of these, one was for invalids, and three solely for those who had misconducted themselves in other gangs. The men worked in coal mines, or raised agricultural produce. Then there were five stations on the coast, in the neighbourhood of D'Entrecasteaux Channel, placed where the land was heavily timbered, all of which, when cleared, was to be devoted to crops; others, also, more inland, and three at which the convicts laboured exclusively at making and repairing roads. In principle, then, probation stations were intended to give convicts, from the first, a certain habit of industry and subordination, and if they had come from the penal settlements, to continue the process. The probation stations were abundantly furnished with religious instructors, and a minute system of notation was introduced to record exactly the conduct of the prisoners from day to day. It was according to his attitude while thus in probation that the next step in the relaxation of his condition was to be regulated. No doubt in many places the work accomplished by these probation parties was not inconsiderable. Naturally the first aim was that they should raise crops enough to suffice for their own support; but after that, their labour was directed into many channels that brought direct advantage to the colony. So far, too, as there were means available, the administration was conducted intelligently. But the entire number poured into Van Diemen's Land was so far in excess of the resources of the colony that adequate lodgment could not be provided. From this, and the difficulty of obtaining respectable supervisors in anything like due proportion, there resulted such a state of things that in course of time the probation gangs were not less a reproach than the penal settlements.

The third stage was reached as soon as the convict had given, as it were, an earnest of his improvement. The comptroller-general of convicts was constituted the judge, and it rested with that functionary whether the convict, after a certain period, should receive the boon of a "probation pass." The holder of this was privileged to hire himself out: to enter private service, and make his own terms with his future master. But there were certain distinctions among pass-holders. Those in the lowest class had to ask the governor's sanction to the employment they chose; they had to be contented with half their wages, while the other half was paid into a savings bank. Other classes could engage themselves without sanction, and got certain larger proportions—half, two-thirds, or in the last class, all their wages. These passes were liable to forfeiture for misconduct, and the holder was then sent back to the gangs. The chief distinction between these pass-holders and the men on ticket-of-leave, to whom I shall come directly, was, that the latter were free to roam where they pleased within certain districts, while the pass-holders were retained at hiring depots till they had found employment for themselves; and even when in service they were under the direct control of a local magistrate, by whom they were inspected every month. These hiring depots were at the chief towns—Hobart Town, Launceston, and elsewhere. The numbers thus on pass came to be considerable; and, later on, when work was slack and labour scarce, they grew to be the most serious difficulty which colonial legislators were called upon to face.

The last two stages, of ticket-of-leave and pardon, were not peculiar to the new system, and differed in no respect to the same named condition of existence under other rules, except that both were to be gained less easily now, and in no case as a matter of right.

I have given now an outline of the system introduced by Lord Stanley's despatch of 1842, and, advancing a year or two where it was necessary, have shown how it was carried out. Extraordinary and deplorable results followed and will be duly set forth in a future chapter.

CHAPTER VI CONVICT SHIPS

Conveyance of convicts beyond seas—Early abuses—Neglect and starvation on board—Large mortality—Question of command—Weak discipline maintained—Constant dread of outbreak—Military guard—Notable conspiracies—Barrington's conduct—Fears of mutiny groundless—Epidemic of scurvy on board the *Waterloo*—Loss of the *Waterloo*—*Amphitrite* cast away at Boulogne—Arrangements for embarking convicts—Millbank stairs—Reforms introduced—Horrors of convict ships beyond description—Dr. Browning—His labours and influence over his charges.

No account of deportation beyond the seas would be complete without some reference to the passage out to the antipodes, which naturally was an integral part of the whole scheme. From first to last many hundreds of ships were employed on this service. Those that composed the "first fleet" under Captain Phillip, R. N., in 1788, head the list; last of all comes the steamer *London*, which went to Gibraltar in November, 1871. The *London* was the last prison ship that has left our shores. In the long interval between these dates the conditions under which deportation was carried out have varied not a little. Abuses in the earliest days were many and flagrant. As time passed there came all that was possible in the way of reform, and those charged with the execution of the system did their utmost to reduce the evils inseparable from it. But even to the last they were hardly obviated altogether; and this difficulty of carrying out under proper restrictions the removal of convicts by sea-passage to a distant land, is one—and by no means the weakest—of the many arguments against transportation.

At the close of the eighteenth century, and during the early years of the nineteenth, when the whole system was still somewhat new and untried, the arrangements were about as bad as it was possible for them to be. Great horrors were perpetrated in one particular convoy: the neglect and starvation produced epidemic sickness and terrible mortality. These shameful proceedings were due entirely to the rapacity and dishonesty of the ship-captains, who sought to increase their profits by improper means. Happily when their misconduct was brought to light, repetition was prevented by new and salutary regulations. The ships were no longer victualled by the contractors, but by the commissioners of the navy, and certain checks and safeguards were introduced to insure the issue to every man of his proper allowance. Nevertheless, the mortality continued at times to be disproportionately large. Especially was this the case in the ships *General Hewitt*, *Surrey*, and *Three Bees*; and, aroused thereby to the necessity of further reform, Governor Macquarie instituted at Sydney, in 1814, a full inquiry into the conduct of convict ships in general. Great alterations were recommended by Dr. Redfern, at that time assistant surgeon of the colony. His suggestions embraced principally the points on which he was specially competent to speak—the necessity, that is to say, for the proper issue of clothing, sufficient diet and air space, with proper medical assistance if required. Most of his recommendations were adopted, and they were all amply justified by the diminished mortality in subsequent voyages. Previous to this period the owners usually provided a surgeon, who was paid by them, receiving only a reward from government, after the completion of his duty; but this reward was dependent on the production by him of a certificate from the governor of New South Wales, to the effect that the latter was perfectly satisfied. The surgeon's letter of service stated that, on the production of this certificate, he would be recompensed for his "assiduity and humanity by a present at the discretion of His Majesty's Secretary of State. On the other hand, any neglect of essential duties will not fail to be properly noticed."

Full instructions were issued for the guidance of the surgeon. He was to inspect the "people"—this term seems to have been adopted from the earliest times to describe the convict passengers—daily; the sick twice a day, those in health once. The former he was to treat according to his judgment; the latter were to be examined closely for signs of fever, flux, or scurvy, in order that "early and effectual means may be taken to stop the progress of these diseases." He was moreover to keep a diary for the entry of everything connected with the sick, noting also the "daily number of convicts admitted upon deck, the times when the decks were scraped, the ship fumigated, the berths cleaned and ventilated, and all other circumstances which may, immediately or remotely, affect the health of the crew or convicts." How closely he performed his duties may be judged by the fact that Mr. Commissioner Bigge advances as one reason for keeping the hospital in the fore part of the ship, that "any arrangement by which the personal inspection of the surgeons is frequently directed to the whole of the prison (which must be the case if they have to traverse it on their visits to the hospital), ought not to be exchanged for another and more commodious position of that apartment, unless the advantages of such a change are clear and decisive." This does not look as if these surgeons were over zealous, at least in the duty of frequently visiting and inspecting the prison decks.

Similarly, precise rules governed the conduct of the master of the ship. He also was promised a reward if his conduct gave satisfaction. He was especially desired to see to the preservation of health, by keeping his ship constantly sweet and clean, and by taking on board before departure everything necessary for the purpose. The master was especially charged with the care of provisions, and in this respect his conduct was to be closely watched. The fear was not so much lest the convicts should receive short allowance, although this happened too, in spite of all precautions, but that there should be a substitution of inferior stores for those of government, which were always supposed to be good of their kind. The former fraud was to some extent guarded against, chiefly by publishing plainly, in several parts of the prison, the scale of diet to which every convict was entitled; but even this was sometimes upset by the captain giving money compensation at the end of the voyage for food not issued. Another precaution lay in making every man of each convict "mess" attend in rotation to receive the rations, instead of having one standing delegate for the whole voyage as heretofore. It was found that imposition and corruption were less frequently tried with many than with few. As to the other kind of dishonesty, it was provided for by requiring the surgeon's attendance at the opening of each new cask of provision—a sufficient check, no doubt, so long as the interests of captain and surgeon were not identical. It was just possible, however, that they might play into each other's hands.

But one of the wisest steps taken after 1814, was when the government itself appointed the medical officers, giving the preference, as far as possible, to surgeons of the Royal Navy. On this point Bigge says, "A great improvement has undoubtedly arisen in the transportation of convicts from the appointment of naval surgeons to the superintendence of the ships taken up for this service. Much attention has been paid by them to the instructions of the navy board, that enjoin an attention to the performance of religious duties; and their efforts in preserving health have been no less conspicuous and successful." There was every reason to expect that the government would be better served by an officer of its own, than by some one taken indiscriminately from outside. But equally probable was it that there would be a conflict of authority between the master, who had been hitherto practically supreme, and the new style of official, who might be said to possess, to some extent, the confidence of the crown. This came to pass; and the difficulty was not smoothed away by the tenor of the early acts regulating transportation in which had been incorporated the provisions of the 4 Geo. I, cap. II, whereby a property in the services of the convict was vested (or assigned) to the persons who contracted to transport them.

The master of the ship, as representing the contractors, had this property with all its responsibilities; but he was bound also to obey all orders from the commissioners of the navy and attend all requisitions from the surgeon-superintendent. This apparent contradiction led to frequent altercations between these two modern Kings of Brentford. Where one looked only to the preservation of health, the other thought chiefly of safe custody. If the doctor wished to fumigate the prison, or send the "people" all on deck, the captain demurred, and talked of the danger he ran of losing his ship and his cargo, too, by one and the same blow. Being thus personally concerned in the security of all they had on board, the masters of convict ships for a long time maintained that they must be the fittest persons to hold the supreme power. On the other hand, many of the higher authorities leaned toward entrusting the real command to the surgeon. This, which was clearly the proper decision, did in time become the rule. The reasons for it yearly became more apparent. In the first place, the naval surgeon, as a commissioned officer, was more under the control of the crown; besides which, by degrees these surgeon-superintendents could fairly claim that they had gained experience, and had proved their aptitude for the service in which they were employed. As ship after ship was chartered the captains came and went. There was no certainty that the same vessel with the same master would be taken up twice over for the conveyance of convicts. But the surgeons remained, and sailed voyage after voyage to the penal colonies. Ere long, the power which had been at first contested rested altogether in their hands.

All contemporary authorities give but a sorry account of the condition of the convicts during the passage. Even when everything possible had been done to reduce the death-rate, by insuring a sufficient supply of food and proper medical attendance, the plain fact remained that here were a couple of hundred felons (or more) boxed up together for months, with no other employment or object in life than that of contaminating one another. As a rule all of the convict passengers remained idle throughout the voyage. A few might assist in the navigation of the ship so far as was possible without going aloft. Others who were mechanics found it to their interest to make themselves useful in their particular trades, gaining in return greater freedom as to coming up on deck, and perhaps some additional articles of food. "But the greater proportion of the convicts," says Bigge, "are sunk in indolence, to which the ordinary duties of washing and cleansing the prisons, though highly salutary in themselves and performed with great regularity, afford but slight interruption."

They spent their time in gambling, quarrelling, and thieving from one another. In these relaxations the crew generally joined, as it was impossible to prevent intercommunication between convicts and sailors. The latter were not always immaculate, and were not seldom charged with purloining the private property of the prisoners, which had been provided by friends when leaving England. The medium for gambling was chiefly the wine and lime juice issued as part of the daily rations. If the convicts had money—which was unusual, except in small quantities—then they played for cash, but this was prevented by taking all money from them, as far as possible, on embarkation, to be kept for them till the voyage was at an end. The other method of speculation was also checked to some extent by "strictly observing that the allowance of wine and lime juice is taken by every convict in the presence of an officer at the time of distribution." Another plan was to deprive the offenders of their allowance, but to compel them to attend at the "grog-tub," and administer that which they had thus forfeited to some other prisoner who had behaved well.

The only discipline enforced on board was just so much as was necessary to insure a moderate amount of repression. For this purpose the people were all for a time in irons; for the same reason, only certain fixed proportions of the whole number were allowed upon deck at one time. As a final bulwark behind all, should an ultimate appeal to the strong arm be at any time needed, stood the military guard. Every ship carried a detachment of soldiers: recruits sometimes, going out as drafts to join their regiments in Australia; at others, part of a battalion, which embarked in instalments on ship after ship, ending, according to one writer, with the commanding officer and the band. The guard, or the portion of it actually on duty, always carried loaded firearms; from it came sentries forever on the watch, some at the doors of the prisons, others upon the poop. As a general rule, ships with poops were preferred for convict ships, because the soldiers stationed thereon were sufficiently elevated above the deck to be able to control the movements of the convicts at exercise below, though altogether separated from them.

The dread of some outbreak among the "people," or convicts, seems to have been an ever present sensation with those in authority on board these ships. Nor was the alarm confined to those connected with the ship itself. Whenever a strange sail, in those days of profound peace, appeared above the horizon, she was set down always as a convict ship seized by its felon passengers, who were supposed to have turned pirates and to have hoisted the black flag to range the high seas in search of plunder. I suppose there was not one among the hundred ships that left the Nore or the Mother Bank, through the long years that transportation lasted, in which rumours of conspiracy did not prevail at some time or other during the passage. Yet nine times out of ten these fears were absolutely groundless. Outbreaks did occur, of course; but few of them were serious in nature, and nearly all were forestalled by the timely perfidy of one of the conspirators. Colonel Breton, in his evidence before the parliamentary committee of 1837, said that he had heard of one ship with female convicts which had been captured by the crew and carried into Rio. But I can find no corroboration of this statement elsewhere. The same authority talks vaguely of another plot in his own ship, which came to nothing, because another and a more desperate character turned informer. Convict ships with females on board were as a rule more easily managed than those with males. But the following extract from a letter from the matron on board the convict ship *Elizabeth and Henry*, in 1848, relates a curious incident:—

"*Off Cape of Good Hope (April 30th)*.—We were likely to have a mutiny on board a few weeks since. The [female] prisoners laid a plan for strangling the doctor, but providentially it was made known by M. A. Stewart, a convict, just before it was executed. McNalty and Brennan were the ringleaders in the affair. When it was known, the officers of the ship went down in the prison with firearms. Fancy the scene! The doctor has now promised to forgive them if they conduct themselves well the rest of the voyage."

More serious was the conspiracy which was discovered in a ship of which Doctor Galloway, R. N., was the surgeon-superintendent. This was brought to light just after the ship had left Plymouth Sound—as a general rule all such attempts are made in the early part of a voyage—and it was discovered by a sentinel who overheard a fragment of a conversation by the hatchway during the morning watch. The plot was cleverly laid. The convicts had observed that the old guard discharged their firelocks always at sunrise, and that the new guard did not reload till eleven o'clock. They planned therefore to mutiny in the early morning, just after the guard had fired, resolving to seize these weapons, and then overpower the captain, the rest of the soldiers, and the crew. The total strength of the military detachment was forty, and the convicts were two hundred and fifty. The plotters of this outbreak were promptly punished on proof of their guilt, twelve of them being carried in double irons for seven or eight weeks.

In one of the earliest ships the opposing parties actually came to blows—so says one Barrington, at least, who went as a convict in 1790 to Botany Bay. The memoirs of this man (a very different person from Sir Jonah Barrington) were widely successful, and soon ran through several editions. His career of crime was more than curious. His London hunting-grounds were royal levées, court balls, Ranelagh, and the opera-house. At the palace he found it easy in the crush to cut the diamonds out of orders and stars. At the opera he picked Prince Orloff's pocket of a snuff-box worth £30,000, but being collared by the owner he restored the booty. He was eventually transported for stealing a gold watch at Enfield races from Mr. H. H. Townshend. According to Barrington's account two Americans among the people persuaded the others to conspire to seize the ship. They declared that the capture effected, it would be easy to carry the prize into some American port, where all would receive a hearty welcome. Not only would all obtain their liberty as a matter of course, but Congress would give them also a tract of land, and a share of the money accruing from the sale of the ship and her cargo.

The plan of action was to seize the arm-chest while the officers were at dinner. This was kept upon the quarter-deck, under the charge of sentries. The latter were to be engaged in conversation till the supreme moment arrived, and then, at a signal given, seized. This was to be followed by a general rush on deck of all the convicts from below. Barrington relates that he was standing with the man at the wheel when the mutiny actually broke out. Hearing a scuffle upon the main deck, he was on the point of going forward, when he was stopped by one of the Americans, who made a stroke at his head with a sword taken from a sentry. "Another snapped at me a pistol. I had a handspike, and felled the first to the ground." Meanwhile the man at the wheel ran down and gave the alarm. The captain was below, seeing to the stowage of some wine; but Barrington held the mutineers at bay, at the head of the companion ladder, till the captain came up with a blunderbuss in his hand and fired. This dispersed the enemy, and they thereupon retired. An immediate example was made of the ringleaders in this affair. Two were forthwith hanged at the yard-arm, and a number flogged. To Barrington, the captain and his officers were profuse in thanks, and at the end of the voyage they made him a substantial present. Told in Mr. Barrington's own words, the story of this mutiny tends rather to his own glorification. It is just possible that he may have exaggerated some of the details—his own valiant deeds with the rest. This trusty convict was received into high favour on landing in New South Wales and after holding several subordinate appointments became at length a police officer and gained high rank.

But as a rule the efforts made by the convicts to rise against their rulers on shipboard were futile in the extreme. Even Mr. Commissioner Bigge, in 1822, laughs at all notion of the convicts combining to capture the ships. He is commenting on the different practice of different doctors and captains, as to allowing the people upon deck and removing their irons. Some, he says, who are inexperienced and timid, dread the assemblage of even half on the upper deck, and they would not for worlds remove the irons till the voyage is half over. Others do not care if all the people come up together, and they take off all irons before the ship is out of the Channel. But he considers free access to the deck so important in preserving discipline, as well as health, during the voyage, that "no unwarrantable distrust of the convicts" ought to interfere with it, and "no apprehension of any combined attempt to obtain possession of the ship." He thus continues:—

"The fear of combinations among the convicts to take the ship is proved by experience of later years to be groundless; and it may be safely affirmed, that if the instructions of the navy board are carried into due effect by the surgeon-superintendent and the master, and if the convicts obtain the full allowance of provisions made to them by government, as well as reasonable access to the deck, they possess neither fidelity to each other, nor courage sufficient to make any simultaneous effort that may not be disconcerted by timely information, and punished before an act of aggression is committed. A short acquaintance with the characters of the convicts, promises of recommendation to the governor on their arrival in New South Wales, and an ordinary degree of skill in the business of preventive police, will at all times afford means of obtaining information."

The passage out of all these convict ships was upon the whole exceedingly prosperous. The voyage could be performed with perfect safety. Mr. Bigge says that up to his time no ships had arrived disabled; more than this, no disasters had occurred to any in Bass Straits, where serious mishaps so frequently happened. The chief and only difficulty really was the tendency to delay upon the road. There was a great temptation to both master and surgeon to call at Rio. All sorts of excuses were made to compass this— that the ship was running short of water, for instance, or that the passengers absolutely required a change of diet. Sugar was to be bought at Rio, and tobacco, and with a freight of these the officials could make a profitable speculation on reaching Sydney. For the doctor the temptation was especially strong, because he was for years allowed to land his goods at New South Wales duty-free. But if the superiors thus benefited themselves, it was at the cost of the discipline of the convicts, such as it was. The ship was for the time neglected utterly; the captain was busy and so was the doctor with their commercial enterprises. The convicts, for security's sake, were relegated to irons; but they found means to obtain spirits from shore, and wholesale intoxication and demoralisation naturally followed. In view of all this the masters of convict ships were ordered to make the run outwards direct. The requisite supplies might be calculated with care in advance, so as to preclude the chance of any scarcity before the end of the voyage. But if it so happened that to touch at some port or other was imperative, then the Cape of Good Hope was to be invariably chosen instead of Rio.

These orders to bear up for the Cape in case of necessity were clearly right and proper, but in one case they were attended with very serious consequences. I allude to the loss of the *Waterloo* convict ship in Table Bay, in September, 1842. In this case scurvy had appeared on board, and therefore the surgeon-superintendent gave the master a written order to change his course. It was necessary to touch at the Cape to obtain supplies of vegetables and fresh meat. To Table Bay they came in due course, and there remained—ignorant, seemingly, of the danger they ran, of which they would have been duly warned had the naval authorities been aware of their arrival. But the surgeon-superintendent failed to report it; and "in this omission," says Vice-Admiral Sir E. King when animadverting upon the whole occurrence, "he has only followed the common and very reprehensible neglect of duty in this respect of surgeon-superintendents of convict ships." Ill-luck followed the *Waterloo*. The master went on shore and left his ship to the care of his chief mate, a young and inexperienced seaman, who showed himself when the moment of emergency came either utterly incompetent or culpably negligent—probably both. One of those sudden gales which frequently ravage Table Bay rose without warning, and the *Waterloo* went straight on the rocks. Nothing was done to save her. The masts were not cut away, and everybody on board seemed helpless. Another ship, the transport *Abercrombie Robinson*, which was lying in Table Bay at the time, was also driven ashore; but her people were rescued, and she did not become an entire wreck. But the moment the *Waterloo* struck she broke up, and went to pieces. Terrible loss of life followed: 188 out of a total of 302 on board were drowned, and but for the merest chance not a soul among the convict passengers would have reached the land alive. The prisoners had been at first set free, but they were then ordered below again by the surgeon-superintendent, who feared they would rush violently into the surf boats coming to the rescue, and so swamp them. The poor creatures went below—obediently enough, and then followed one of those fatal but inexplicable mistakes which might have led to the most terrible consequences. The doctor as a matter of precaution had ordered the prisons to be bolted down, but the bolts in the hatches could have been easily at any moment withdrawn. However, the officious corporal in command of the military guard *proprio motu* affixed a padlock to the bolt to make it secure, and forgot to take it off again. The excuse made for him was that he was "under the influence of the panic incident to the unexpected and almost instantaneous demolition of the ship." Thus several hundred men were in momentary danger of being drowned like rats in a hole. "Most providentially," says the report from which I quote, "the awful consequences of the unaccountable conduct of the corporal were averted by one of the prisoners striking off the padlock with a hammer that had accidentally been left in the prison early that morning, it having been used to remove the irons from the only prisoners who wore them for some offence." So the convicts reached the deck in time to avail themselves of such means of escape as offered. But these were few. Had the masts been cut down, when the long boat was lowered, they might have formed a temporary bridge over which the people might have passed in comparative safety to the surf boats. As it was, nearly two-thirds of them were drowned.

This catastrophe attracted great attention at the time. At Cape Town the sudden and apparently unaccountable destruction of the ship led to great excitement in the public mind. A very searching inquiry was therefore set on foot. The *débris* of the wreck having been carefully examined by Captain Sir John Marshall, R. N., he reported unhesitatingly that the *Waterloo* must have been unseaworthy when she left England. "General decay and rottenness of the timbers appeared in every step we took." She had been repeatedly repaired at considerable outlay, but she had run so long that she was quite beyond cure.

As a further explanation of the disaster the mate and crew were charged with being drunk at the time the ship struck. But the only evidence in support of this was an intercepted letter of one of the convicts who had been saved. He asserted that the chief mate could not keep his legs; that in trying to drive in a nail he staggered and fell. The rolling of the vessel was deemed a more than sufficient explanation of this. Another charge was made against one of the seamen who swam back to the ship after he had once actually reached the shore. No man in his sober senses, urged the convict witness, would have risked his life in this way; whereas it was clearly proved that no man otherwise than sober could possibly have battled successfully with the surf.

It is but fair to add that the unseaworthy condition of the *Waterloo* was distinctly denied at Lloyd's. They certified that at the time of sailing she was "in an efficient state of repair and equipment, and fully competent for the safe performance of any voyage to any part of the world." And as the credit of the transport office had been more or less impugned, a return was about this time called for by the House, of the number of convict-ships which had foundered at sea, or not been heard of, between 1816 and 1842. It was satisfactorily shown that in this way not one single ship had been lost through all those years.

But there had been other shipwrecks, and among these none with more fatal results than that of the *Amphitrite*, which went ashore at Boulogne, in September, 1833. The story of this mishap is an instructive homily in more ways than one. The ship was proceeding gaily down channel, with a freight of one hundred and eight female convicts, when she was met by a violent and unexpected gale, accompanied by a very heavy sea. She was on a lee shore. The conduct of the master in presence of danger is described as seamanlike, judicious, and decisive. Seeing no help for it, and that he could not save his vessel from the land, he said openly to the mate that he must look for the best berth and run her straight on shore. They ran her up as high as possible, hoping the tide as it rose would drive her higher. Then with as much complacency as if they were safely lodged in a secure harbour, the crew went below, had supper, and turned in. Before daybreak the ship was smashed to atoms and only three lives were saved. The ship's fate was indeed sealed from the moment she went ashore. Nothing possibly could have saved her, and it was a matter of surprise to all who witnessed the catastrophe that she was not deserted while there was yet time. "All might have been saved, but for the deplorable error in judgment on the part of the crew."

More than this, the lives of the female convicts, at least, might have been preserved but for the strange obstinacy of the surgeon's wife. According to the evidence of one of the survivors, the doctor ordered the long boat to be lowered soon after the ship struck. He was not in the least afraid of losing his prisoners, and meant to put them all forthwith on shore. Here, however, his wife interposed. She would not go ashore in the boat. Nothing would induce her to sit in the same boat with the convicts. "Her pride," says the narrator, "revolted at the idea." Whether her husband expostulated does not appear; in the end he gave way. No boat should leave the ship that night. Next morning it was too late. Complete destruction, as I have said, followed the rising of the tide.

Upon the introduction of the new régime by the Act of 1843, embarkation of drafts for Australia took place every week or two from the stone steps on the river bank, opposite the main entrance of Millbank prison. As the dawn broke the convicts filed silently across the deserted roadway, and aboard the tug that was to convey them to the Nore. Only the night previous were they made aware that the hour of their departure had arrived. Then had followed such necessary preparations as a close medical inspection, to guard against the propagation of infectious disease; shaving, bathing, and the issue of the necessary clothing and kit bags. Every convict was furnished with a new suit, which was to last him all the voyage; but they carried a second suit in their bags, with underclothing, and, in some cases, an outfit to serve on landing at their journey's end. Substantial shoes and gray guernsey nightcaps completed their attire.

The next morning the whole draft was wakened about three o'clock, and breakfasted. They were then marched to the reception ward, where their names were called over by the chief warder. Next came the "shackling," or chaining them together in gangs of ten men upon one chain, the chain passing through a bracelet on each man's arm. The same plan is pursued to this day in ordinary removals from prison to prison, except that a D lock is now introduced between every two prisoners. This practically handcuffs the men together two and two. Under the old system, if one link in the chain was cut, the whole ten were free; now, when a link goes five *couples* only are set loose. As soon as these precautions were completed, the side door of the reception ward was opened, and the prisoners passed on to the outer gate, and so to the river side.

If the embarkation was to be at low tide, old Collins, a well-known bargee, who had permission to make his boats fast opposite the Millbank steps, had brought them some hours before and run them aground so as to form a passage or gangway to the steam-tug. This Collins was a well-known character in his time and later served as the model for Rogue Riderhood in "Our Mutual Friend." His spare hours were devoted to gathering up the bodies of people drowned in the Thames. It was said that he had secured in this way no fewer than two hundred corpses. The parish authorities paid him at the rate of ten shillings per head. It was his invariable custom, so he assured the coroner, to wash the face of every corpse he picked up and kiss it. But he did other jobs, such as dredging for sand, which he sold to the builders, and anything else that he might pick up. It was all fish that came to his net. On one occasion he found a bag full of sovereigns, upon which, so the story runs, both he and his family lived gloriously till the money was all gone. This piece of luck proved fatal to his wife. Returning from one of her drinking bouts to their home on board a barge—for Collins occupied the oldest of his boats, roofed in—Mrs. Collins slipped off the plank into the Thames, and was picked up by her husband next day. He had lived all his life in this barge, rearing there a large family, most of whom, I believe, turned out ill. His daughters were, however, known as the best oarswomen on the river. Poor old Collins himself came to a bad end. He was caught in his old age, in the act of stealing coals from a neighbouring barge, and for this he was sentenced to six months' imprisonment. When he came out his barges were sold, and the place knew him no more. But for many years he actively assisted in all embarkations from Millbank stairs.

Of course there was a large staff of officials who were really responsible. In charge of all generally went the deputy-governor, and under him were sometimes as many as thirty warders. Their duties were principally to insure safe custody, and to enforce silence and soberness of demeanour on the passage down stream. Occasionally the tug halted at Woolwich, to take in more passengers from the hulks; more often it made the run direct to Gravesend or the Nore. Here, with blue peter flying and anchor atrip, was the prison ship waiting for its living cargo. The surgeon-superintendent was on board, ready to sign receipts for the bodies of all committed to his charge; the convicts climbed the sides, were unshackled, told off to messes, and sent below. Before mid-day the ship had got under weigh, and had taken her place among the rest of the outward bound.

The interior fittings of all the old convict ships varied little. The "prison" occupied the main deck. It was separated fore and aft by strong bulkheads, sheeted with iron. In the forward part the crew lodged as usual; aft, the military guard. The only access from the prison to the deck was by the main hatchway. This was secured by barred gates at the foot of the ladder, so that the prison within looked like a huge cage. A substantial bulkhead ran across the upper deck, dividing the part used by the prisoners from the poop. There were doors in this, at each of which a sentry was always stationed. The hatches were also provided with stout padlocks. The "prison" was divided into "bunks" or "bays," as in a troop-ship, each of which had a table for eight men, and at night eight hammocks. For a long time prison ships sailed always without any special staff for supervision. Later a small proportion of warders embarked in each. During the day these officers took turns to patrol the deck and keep a general look-out. But on the whole, they preferred to interfere as little as possible with the "people." At night five convict sentries kept watch on deck, and were held responsible that no others came up; but below, the prisoners were left entirely to themselves. This, of itself, was one of the chief blots in the whole plan of deportation. To permit men of this class to herd together just as they please, is the surest way to encourage the spread of wickedness and vice. The tendency of any collection of human beings, it is to be feared, is rather to sink to the level of the worst than to rise to that of the best. In a ship load of convicts, free to talk and associate at all hours of the day and night, the deterioration is almost inevitable. For this reason, the elaborate machinery for providing for the religious wants and teaching of the ships sent out in later years was rendered nearly useless. A slight veneer of propriety in diction and demeanour might lie on top, but beneath, the real stuff was as bad as ever. It could not be denied even in after years, when every possible precaution had been taken. It was admitted, before the parliamentary commission on transportation in 1861, that "the horrors of convict ships were really past description." The arrangements for the conveyance of convicts by sea were never really put on a satisfactory footing until 1870, when the steamship *London* was especially fitted up for the purpose of taking convicts to Gibraltar; a portion of her forward hold was turned into a "prison," in every respect the same as a separate prison on shore. Here officers patrolled on duty day and night. This, with the rapidity of the voyage, reduced the chances of contamination to the lowest.

The Convict Ship "Success;" Tasmania

On the convict ship transporting prisoners to the Antipodes it was necessary in order to maintain discipline to put them all in irons for a part of the voyage. The worst class of convicts were sent to Tasmania from the prisons of England, where they remained until by good conduct they were removed to the probation gang; the second stage in the elaborate scheme for convict colonies which ended so disastrously.

I cannot refrain, however, from paying a tribute here to one who appears to have worked wonders in the various ships he had in charge. I allude to Dr. C. A. Browning, R. N., who has himself, in "The Convict Ship and England's Exiles," given us an interesting account of his labours, and the success that attended them. He was clearly a man of great piety, gifted also with singular earnestness of character. The influence of such a person cannot fail to be soon felt, especially in a society of which he is himself the recognised head. Wonderful as were the results obtained by Dr. Browning, they are substantiated by the testimony of high colonial officials. Writing on the subject, Sir George Arthur, the lieutenant-governor of Van Diemen's Land, says, "The convicts brought out in the *Arab*, in 1834, were put on board, I have every reason to believe, as ignorant, as profane, and in every respect as reckless as transported criminals usually are. But when they were disembarked, it was evident the character of many of them had undergone a most remarkable change. Their tempers had been subdued; they had been induced to think and reflect; and they had been instructed, so as to know them familiarly, in the principles of religion." It was said that in after years the convicts whom Dr. Browning reformed, seldom if ever fell away; but on this point I can find no reliable evidence. That quoted above refers only to these men at the moment they landed on shore, when Dr. Browning's impressive lessons were still ringing in their ears. An examination of the parliamentary returns, however, leads me to conclude that instances of after misconduct, as proved by the number of convictions, summary and otherwise, were just as plentiful among the men of Dr. Browning's ships as of any others.

But I should be loath to detract from Dr. Browning, who, besides being a preacher of some power, was also a practical man with considerable talent for organisation. His ships must have been patterns of propriety and cleanliness. Yet he worked single-handed. The only officials under him were convicts chosen among the "people," according to character received with them, and "the impression," to use his own words, "formed on my own mind by the expression of their countenances, and general demeanour." At the doctor's right hand was the first captain, who was at the head of the whole establishment; next to him came a second captain; and below them the captains of divisions. Each had his duties prescribed according to a carefully prepared scale. There were also appointed cooks, barber, delegates, head of messes, a clerk, librarian, hospital steward, and, last, not least, schoolmasters and inspectors of schools. The routine of work for every day of the week was also laid down, and was punctually carried out. As a rule, after the necessary cleaning operations, it resolved itself almost entirely into school instruction, and constant exhortation from the surgeon himself. Dr. Browning was apparently much beloved even by the convicts; and his orders are said to have been readily and implicitly obeyed. In return his confidence in them was so great that when he was attacked with serious illness he had his hammock hung inside on the prison deck, and gave himself up to be nursed altogether by the convicts.

In after years the example set by Dr. Browning was so far followed that every ship carried a religious instructor to teach, and perform the services—duties which every surgeon-superintendent could not be expected to perform, as did Dr. Browning. These instructors were selected from among the Scripture readers and schoolmasters at Millbank or Pentonville, and no doubt they were conscientious men, fairly anxious to do their best. But this best fell far short of that which an enthusiast of superior education like Dr. Browning could accomplish; and in most of the ships, in spite of all the efforts of the instructors, wickedness reigned supreme to the last.

CHAPTER VII THE EXILES OF CRIME

Notorious individuals exiled—Murderous assaults on the Queen—Bank frauds—Burgess and the Bank of England—Robbery of Rogers' Bank—Fraud and embezzlement—Walter Watts—Robert F. Pries—Joseph Windle Cole—Strahan, Paul and Bates—Aristocratic bankers—Robson—Redpath—Enormous stealings—Great gold robbery on the South-Eastern Railway—Agar, Pierce and Tester—Extensive forgeries—Saward or "Jim the Penman"—Vicissitudes of a convict's life—Journeys round the world.

So long as the law ordained that removal to a far-off land should be the invariable fate of every offender who escaped "vertical punishment," as hanging was sometimes styled, we must certainly find the most notable criminals in the stream setting unceasingly southward. It will be interesting and instructive to present here some of the most notable or notorious individuals who thus left their country "for their country's good" and still more for their own, as shown in many remarkable instances on preceding pages. For a long time the great mass of passing criminality hardly rises above the commonplace, for the simple reason that the worst individuals, under the sanguinary British code of those days, were peremptorily "finished" on the scaffold. But as death penalties diminished, expatriation overtook many vicious criminals and it is with some of these that I now propose to deal.

The assassination of or the murderous assault on crowned heads and chief magistrates has been too sadly characteristic of modern crime. One tried in England upon the person of the young Queen Victoria in 1842 created a great sensation in London. The perpetrator was a certain John Francis who, moved, as was supposed, by a thirst for notoriety, fired a shot at the Queen as she was driving back to Buckingham Palace. The deed was premeditated and would have been put into execution a day earlier had not his courage failed him. A youth had seen him point a pistol at the Queen's carriage, but drop it exclaiming, "I wish I had done it." The boy weakly allowed Francis to go off without securing his apprehension, but later gave full information. The Queen was apprised of the danger, and was implored to remain within doors; but she declared she would not remain a prisoner in her own palace, and next day drove out as usual in an open barouche. Nothing happened until Her Majesty returned to Buckingham Palace about six o'clock, when, on descending Constitution Hill, with an equerry riding close on each side of her carriage, a man who had been leaning against the palace garden wall suddenly advanced, levelled a pistol at the Queen and fired. He was so close to the carriage that the smoke of his pistol enveloped the face of Colonel Wylde, one of the equerries. The Queen was untouched and at first, it is said, hardly realised the danger she had escaped. Francis had already been seized by a policeman named Trounce, who saw his movement with the pistol too late to prevent its discharge. The prisoner was conveyed without delay to the Home Office and there examined by the Privy Council, which had been hastily summoned for the purpose. On searching him the pistol was found in his pocket, the barrel still warm; also some loose powder and a bullet. There was some doubt as to whether the pistol when fired was actually loaded with ball, but the jury brought in a verdict of guilty of the criminal intent to kill. Francis was sentenced to be hanged, decapitated and quartered, the old traitor's doom, but was spared, and subsequently transported for life. The enthusiasm of the people at the Queen's escape was intense, and her drive next day was one long triumphal progress. At the Italian Opera in the evening, the audience on the Queen's appearance, greeted her with loud cheers and called for the national anthem. This was in May, 1842.

Not long afterwards, a gentleman, for some occult reason of his own, committed the atrocity of striking the young Queen in the face just as she was leaving the palace. The weapon he used was a thin cane, but the blow fell lightly, as the lady-in-waiting interposed. No explanation was offered, except that the culprit was out of his mind. This was the defence set up by his friends, and several curious facts were adduced in proof of insanity. One on which great stress was laid, was that he was in habit of chartering a hansom to Wimbledon Common daily, where he amused himself by getting out and walking as fast as he could through the furze. But this line of defence broke down, and the jury found the prisoner guilty. When he came to Millbank he declared that he had been actuated only by a desire to bring disgrace on his family and belongings. In some way or other he had seriously disagreed with his father, and he took this curious means to obtain revenge. The wantonness of the outrage called for severe punishment, and the man was sentenced to seven years' transportation; but the special punishment of whipping was omitted, on the grounds of the prisoner's position in life. Whether the mere passing of this sentence was considered sufficient, or the Queen herself interposed, the prisoner at Millbank was treated with exceptional leniency and consideration. By order of the Secretary of State he was exempted from most of the restrictions to which other prisoners were subjected. He was not lodged in a cell, but in two rooms adjoining the infirmary, which he used as sitting and bedroom respectively. He did not wear the prison dress, and he had, practically, what food he liked. He seems to have awakened a sort of sympathy on the part of the warders who attended him; probably because he was a fine, tall fellow of handsome presence and engaging manners and because also they thought his offence was one of hot-headed rashness rather than premeditated wickedness. Eventually he went to Australia.

Frauds upon banks and large financial institutions became prevalent about 1844. In that year the Bank of England suffered at the hands of one of its clerks named Burgess who robbed it of £8,000 in conjunction with an accomplice named Elder. Burgess fraudulently transferred consols in the above amount to another party. Elder impersonated the owner and attended at the bank to complete the transfer and sell the stock. Burgess, who was purposely on leave from the bank, effected the sale, which was paid for with a cheque for nearly the whole amount on Lubbock's Bank. Burgess and Elder proceeded in company to cash this, but as they wanted all gold, the cashier gave them eight Bank of England notes for £1,000 each, saying that they could get so much specie nowhere else. Thither Elder went alone, provided with a number of canvas bags and one large carpet bag. When the latter was filled with gold it was too heavy to lift and Elder had to be assisted by two bank porters, who carried it for him to a carriage waiting near the Mansion House. Elder was soon joined by Burgess and they drove together to Ben Caunt's, the pugilist's public house in St. Martin's Lane, where the cash was transferred from the carpet bag to a portmanteau. The same evening both started for Liverpool and, embarking on board the mail steamer *Britannia*, escaped to the United States.

Burgess' continued absence was soon noticed at the bank. Suspicions were aroused when it was found that he had been employed in selling stock for Mr. Oxenford, owner of the stolen consols, which developed as soon as that gentleman was referred to. Mr. Oxenford having denied that he had made any transfer of stock, the matter was at once put in the hands of the police. A smart detective, Forrester, after a little inquiry, established the fact that the man who had impersonated Mr. Oxenford was a horse-dealer named Joseph Elder, an intimate acquaintance of Burgess's. Forrester next traced the fugitives to Liverpool and thence to Halifax, whither he followed them, accompanied by a confidential clerk from the bank. At Halifax, Forrester learned that the men he wanted had gone on to Boston, thence to Buffalo and Canada, and back to Boston. He found them at length residing at the latter place, one as a landed proprietor, the other as a publican. Elder, the former, was soon apprehended at his house, but he evaded the law by hanging himself with his pocket-handkerchief. The inn belonging to Burgess was surrounded, but he escaped through a back door on to the river, and rowed off in a boat to a hiding place in the woods. Next day a person betrayed him for the reward and he was soon captured. The proceeds of the robbery were lodged in a Boston bank, but four hundred sovereigns were found on Elder, while two hundred more were found in Burgess's effects. Burgess was eventually brought back to England, tried at the Central Criminal Court and sentenced to transportation for life.

Within a month or two the bank of Messrs. Rogers and Co. in Clement's Lane was broken into. Robberies as daring in conception as they were boldly executed were common enough. One night a quantity of plate was stolen from Windsor Castle; another time Buckingham Palace was robbed. Of this class of burglaries was the ingenious yet peculiarly simple one effected at the house of Lord Fitzgerald, in Belgrave Square. The butler on the occasion of a death in the family, when the house was in some confusion, arranged with a burglar to come in, and with another carry off the plate-chest in broad daylight and as a matter of business. No one interfered or asked any questions. The thief walked into the house in Belgrave Square and openly carried off the plate-chest, deposited it in a light cart at the door and drove away. Howse, the butler, accused the other servants, but they retorted, declaring that he had been visited by the thief the day previous, whom he had shown over the plate closet. Howse and his accomplice were arrested; the former was found guilty and sentenced to fifteen years, but the latter was acquitted.

In 1850 occurred the first of a series of gigantic frauds, which, following each other at short intervals, had a strong family likeness in that all of them meant to make money easily, without capital and at railroad speed. Walter Watts was an inventor, a creator, who struck an entirely new and original line of crime. Employed as a clerk in the Globe Assurance office, he discovered and with unusual quickness of apprehension promptly turned to account an inexcusably lax system of management, which offered peculiar chances of profit to an ingenious and unscrupulous man. It was the custom in this office to make the banker's pass-book the basis of the entries in the company's ledgers. Thus, when a payment was made by the company, the amount disbursed was carried to account in the general books from its entry in the pass-book, and without reference to or comparison with the documents in which the payment was claimed. This pass-book, when not at the bank, was in the exclusive custody of Watts. The checks drawn by the directors also passed through his hands; to him, too, they came back to be verified and put by, after they had been cashed by the bank. In this way Watts had complete control over the whole of the monetary transactions of the company. He could do what he liked with the pass-book, and by its adoption, as described, as the basis of all entries, there was no independent check upon him if he chose to tamper with it. This he did to an enormous extent, continually altering, erasing, and adding figures to correspond with and cover the abstractions he made of various checks as they were drawn. It seems incredible that this pass-book, which when produced in court was a mass of blots and erasures, should not have created suspicion of foul play either at the bank or at the company's board. Implicit confidence appears to have been placed in Watts, who was the son of an old and trusted employee, and, moreover, a young man of plausible address.

Watts led two lives. In the West End he was a man of fashion, with a town house, a house at Brighton, and a cellar full of good wine at both. He rode a priceless hack in Rotten Row, or drove down to Richmond in a mail phaeton and pair. He played high, and spent his nights at the club, or in joyous and dissolute company. When other pleasures palled he took a theatre, and posed as a munificent patron of the dramatic art. Under his auspices several "stars" appeared on the boards of the Marylebone theatre, and later he became manager of the newly rebuilt Olympic at Wych Street. No one cared to inquire too closely into the sources of his wealth. Some said he was a fortunate speculator in stocks, others that he had had extraordinary luck as a gold-digger. Had his West End and little-informed associates followed him into the city, whither he was taken every morning in a smart brougham, they would have seen him alight from it in Cornhill, and walk forward on foot to enter as a humble and unpretending employee the doors of the Globe Assurance office. His situation, exactly described, was that of check clerk in the cashier's department, and his salary was £200 a year. Nevertheless, in this position, through the culpable carelessness which left him unfettered, he managed between 1844 and 1850 to embezzle and apply to his own purposes some £71,000. The detection of these frauds came while he was still prominently before the world as the lessee of the Olympic. Rumours were abroad that serious defalcations had been discovered in one of the insurance offices, but it was long before the public realised that the fraudulent clerk and the great theatrical manager were one and the same person. Watts' crime was discovered by the secretary of the Globe company, who came suddenly upon the extensive falsification of the pass-book. An inquiry was at once set on foot, and the frauds were traced to Watts. The latter, when first taxed with his offence, protested his innocence boldly, and positively denied all knowledge of the affair; and he had so cleverly destroyed all traces that it was not easy to bring home the charge. But it was proved that Watts had appropriated one check for £1,400, which he had paid to his own bankers, and on this he was committed to Newgate for trial. There were two counts in the indictment: one for stealing a check for £1,400, the second for stealing a bit of paper valued at one penny. The jury found him guilty of the latter only, with a point of law reserved. This was fully argued before three judges, who decided that the act of stealing the bit of paper involved a much more serious offence, and told him they should punish him for what he had really done, and not for the slight offence as it appeared on the record. The sentence of the court, one of ten years' transportation, struck the prisoner with dismay. He had been led to suppose that twelve months' imprisonment was the utmost the law could inflict, and he broke down utterly under the unexpected blow. That same evening he committed suicide in Newgate.

The details of the suicide were given at the inquest. Watts had been in ill-health from the time of his first arrest. In Giltspur Street Compter, where he was first lodged, he showed symptoms of delirium tremens, and admitted that he had been addicted to the excessive use of stimulants. His health improved, but was still indifferent when he was brought up for sentence from the Newgate infirmary. He returned from court in a state of gloomy dejection, and in the middle of the night one of the fellow-prisoners who slept in the same ward noticed that he was not in his bed. This man got up to look for him, and found him hanging from the bars of a neighbouring room. He had made use of a piece of rope cut out from the sacking of his bedstead, and had tied his feet together with a silk pocket-handkerchief. The prison officers were called, but Watts was quite cold and stiff when he was cut down.

In 1853 a second case of gigantic fraud alarmed and scandalised the financial world. It outshone even the defalcations of Watts. Nothing to equal the excitement caused by the forgeries of Robert Ferdinand Pries had ever been known in the city of London. He was a corn merchant who operated largely in grain. So enormous were his transactions, that they often affected the markets, and caused great fluctuations in prices. These had been attributed to political action; some thought that the large purchases in foreign grains, effected at losing prices, were intended by the protectionists to depress the wheat market, and secure the support of the farmers at the forthcoming election; others, that Napoleon III, but recently proclaimed Emperor of the French, wished to gain the popularity necessary to secure the support of the people. Few realised that these mysterious operations were the "convulsive attempt" of a ruined and dishonest speculator to sustain his credit. Pries, although enjoying a high reputation in the city, had long been in a bad way. His extensive business had been carried on by fraud. His method was to obtain advances twice over on the same bills of lading or corn warrants. The duplicates were forged. In this way he obtained vast sums from several firms, and one to which he was indebted upwards of £50,000 subsequently stopped payment. Pries at length was discovered through a dishonoured check for £3,000, paid over as an instalment of £18,000 owing for an advance on warrants. Inquiries were instituted when the check was protested, which led to the discovery of the forgeries. Pries was lodged in Newgate, tried at the Old Bailey, and transported for life.

Another set of frauds, which resembled those of Pries in principle, although not in practice, was soon afterwards discovered. These were the forgeries of Joseph Windle Cole. This clever but unscrupulous trader proposed to gain the capital he needed for business purposes by raising money on dock warrants for imported goods which had no real existence. When such goods arrived they were frequently left at a wharf, paying rent until it suited the importer to remove them. The dock warrant was issued by the wharfinger as certificate that he held the goods. The warrant thus represented money, and was often used as such, being endorsed and passed from hand to hand as other negotiable bills. Cole's plan was to have a wharf of his own, nominally occupied by a creature trading as Maltby & Co. Goods would be landed at this wharf; Maltby & Co. would issue warrants on them deliverable to the importer, and the goods were then passed to be stored in neighbouring warehouses. The owners of the latter would then issue a second set of warrants on these goods, in total ignorance of the fact that they were already pledged. Cole quickly raised money on both sets of warrants. He carried on this game for some time with great success, and so developed his business that in one year his transactions amounted to a couple of millions of pounds. He had several narrow escapes. Once a warrant-holder sent down a clerk to view certain goods, and the clerk found that these goods had already a "stop" upon them, that is, they were pledged. Cole escaped by throwing the blame on a careless partner, and at once removed the "stop." Again, some of the duplicate and fictitious warrants were held by a firm which suspended payment, and there was no knowing into whose hands they might fall. Cole found out where they were, and redeemed them at a heavy outlay, thus establishing business relations with the firm that held them, much to the firm's subsequent anger and regret. Last of all, the well-known bankers, Overend & Gurney, whose own affairs created much excitement some years later, wishing to verify the value of warrants they held, and sending to Maltby & Co.'s wharf, found out half the truth. These bankers, wishing for more specific information, asked Davidson & Gordon, a firm with which Cole was closely allied, whether the warrants meant goods or nothing. They could not deny that the latter was the truth, and were forthwith stigmatised by Overend & Gurney's representative as rogues. But Overend & Gurney took no steps to make the swindle public, and therefore, according to people of principle, became a party to the fraud.

The course of the swindlers was by no means smooth, but it was not till 1854 that suspicion arose that anything was wrong. A firm which held a lot of warrants suddenly demanded the delivery of the goods they covered. The goods having no existence, Cole of course could not deliver them. About this time Davidson & Gordon, the firm above-mentioned, who had out fraudulent warrants of their own to the extent of £150,000, suspended payment and absconded. This affected Cole's credit, and ugly reports were in circulation charging him with the issue of simulated warrants. These, indeed, were out to the value of £367,800. Cole's difficulties increased more and more; warrant-holders came down upon him demanding to realise their goods. Cole now suspended payment. Maltby, who had bolted, was pursued and arrested, to end his life miserably by committing suicide in a Newgate cell. Cole too was apprehended, and in due course tried at the Central Criminal Court. He was found guilty, and sentenced to the seemingly inadequate punishment of four years' transportation. Davidson and Gordon were also sentenced to imprisonment.

A more distressing case stands next on the criminal records—the failure and subsequent sentence of the bankers Messrs. Strahan, Paul & Bates, for the fraudulent disposal of securities lodged in their hands. This firm was one of the oldest banking establishments in the kingdom, and dated back to the Commonwealth, when, under the title of Snow & Walton, it carried on business as pawnbrokers. The Strahan of the firm which came to grief was a Snow who changed his name for a fortune of £200,000; he was a man esteemed and respected in society and the world of finance, incapable, it was thought, of a dishonest deed. Sir John Dean Paul had inherited a baronetcy from his father, together with an honoured name; he was himself a prominent member of the Low Church, of austere piety, active in all good works. Mr. Bates had been confidential managing clerk, and was taken into the firm not alone as a reward for long and faithful service, but that he might strengthen it by his long experience and known business capacity. The bank enjoyed an excellent reputation, it had a good connection, and was supposed to be perfectly sound. Moreover, the partners were sober, steady men, who paid unremitting attention to business. Yet, even as early as the death of the first Sir John Paul, the bank was insolvent, and instead of starting on a fresh life with a new name, it should then and there have closed its doors. In December, 1851, the balance sheet showed a deficiency of upwards of £70,000. The bank had been conducted on false principles; it had assumed enormous responsibilities—on one side by the ownership of the Mostyn collieries, a valueless property, and on the other by backing up an impecunious and rotten firm of contractors with vast liabilities and pledged to impossible works abroad. The engagements of the bank on these two heads, amounting to nearly half a million of money, produced immediate embarrassment and financial distress.

The bank was already insolvent, and the partners had to decide between suspending payment or continuing to hold its head above water by flagitious processes. They chose, unhappily for themselves, the latter alternative. Money they must have, and money they raised to meet their urgent necessities upon the balances and securities deposited with them by their customers. This borrowing continued, and on such a scale that their paper was soon at a discount, and the various discount houses would not advance sufficient sums to relieve the necessities of the bank. Then it was that instead of merely pledging securities, the bank sold them outright, and thus passed the Rubicon of fraud. This went on for some time, and might never have been discovered had some good stroke of luck provided the partners with money enough to retrieve the position of the bank. But that passed from bad to worse; the firm's paper went down further and further; an application to the Committee of Bankers for assistance was peremptorily refused; then came a run on the bank, and it was compelled to stop payment. Its debts amounted to three-quarters of a million, and the dividend it eventually paid was three and twopence in the pound. But worse than the bankruptcy was the confession made by the partners in the court. They admitted that they had made away with many of the securities intrusted to their keeping. Following this, warrants were issued for their arrest, the specific charge being the unlawful negotiation of Danish bonds and other shares belonging to the Rev. Dr. Griffiths, of Rochester, to the value of £20,000.

Bates was at once captured in Norfolk Street, Strand. Police officers went down at night to Nutfield, near Reigate, and arrested Sir John Paul, but allowed the prisoner to sleep there. Next morning they barely managed to catch the train to town, and left Sir John behind on the platform, but he subsequently surrendered himself. Mr. Strahan was arrested at a friend's house in Bryanston Square. All three were tried at the Central Criminal Court, and sentenced to fourteen years' transportation, passing some time in Newgate *en route*. Bates, the least guilty, was pardoned in 1858.

Two cases of extensive embezzlement which were discovered almost simultaneously, those of Robson and Redpath, will long be remembered both within and without the commercial world. They both reproduced many of the features of the case of Watts, already described, but in neither did the sums misappropriated reach quite the same high figure. But neither Robson nor Redpath would have been able to pursue their fraudulent designs with success had they not, like Watts, been afforded peculiar facilities by the slackness of system and the want of methodical administration in the concerns by which they were employed. Robson was of humble origin, but he was well educated, and he had some literary ability. His tastes were mainly theatrical, and he was the author of several plays, one of which, at least, "Love and Loyalty," with Wallack in a leading part, achieved a certain success. He began life as a law-writer, earning thereby some fifteen or eighteen shillings a week; but the firm he served got him a situation as clerk in the office of the Great Northern Railway, whence he passed to a better position under the Crystal Palace Company. He now married, although his salary was only a pound a week; but he soon got on. He had a pleasant address, showed good business aptitude, and quickly acquired the approval of his superiors. Within a year he was advanced to the post of chief clerk in the transfer department, at a salary of £150 a year. His immediate chief was a Mr. Fasson, upon whose confidence he gained so rapidly, through his activity, industry, and engaging manners, that ere long the whole management of the transfer department was intrusted to him.

Some time elapsed before Robson succumbed to temptation. He was not the first man of loose morality and expensive tastes who preferred the risk of future reputation and liberty to the present discomfort of living upon narrow means. The temptation was all the greater because the chances of successful fraud lay ready to hand. Shares in the company were represented by certificates, which often enough never left the company's, or more exactly Robson's, hands. He conceived the idea of transferring shares, bogus shares from a person who held none, to any one who would buy them in the open market. He took it for granted that the certificates representing these bogus shares, and which practically did not exist, would never be called for. This ingenious method of raising funds he adopted and carried on without detection, till the defalcations from fraudulent transfers and fraudulent issues combined amounted to £27,000. With the proceeds of these flagitious frauds Robson feasted and made merry. He kept open house at Kilburn Priory; entertained literary, artistic, and dramatic celebrities; had a smart "turn out," attended all the race-meetings, and dressed in the latest fashion. To his wife, poor soul, he made no pretence of fidelity, and she enjoyed only so much of his company as was necessarily spent in receiving guests at home, or could be spared from two rival establishments in other parts of the town. To account for his revenues he pretended to have been very lucky on the Stock Exchange, which was at one time true to a limited extent, and to have succeeded in other speculations. When his friends asked why he, a wealthy man of independent means, continued to slave on as a clerk on a pittance, he replied gaily that his regular work at the Crystal Palace office was useful as a sort of discipline, and kept him steady.

All this time his position was one of extreme insecurity. He was standing over a mine which at any moment might explode. The blow fell suddenly, and when least expected. One morning Mr. Fasson asked casually for certain certificates, whether representing real or fictitious shares does not appear; but they were certificates connected in some way with Robson's long-practised frauds, and he could not produce them. His chief asked sternly where they were. Robson said they were at Kilburn Priory. "Let us go to Kilburn for them together," said Mr. Fasson, growing suspicious.

They drove there, and Robson on arrival did the honours of his house, rang for lunch to gain time, but at Mr. Fasson's pressing demands went up-stairs to fetch the certificates. He came back to explain that he had mislaid them. Mr. Fasson, more and more ill at ease, would not accept this subterfuge, and declared they must be found. Robson again left him, but only to gather together hastily all the money and valuables on which he could lay his hands, with which he left the house. Mr. Fasson waited and waited for his subordinate to reappear, and at last discovered his flight. A reward was forthwith offered for Robson's apprehension. Meanwhile the absconding clerk had coolly driven to a favourite dining-place in the West End, where a fish curry and a brace of partridges were set before him, and he discussed the latter with appetite, but begged that they would never give him curry again, as he did not like it. After dinner he went into hiding for a day or two. Then, accompanied by a lady not Mrs. Robson, he took steamer and started for Copenhagen. But the continental police had been warned to look out for him, and two Danish inspectors got upon his track, followed him over to Sweden, and arrested him at Helsingfors. Thence he was transferred to Copenhagen and surrendered in due course to a London police officer.

Little more remains to be said about Robson. He appears to have accepted his position, and at once to have resigned himself to his fate. When brought to trial he took matters very coolly, and at first pleaded "Not Guilty," but subsequently withdrew the plea. Sergeant Ballantine, who prosecuted, paid him the compliment of describing him as "a young man of great intelligence, considerable powers of mind, and possessed of an education very much beyond the rank of life to which he originally belonged." Robson was found guilty, and sentenced to two terms of transportation, one for twenty and one for fourteen years. Newgate officers who remember Robson describe him as a fine young man, who behaved well as a prisoner, but who had all the appearance of a careless, thoughtless, happy-go-lucky fellow.

In many respects the embezzlement of which Leopold Redpath was guilty closely resembled that of Robson, but it was based upon more extended and audacious forgeries. Redpath's crime arose from his peculiar and independent position as registrar of stock of the Great Northern Railway Company. This offered him ample facilities for the creation of artificial stock, its sale from a fictitious holder, and transfer to himself. All the signatures in the transfer were forged. Not only did he thus transfer and realise "bogus" stock, but he bought *bonâ fide* amounts, increased their value by altering the figures, and in this way a larger amount was duly carried to his credit on the register, and entered upon the certificates of transfer. By these means Redpath misappropriated vast sums during a period extending over ten years. The total amount was never exactly made out, but the false stock created and issued by him was estimated at £220,000. Even when the bubble burst Redpath, who had lived at the rate of twenty thousand a year, had assets in the shape of land, house, furniture, pictures, and *objets d'art* to the value of £50,000.

He began in a very small way. First a lawyer's clerk, he then got an appointment in the Peninsula and Oriental Company's office; afterwards set up as an insurance broker on his own account, but presently failed. His fault was generosity, an open-handed, unthinking charity which gave freely to the poor and needy the money which belonged to his creditors. After his bankruptcy he obtained a place as clerk in the Great Northern Railway office, from which he rose to be assistant registrar, with the special duties of transferring shares. He soon proved his ability, and by unremitting attention mastered the whole work of the office. Later on he became registrar, and in this more independent position developed to a colossal extent the frauds he had already practised as a subordinate. Now he launched out into great expenditure, took a house in Chester Terrace, and became known as a Mæcenas and patron of the arts. He had a nice taste in *bric-à-brac*, and was considered a good judge of pictures. Leading social and artistic personages were to be met with at his house, and his hospitality was far famed. The choicest wines, the finest fruits, peas at ten shillings a quart, five-guinea pineapples, and early asparagus were to be found on his table. But his chief extravagance, his favourite folly, was the exercise of an ostentatious benevolence. The philanthropy he had displayed in a small way when less prosperous became now a passion. His name headed every subscription list; his purse was always open. Not content with giving where assistance was solicited, he himself sought out deserving cases and personally afforded relief. When the crash came there were pensioners and other recipients of his bounty who could not believe that so good a man had really been for years a swindler and a rogue. Down at Weybridge, where he had a country place, his name was long remembered with gratitude by the poor. During the days of his prosperity he was a governor of Christ's Hospital, of the St. Ann's Society, and one of the supporters and managers of the Patriotic Fund. In his person he was neat and fastidious; he patronised the best tailors, and had a fashionable *coiffeur* from Hanover Square daily to curl his hair.

There was something dramatic in Redpath's detection. Just after Robson's frauds had agitated the minds of all directors of companies, Mr. Denison, chairman of the Great Northern, was standing at a railway station talking to a certain well-known peer of the realm. Redpath passed and lifted his hat to his chairman; the latter acknowledged the salute. But the peer rushed forward and shook Redpath warmly by the hand. "What do you know of our clerk?" asked Mr. Denison of his lordship. "Only that he is a capital fellow, who gives the best dinners and balls in town." Redpath had industriously circulated reports that he had prospered greatly in speculation; but the chairman of the Great Northern could not realise that a clerk of the company could honestly be in the possession of unlimited wealth. It was at once decided at the board to make a thorough examination of all his books. Redpath was called in and informed of the intended investigation. He tried to stave off the evil hour by declaring that everything was perfectly right; but finding he could not escape, he said he would resign his post, and leaving the board-room, disappeared.

The inquiry soon revealed the colossal character of the frauds. Warrants were issued for Redpath's arrest, but he had flown to Paris. Thither police officers followed, only to find that he had returned to London. A further search discovered him at breakfast at a small house in the New Road. He was arrested, examined before a police magistrate, and committed to Newgate. Great excitement prevailed in the city and the West End when Redpath's defalcations were made public. The stock market was greatly affected, and society, more especially the evangelical element of it which frequented Exeter Hall, was convulsed. The Central Criminal Court, when the trial came on, was densely crowded, and many curious eyes were turned upon the somewhat remarkable man who occupied the dock. He is described by a contemporary account as a fresh-looking man of forty years of age, slightly bald, inclined to embonpoint, and thoroughly embodying the idea of English respectability. His manner was generally self-possessed, but his face was marked with "uneasy earnestness," and he looked about him with wayward, furtive glances. When the jury found a verdict of guilty he remained unmoved. He listened without emotion to the judge's well-merited censures, and received his sentence of transportation for life without much surprise. Redpath passed away into the outer darkness of a penal colony, where he lived many years. But his name lingers still in England as that of the first swindler of his time, and the prototype of a class not uncommon in our later days—that of dishonest rogues who assume piety and philanthropy as a cloak for their misdeeds.

In Newgate, Redpath was a difficult man to deal with. From the moment of his reception he gave himself great airs, as a martyr and a man heavily wronged. By and by, when escape seemed hopeless, and after sentence, he suddenly degenerated into the lowest stamp of criminal, and behaved so as to justify a belief that he had been a gaol-bird all his life.

It has been already remarked in these pages that with changed social conditions came a great change in the character of crimes. Highway robberies, for instance, had disappeared, if we except the spasmodic and severely repressed outbreak of "garrotting," which at one time spread terror throughout London. Thieves preferred now to use ingenuity rather than brute force. It was no longer possible to stop a coach or carriage, or rob the postman who carried the mail. The improved methods of locomotion had put a stop to these depredations. People travelled in company, as a rule; only when single and unprotected were they in any danger of attack, and that but rarely. There were still big prizes, however, to tempt the daring, and none appealed more to the thievish instinct than the custom of transmitting gold by rail. The precious metal was sent from place to place carefully locked up and guarded, no doubt; but were the precautions too minute, the vigilance too close to be eluded or overcome? This was the question which presented itself to the fertile brain of one Pierce, who had been concerned in various "jobs" of a dishonest character, and who for the moment was a clerk in a betting office. He laid the suggestion before Agar, a professional thief, who thought it contained elements of success. But the collusion and active assistance of employees of the railway carriers were indispensable, and together they sounded one Burgess, a guard on the South-Eastern Railway, a line by which large quantities of bullion were sent to the Continent. Burgess detailed the whole system of transmission. The gold, packed in an iron-bound box, was securely lodged in safes locked with patent Chubbs. Each safe had three sets of double keys, all held by confidential servants of the company. One pair was with the traffic superintendent in London, another with an official in Folkestone, a third with the captain of the Folkestone and Boulogne boat. At the other side of the Channel the French railway authorities took charge.

The safes while on the line between London and Folkestone were in the guard's van. This was an important step, and they might easily be robbed some day when Burgess was the guard, provided only that they could be opened. The next step was to get impressions and fabricate false keys. A new accomplice was now needed within the company's establishment, and Pierce searched long before he found the right person. At last he decided to enlist one Tester, a clerk in the traffic department, whom he thought would prove a likely tool. The four waited patiently for their opportunity, which came when the safes were sent to Chubbs' to be repaired; and Chubbs sent them back, but only with one key, in such a way that Tester had possession of this key for a time. He lent it to Agar for a brief space, who promptly took an impression on wax. But the safes had a double lock; the difficulty was to get a copy of the second key. This was at length effected by Agar and Pierce. After hanging about the Folkestone office for some time, they saw at last that the key was kept in a certain cupboard. Still watching and waiting for the first chance, they seized it when the clerks left the office empty for a moment. Pierce boldly stepped in, found the cupboard unlocked; he removed the key, handed it to Agar outside, who quickly took the wax impression, handed it back to Pierce; Pierce replaced it, left the office, and the thing was done.

After this nothing remained but to wait for some occasion when the amount transmitted would be sufficient to justify the risks of robbery. It was Tester's business, who had access to the railway company's books, to watch for this. Meanwhile the others completed their preparations with the utmost care. A weight of shot was bought and stowed in carpet bags ready to replace exactly the abstracted gold. Courier bags were bought to carry the "stuff" slung over the shoulders; and last, but not least, Agar frequently travelled up and down the line to test the false keys he had manufactured with Pierce's assistance. Burgess admitted him into the guard's van, where he fitted and filed the keys till they worked easily and satisfactorily in the locks of the safe. One night Tester whispered to Agar and Pierce, "All right," as they cautiously lounged about London Bridge. The thieves took first-class tickets, handed their bags full of shot to the porters, who placed them in the guard's van. Just as the train was starting Agar slipped into the van with Burgess, and Pierce got into a first-class carriage. Agar at once got to work on the first safe, opened it, took out and broke into the bullion box, removed the gold, substituted the shot from a carpet bag, re-fastened and re-sealed the bullion box, and replaced it in the safe. At Redhill, Tester met the train and relieved the thieves of a portion of the stolen gold. At the same station Pierce joined Agar in the guard's van, and there were now three to carry on the robbery. The two remaining safes were attacked and nearly entirely despoiled in the same way as the first, and the contents transferred to the courier bags. The train was now approaching Folkestone, and Agar and Pierce hid themselves in a dark part of the van. At that station the safes were given out, heavy with shot, not gold; the thieves went on to Dover, and by and by, with Ostend tickets previously procured, returned to London without mishap, and by degrees disposed of much of the stolen gold.

The theft was discovered at Boulogne, when the boxes were found not to weigh exactly what they ought. But no clue was obtained to the thieves, and the theft might have remained a mystery but for the subsequent bad faith of Pierce to his accomplice Agar. The latter was ere long arrested on a charge of uttering forged checks, convicted, and sentenced to transportation for life. When he knew that he could not escape his fate, he handed over to Pierce a sum of £3,000, his own, whether rightly or wrongly acquired never came out, together with the unrealised part of the bullion, amounting in all to some £15,000, and begged his accomplice to invest it as a settlement on a woman named Kay, by whom he had had a child. Pierce made Kay only a few small payments, then appropriated the rest of the money. Kay, who had been living with Agar at the time of the bullion robbery, went to the police in great fury and distress, and disclosed all she knew of the affair. Agar too, in Newgate, heard how Pierce had treated him, and at once readily turned informer. As the evidence he gave incriminated Pierce, Burgess, and Tester, all three were arrested and committed to Newgate for trial. The whole strange story, the long incubation and the elaborate accomplishment of the plot, came out at the Old Bailey, and was acknowledged to be one of the most extraordinary on record.

Scarcely had the conviction of these daring and astute thieves been assured, than another gigantic fraud was brought to light. The series of boldly conceived and cleverly executed forgeries in which James Townshend Saward, commonly called "Jim the Penman," was the prime mover, has probably no parallel in the annals of crime. Saward himself is a striking and in some respects a unique figure in criminal history. A man of birth and education, a member of the bar, and of acknowledged legal attainments, his proclivities were all downward. Instead of following an honourable profession, he preferred to turn his great natural talents and ready wits to the most nefarious practices. He was known to the whole criminal fraternity as a high-class receiver of stolen goods, a negotiator more especially of stolen paper, checks and bills, of which he made a particular use. He dealt too in the precious metals, when they had been improperly acquired, and it was to him that Agar, Pierce, and the rest applied when seeking to dispose of their stolen bullion. But Saward's operations were mainly directed to the fabrication and uttering of forged checks. His method was comprehensive and deeply laid. Burglars brought him the checks they stole from houses, thieves what they got in pocket-books. Checks blank and cancelled were his stock in trade. The former he filled up by exact imitation of the latter, signature and all. When he could get nothing but the blank check, he set in motion all sorts of schemes for obtaining signatures, such as commencing sham actions, and addressing formal applications, merely for the reply. One stroke of luck which he turned to great account was the return from transportation of an old "pal" and confederate, who brought with him some bills of exchange.

Saward's method of negotiating the checks was equally well planned. Like his great predecessor "Old Patch," he himself never went to a bank, nor did any of his accomplices. The bearer of the check was always innocent and ignorant of the fraudulent nature of the document he presented. In order to obtain messengers of this sort, Saward answered advertisements of persons seeking employment, and when these presented themselves, intrusted them as a beginning with the duty of cashing checks. A confederate followed the emissary closely, not only to insure fair play and the surrender of the proceeds if the check was cashed, but to give timely notice if it were not, so that Saward and the rest might make themselves scarce. As each transaction was carried out from a different address, and a different messenger always employed, the forgers always escaped detection. But fate overtook two of the gang, partly through their own carelessness, when transferring their operations to Yarmouth. One named Hardwicke assumed the name of Ralph, and, to obtain commercial credit in Yarmouth, paid £250 to a Yarmouth bank as coming from a Mr. Whitney. He forgot to add that it was to be placed to Ralph's credit, and when he called as Ralph, he was told it was only at Mr. Whitney's disposal, and that it could be paid to no one else. Hardwicke, or "Ralph," appealed to Saward in his difficulty, and that clever schemer sent an elaborate letter of instructions how to ask for the money. But while Hardwicke was in communication with Saward, the bank was in communication with London, and the circumstances were deemed sufficiently suspicious to warrant the arrest of the gentlemen at Yarmouth on a charge of forgery and conspiracy.

Saward's letter to Hardwicke fell into the hands of the police and compromised him. While Hardwicke and Atwell were in Newgate awaiting trial, active search was made for Saward, who was at length taken in a coffee-shop near Oxford Street, under the name of Hopkins. He resisted at first, and denied his identity, but on being searched, two blank checks of the London and Westminster Bank were found in his pocket. He then confessed that he was the redoubtable Jim Saward, or Jim the Penman, and was conveyed to a police court, and thence to Newgate. At his trial Atwell and Hardwicke, two of his chief allies and accomplices, turned informers, and the whole scheme of systematic forgery was laid bare. The evidence was corroborated by that of many of the victims who had acted as messengers, and others who swore to the meetings of the conspirators and their movements. Saward was found guilty, and the judge, in passing sentence of transportation for life, expressed deep regret that "the ingenuity, skill, and talent, which had received so perverted and mistaken direction, had not been guided by a sense of virtue, and directed to more honourable and useful pursuits." The proceeds of these forgeries amounted, it was said, to some thousands per annum. Saward spent all his share at low gaming houses, and in all manner of debaucheries. He was in person a short, square-built man of gentlemanly address, sharp and shrewd in conversation and manner. He was fifty-eight at the time of his conviction, and had therefore had a long criminal career.

The vicissitudes of the felon transport who ventured to return before his sentence of exile had expired, has been told by one of their number. His statement bears date of 1852 and runs as follows:

"At the time of the offence for which I was convicted I was suffering from the most acute pecuniary distress, with a wife and large family of children.

A series of misfortunes—the most heavy was the death of my second wife, by which I lost an annuity of £150, with a great falling off, notwithstanding all my exertions, in my occupation as reporter to the public press—brought about mainly the distress in question. Previous to the commission of the offence I had through life borne an irreproachable character. In early life, from 1818 to 1822, I held some most responsible appointments in Jamaica and other West India Islands; from 1829 to 1834, I held the appointment of Magistrate's Clerk and Postmaster at Bong Bong in New South Wales; afterwards was superintendent of large farms in Bathurst, over the Blue Mountains, in the same colony. At the later period I had a wife and family of young children; the former, a most amiable partner, I had the misfortune to lose in 1838, leaving me with seven young children. My connections are most respectable. My late father was an officer of rank, and of very meritorious services. My eldest brother is at present a major in the Royal Marine Corps. I was convicted in October, 1846; was three months in Millbank Penitentiary, at which period fears were entertained that my intellect would become impaired in solitary confinement; subsequently I was three years and two months in the *Warrior* convict ship at Woolwich, during which period I was employed on the government works in the dockyard; and was sent abroad in March, 1850. At Millbank and the hulks I had the best possible character, as also on my arrival at Hobart Town, Van Diemen's Land, after a passage of four months. On my arrival I received a ticket-of-leave, which I retained until I left the colony, never having forfeited the same for a day by any kind of insubordinate conduct. My motive in leaving Van Diemen's Land was to proceed to the gold-diggings, in the hope that I might be successful and better the condition of my family at home, who were in very impoverished circumstances; but although my exertions were very great in California, Victoria, and New South Wales, I was unsuccessful. It is true I made, occasionally, some money; but I was robbed of it on the road by armed bushrangers, and frequently ill-used and robbed at Melbourne and Geelong by the worst of characters. I was shipwrecked twice, and once burnt out at sea: the first time in Torres Straits, between New Holland and New Guinea on a reef of coral rocks. Upon this occasion I lost between £70 and £80 in cash, and all my luggage. Eleven only of us got ashore, out of a ship's company of twenty-seven, chiefly Lascars, Malays, and Chinamen. After thirty days' great suffering and privation we were picked up by an American whaler, and ultimately reached Sydney, New South Wales.

"I was subsequently wrecked in a brigantine called the *Triton*, going from Melbourne to Adelaide, and lost all I possessed in the world, having another very narrow escape of my life. In returning from San Francisco to Melbourne in a vessel called the *White Squall*, she caught fire about three hundred and fifty miles from Tahiti (formerly called Otaheite). We were obliged to abandon her and take to the boats; but a great number of the crew and passengers perished by fire and water. The survivors in the boats reached Tahiti in about eight days, in a state of great exhaustion; many of them died from the effects of the same. I had the misfortune to lose nearly all I possessed upon this occasion. On reaching Melbourne I was very ill and went into the hospital. I left in about five weeks, intending to go again to Mount Alexander diggings; but, owing to ill-health, bad state of the roads from the floods, and limited means, I abandoned such intention. I had a twelvemonth before been to Ballarat, Mount Alexander, Forest Creek, Bendigo, and many other diggings: but at this time there were no police or gold escort troopers, consequently nearly all the unfortunate diggers were robbed of what they got by hordes of bushrangers, well mounted, and armed with revolvers and other weapons to the teeth. In returning to Melbourne from Forest Creek the last time, I was beat, stripped, and robbed of all I had, in the Black Forest, about halfway between Melbourne and Mount Alexander.

"I left Melbourne in the brig *Kestrel* for Sydney, New South Wales, at which place I was acquainted with many respectable parties, some of whom I had known as far back as 1829, when I first went to Sydney with my wife and children. The *Kestrel* put in at some of the settlements of New Zealand, at one of which (Auckland) was lying a barque, bound for England, in want of hands. The temptation was great to reach my dear family, for which I had mourned ever since I met with my misfortune. I shipped myself as ordinary seaman and assistant steward. We left the settlement in July, with a miserably crippled ship's company, and made a very severe passage round Cape Horn, in the winter season, which carried away masts, sails, rigging, boats, bulwarks, stanchions, etc., etc. Some of the crew were lost with the yards, and most of us were frost-bitten. We put into Rio de Janeiro to refit and provision. We proceeded on our passage, crossed the equator, touched at Funchal—one of the Azores—for two days, and reached England in September, after a severe passage of four months and twenty-six days from New Zealand.

"Under all the circumstances of my present unhappy condition, I humbly hope the legislature will humanely consider the long, severe, and various descriptions of punishment I have undergone since my conviction. I would also most respectfully call the attention of the authorities to the fact that the offence for which I have so severely suffered was the first deviation from strict rectitude during my life; and that I have never since, upon any occasion whatever, received a second sentence even of the most minor description. It was only required of me by the then regulation of the service, that I should serve five years upon the public works at Woolwich. On my embarkation for Van Diemen's Land I had done three years and four months: if I had completed the remaining twenty months I should have been discharged from the dockyard a free man. I also humbly beg to state, at the time I left Van Diemen's Land, six years after my conviction, I was entitled by the regulations of the service to a conditional pardon, which would have left me at liberty to leave the colony without further restraint. I beg to state that during the period of three years and four months I was at the hulks I worked in all the gangs in the dockyard. Upon several occasions I received severe injuries, some of which required me to be sent to the hospital ship. I was ruptured by carrying heavy weights, the effect of which I have frequently felt since, and do to the present day. During the two periods when the cholera raged in the hulks, I attended upon the sick at the hospital ships. I humbly implore the government will have compassion upon me for the sake of my numerous and respectable family, for my great mental and bodily sufferings since my conviction, and for my present weakly, worn-out debilitated state of health, and award me a mild sentence. During my captivity and absence my unfortunate wife has suffered from great destitution, and has buried two of her children. She is again bereaved of me in a distressed condition with her only surviving child, a little girl of ten years of age."

This man was set at large without punishment.

CHAPTER VIII THE COLLAPSE OF DEPORTATION

>Lamentable state of Van Diemen's Land—Colony on the brink of ruin—Latest convict schemes a complete failure—Glut of labour and deadlock in employment—Terrible state of Norfolk Island—Convicts rule—Report of special commissioner—Ill-advised leniency—Severer discipline introduced—Interference with so-called rights aggravates misconduct—Many murders committed—New commandant appointed—Offenders brought to trial—Fourteen hanged—Norfolk Island condemned—Creation of new Colony in Northern Australia Gladstone's scheme—Change of Ministry and new measures—Exile to Van Diemen's Land checked—The new Colonies refuse to receive convicts—Western Australia alone admits them—An insufficient outlet—New ideas.

Within three years of the establishment of the new system, already described at length, by which transportation was to be robbed of all its evils, the most deplorable results showed themselves. The condition of Van Diemen's Land had become most lamentable. It was filled to overflowing with convicts. There were in all 25,000, half of whom were still in the hands of government; and besides these numbers there were three thousand pass-holders waiting for hire, but unable to obtain employment. The latter would be reinforced by as many more in the year immediately following. The colony itself was on the verge of bankruptcy: its finances embarrassed, its trades and industries depressed. With all this was a wholesale exodus of all classes of free people—the better class, to avoid the ruin that stared them in the face, and working men, because higher wages were offered elsewhere in the neighbouring colonies. Already, in fact, the new system of probation had broken down. It had given rise to evils greater than any which it had been expected to replace. Not only was Van Diemen's Land itself on the brink of ruin, but the consequences to the convicts were almost too terrible to be described. Mr. Pitcairn, a resident of Hobart Town, raised an indignant protest, in which he urges that "all that the free colonists suffer, even the total destruction of Van Diemen's Land as a free colony, is as nothing to what the wretched convicts are forced to submit to. It is not bodily suffering that I refer to: it is the pollution of their minds and hearts which is forced upon them and which they cannot escape from. Loathsome as are the details of their miserable state, it is impossible to see thousands of men debased and depraved without at least making an attempt to save others from the same fate." The congregation of criminals in large numbers without due supervision, meant simply wholesale, wide-spread pollution. Assignment, with all its faults, had at least the merit of dispersing the evil over a wide area.

Not only in its debasing effects upon the convicts themselves was the system quite a failure. Half the scheme became a dead letter from the impoverished condition of the colony. Of what avail was it to prepare prisoners gradually for honest labour when there was no labour upon which they could be employed? The whole gist and essence of the scheme was that after years of restraint the criminal, purged of his evil propensities, would gladly lend himself out for hire. But what if there were no hirers? Yet this was practically the state of the case. Following inevitably from the unnatural over-crowding of Van Diemen's Land, there came a great glut in the labour market. Had the colony been thoroughly prosperous, and as big as the neighbouring island-continent, it could hardly have found employment for the thousands of convicts poured in year by year. Being quite the reverse—small and almost stagnant—a species of deadlock was the certain result of this tremendous influx. To make matters worse, goaded, doubtless, by the excessive costliness of the whole scheme, the imperial government insisted that all hirers should pay a tax over and above the regular wages for every convict engaged, and this whether the hirer was a private person or the public works department of the colony. Neither private nor public funds could stand this charge. In the general distress, employers of labour could hardly afford the moderate wages asked; while the local revenues were equally impecunious. Yet there were many works urgently needed in the colony, which the colonial government was quite disposed to execute—provided they got their labour for nothing. But to pay for it was impossible. In fact, this imperial penuriousness defeated its own object. The home government would not let out its labour except at a price which no one would pay; so the thousands who might at least have lived at their own expense, remained at that of the government. They were put to raise produce for their own support; but they earned nothing, and ate their heads off into the bargain. They had, moreover, a grievance. They were denied all fruition in the status to which, by their own conduct and according to prescribed rules, they arrived. They had been promised that after a certain probationary period they would pass into a stage of semi-freedom. Yet here, after all, they were in a condition little superior to the convicts in the gangs—in the very stage, that is to say, which the pass-holders had left behind them. The authorities had, in fact, broken faith with them. This was a fatal flaw in the scheme; a link broken in the chain; a gap in the sequence of progressive probation enough to bring the whole to ruin.

But at any rate the pass-holders were better off than the "conditional-pardon" or "ticket-of-leave" men. The first named had still a lien on the government. They were certain of food, and a roof over their heads at the various hiring depôts. But those who were in a stage further ahead towards freedom were upon their own resources. These men were "thrown upon the world with nothing but their labour to support them." But no labour was in demand. What, then, was to become of them? They must steal, or starve; and as the outcome of either alternative, the community might expect to be weighted with a large and increasing population of thieves and paupers.

Nor would any description of the main island alone suffice to place in a proper light the actual state of affairs. Norfolk Island, the chief penal settlement, had deteriorated so rapidly, that what was bad before, had grown to be infinitely and irremediably worse. Naylor, a clergyman, writing about this time, paints a terrible picture of the island. Rules disregarded; convicts of every degree mingled indiscriminately in the settlement. Some of the prisoners had been convicted, and reconvicted, and had passed through every grade of punishment in hulks, chain-gangs, or penal settlements. Among them were "flash men," who kept the island in awe, and bearded the commandant himself; bodies of from seventy to one hundred often in open mutiny, refusing to work, and submitting only when terms had been arranged to their satisfaction. The island was kept in perpetual alarm; houses were robbed in open day; yet no successful efforts were made to bring the culprits to justice. An official long resident on the island tells the following incident: that a favourite parrot, with its cage, was stolen from his house, and the thief was known, and seen with the bird. He kept it in his barrack-room, and took it daily with him to his work. Yet no one dared to interfere with him! The bird was left in his possession, and he altogether escaped punishment. The commandant was deliberately knocked down by one of these ruffians and received severe contusions. The state of the island might well awaken alarm.

In 1846 a special commissioner was despatched from headquarters at Hobart Town, to report from personal observation on the state of the settlement. It is abundantly evident from his report, which will be found *in extenso* in a Blue-Book on convict discipline, issued in February, 1847, that some terrific explosion of the seething elements collected together at Norfolk Island might be looked for at any early day. Mr. Stewart, the commissioner, attributed the condition of the settlement chiefly to the lax discipline maintained by its commandant. This gentleman certainly appears to have been chosen unwisely. He was quite the wrong man for the place, utterly unfitted for the arduous duties he was called upon to perform. Of a weak and vacillating disposition, he seldom had the courage to act upon his own judgment. It was openly alleged that his decisions rested with his chief clerk. Most of his subordinates were at loggerheads with one another, but he never dared to settle their quarrels himself. Points the most trivial were referred always to headquarters. He was equally wanting in resolute determination in dealing with the great mass of convicts who constituted the bulk of his command. With them he was forever temporising and making allowances; so that rules, never too severe, came by degrees to be sensibly relaxed, till leniency grew into culpable pampering and childish considerateness. As might have been expected, the objects of his tender solicitude were utterly ungrateful. He interfered sometimes to soften the sentences of the sitting magistrate, even when they were light enough; but his kindness was only mistaken for weakness, and the men in his charge became day by day more insolent and insubordinate. Where firmness was required in almost every particular, in order to maintain anything like a controlling supervision, it was altogether wanting. This commandant was considered by his supreme chief, to be "totally unfitted for the peculiar situation in which he is placed, either from want of experience, or from an absence in his own character of the qualifications necessary to control criminals."

Of a truth, Norfolk Island was a government that could not be entrusted to any but iron hands. That this commandant was clearly the wrong man for the post cannot be questioned; nevertheless, he was not altogether to blame for the terrible state of affairs existing. No doubt by his wavering incompetence the original condition of the island was greatly aggravated, but all these evils which presently broke out and bore such noxious fruit, had been germinating long before his time. It had been the custom for many years to treat the convicts with ill-advised leniency. They had been allowed practically too much indulgence, and were permitted to forget that they owed their location on that island solely to their own grievous crimes and offences. They had been kept in order by concession, and not by stern force; persuaded to be good, rather than coerced when bad. Such a method of procedure can but have one result with criminals. It is viewed by them as weakness of which they are quick to take every advantage. Here, at Norfolk Island, under a loose régime, the convicts had always been allowed their own way; half the officers placed over them trafficked with them, and were their free-and-easy familiar friends. On the introduction of the new system, no attempt was made to sweep the place clean before the arrival of greatly increased numbers. Old officers remained, and old convicts; enough of both to perpetuate the old evils and to render them twice as harmful under the new aspect of the settlement. Gardens were still allowed; great freedom to come and go hither and thither, with no strict observance of bounds; any number of private shops existed whereat the convicts bought and sold, or bartered with each other for pork and vegetables and other articles of general use. Worse than this, the "Ring" was left untouched, and grew daily more and more powerful, till a band of some forty or fifty cut-throat scoundrels ruled the whole convictdom of the settlement. The members of this "Ring" were in league with the cooks, from whom they obtained the best portions of the food, abstracted from their fellow-prisoners' rations; but no one dared to complain. Such was the malignant terrorism inspired by these fifty ruffians, that they kept the whole body of the convicts in awe, and their wholesale plunderings and pilferings flourished unchecked long before any attempt was made to put them down. Under such conditions as these, the management of the convicts in Norfolk Island was certainly a disgrace to the authorities.

Following Mr. Stewart's visit, a more stringent system was attempted, although not entirely carried out. The commandant was informed that he must tighten the reins. One by one the highly prized privileges disappeared: trafficking was now for the first time openly discountenanced, and the prisoners at length saw themselves debarred from many little luxuries and indulgences. A strictly coercive labour-gang was established; the gardens were shut; the limits of bounds rigorously enforced; and, last but not least, a firm attack was made upon the method of messing, to check, if possible, the unlawful misappropriation of food. In this last measure lay the seed of serious trouble. It interfered directly with the vested interest of a small but powerful oligarchy, the members of which were not disposed to surrender lightly the rights they had so long arrogated to themselves. From the moment that the robberies in the cook-house had been discovered, a growing spirit of dissatisfaction and discontent was observable among the more influential prisoners.

A second authorised attack in the same direction brought matters to a crisis. Not the least of the evils attending the old plan of messing was, that the prisoners themselves, one by one, were allowed access to the kitchen, where they might cook anything they happened to have in possession, whether obtained by fair means or foul. To meet these culinary requirements, most of the "flash men" had collected pots and pans of various sorts, constructed chiefly from the regulation mess-tins and platters. It was decided as a bold stroke against illicit cookery, to seize every *batterie de cuisine* in the place. Accordingly, one evening, after the convicts had been locked up for the night, a careful search was made through the lumber-yard (the mess-room, so to speak), and everything of illegal shape was seized. All these collected articles were then and there removed to the convicts' barrack store. It must be remarked here that several of the officials shrunk from executing this duty. One free overseer, named Smith, who was also superintendent of the cook-house, urged that he was all day among the prisoners, and felt his life hardly safe if it were known that he had taken part in the search. Others demurred also; but eventually the work was done.

Next morning, when the convicts went to breakfast, they missed their highly prized kitchen utensils. A storm quickly gathered, and broke forth with ungovernable fury. A great mass of men, numbering several hundreds, streamed at once out of the lumber-yard, and hurried towards the barrack stores. Everything fell before them: fastenings, woodwork, doorposts. There within were the cans, the cause of all this coil. These they gathered up at once, and then turned back, still *en masse*, to the lumber-yard. They were in search now of victims. Their thirst was for blood, and nothing less would quench it. They sought first the officers they hated most; and chief among these was Smith, the overseer of the kitchen. A convict named Westwood, by birth a gentleman, and having received a superior education, commonly called "Jacky-Jacky," was ringleader, and marched at the head of the mutineers. All were armed—some with long poles, others with axes, most with knives. It was a case of *sauve qui peut* with the officers. There were not more than half a dozen constables on duty, and warning came to four of them too late. Smith, who had remained in the cook-house, was caught and murdered on the spot. Another officer, Morris, was also killed. Two others were struck down with mortal hurts. All the wounds inflicted were about the head and face. One man had his forehead cut open deep down into the cavity of the head. He had also a frightful gash from the eye down the cheek, through which the roof of the mouth was visible. Another had the whole of one side of his face completely smashed in, from the temple to the mouth. A third unfortunate man had his skull fractured. All this had happened in less time than it takes to tell it. Then the mutineers cried out for more blood. Leaving the lumber-yard, they made for the police huts, driving the few remaining constables before them, and striking down all they overtook. At the police huts they smashed the windows and did what damage they could. They were then for proceeding onward. "Let's get that villain Barrow," was now the cry—Mr. Barrow being the stipendiary magistrate, whom they hated with especially keen hatred. They were determined, so it was afterwards said, to murder every official on the island, and then to take to the bush.

By this time active opposition was close at hand. First came a military guard, which formed across the road, and checked all further advance of the mutineers. Presently Mr. Barrow himself appeared upon the scene with a larger detachment of troops, and in the presence of this exhibition of force the convicts retired quietly enough to their barracks.

The strength of the storm therefore was now spent. The mutineers were either for the moment satisfied with their efforts, or—which is more probable—they were cowed by the troops, and felt that it was now the turn for authority to play its hand. Accompanied by a strong escort of soldiers, the stipendiary magistrate went in amongst the convicts, examined all carefully, and then and there arrested every one who bore a single spot or stain of blood. Seven were thus singled out at once, among them Jacky-Jacky and several members of the "Ring." Forty-five others, who were strongly suspected of complicity in the murders, were also arrested; and all these, heavily ironed, were for immediate security chained together in a row to the iron runners of the boat-shed. But such was the alarm on the island, that the commandant was strenuously urged to remove these ringleaders at once to Van Diemen's Land.

Indeed it was felt on all sides that there was no longer any safety for either life or property. The convict population had reached the pitch of anarchy and insubordination. It was indeed thought that the storm would soon break out with renewed fury. The success which the mutineers had won would doubtless tempt them to fresh efforts. They gave signs, too, that they were ready to recommence. When the corpses of the murdered men were carried past the barracks, the convicts within yelled in derision, and cried that these victims should not be the last. The apprehension was so great, that some officials maintained that the convicts ought to remain immured in their barracks until a reinforcement of troops arrived. There were some, too, who doubted the loyalty of the soldiers, saying that the troops would yet make common cause with the convicts. But this was never proved. What was really evident, was that the soldiers were harassed and overworn by the incessant duties they had been called upon recently to perform. They had been continually under arms, and were often on guard six nights out of the seven. Fortunately Sir Eardly Wilmot, Governor of Van Diemen's Land, had acted on Mr. Stewart's representations, and had despatched reinforcements long before this, which landed on the island a day or two after the actual outbreak. The most serious dangers were therefore at an end.

But the state of Norfolk Island called for some radical reformatory measures. If anything further had been needed to prove the incompetence of the commandant, it was to be found in his latest proceedings. Sudden changes, passing from laxity to strictness, had been made in the regulations; yet no precautionary measures were taken to meet that violent resistance which the convicts had long openly threatened. The last act of authority, the removal of the cooking utensils, should at least have been backed by an imposing exhibition of armed force. It was, indeed, time to substitute new men and new measures. The Hobart Town executive council resolved unanimously to suspend the commandant and to replace him by Mr. Price, the police magistrate of Hobart Town, a gentleman of knowledge, firmness, and long experience with the convict population in the island. His instructions were precise. He was to disarm the convicts and take from them the knives they habitually carried; to make all wear, without distinction, the convict dress; to compel close attendance on divine service; to institute messes, regulate the muster, insist upon exact obedience to all rules, and above all, to enforce the due separation of the convicts at night. By close attention to these regulations it was hoped that peace and good order would soon be restored to the settlement.

At the same time condign punishment was meted out to the mutineers. A judge went down posthaste to the island, a court was formed immediately on his arrival, trials proceeded with, and fourteen were hanged the same day. This salutary example, with the measures promptly introduced by Mr. Price, soon restored order to the island. The new commandant was undoubtedly a man of great courage and decision of character. He acted always for himself, and looked into everything with his own eyes. Being perpetually on the move about the settlement, nothing escaped him. Frequently when he met convicts, though he might have with him only one constable as orderly, he would halt them, and search them from head to foot. If they had knives or other forbidden articles, he impounded them forthwith; saying as often as not, "I'll have you to understand, my men, that in twelve months you shall see a gold watch upon the road and yet not pick it up." Under his able government the evils of Norfolk Island were sensibly lessened; but nothing could wash the place clean. So convinced was the imperial government of this, that they had resolved, even before the news of the mutiny, to break up the settlement. But after that, positive instructions were sent out to carry this into effect, and by degrees the place was altogether abandoned.

Indeed, the results of "probation," as they had shown themselves, were far from ignored at home, and the members of successive administrations had sought anxiously to provide some remedy for evils so plainly apparent. Mr. Gladstone among others, when Under Secretary of State for the Colonies, propounded an elaborate scheme for the establishment of a new settlement in North Australia. This new colony was to provide an outlet for the overplus in labour, which at that time in Van Diemen's Land choked up every avenue to employment. "It is founded"—to use Mr. Gladstone's own words—"as a receptacle for convicts who, by pardon or lapse of time, have regained their freedom, but who may be unable to find elsewhere an effective demand for their services." It was to be a colony of emancipists. The earliest settlers would be exiles sent out from England, with whose assistance the governor of the new colony was to prepare for the arrival of the rest from Van Diemen's Land. The first points which would require attention, were the selection of the best sites for a town and harbour, the reservation of certain crown lands, and the distribution of the rest to the various sorts of settlers. All these points were fully discussed and provided for minutely by Mr. Gladstone. Every other detail was equally well arranged. As economy was to be the soul of the new settlement, its officials were to rank lower than those of other colonies. The governor was to be styled only superintendent, and the judge, chairman of quarter sessions. The whole settlement was to be subordinate to New South Wales. And, as the word "convict" was somewhat unsavoury to the Australian colonists, Mr. Gladstone provided also for this.

Ruins of Prison Church, Tasmania

The settlements in Tasmania formed an important feature of the English system of progressive penal servitude. Religious instruction was abundantly furnished, and a record of each prisoner's daily conduct was carefully kept, so that attendance at the regular church services naturally assisted the convict in his progress toward the last two stages of ticket-of-leave and pardon.

In anticipation of the possible objections of the people of New South Wales to the establishment of a new convict settlement on the continent of Australia, Mr. Gladstone put his foot down firmly, and declared he would admit no such protest. "It would be with sincere regret," he says, "that I should learn that so important a body of Her Majesty's subjects were inclined to oppose themselves to the measures I have thus attempted to explain. Any such opposition must be encountered by reminding those from whom it might proceed, in terms alike respectful and decided, that it is impossible that Her Majesty should be advised to surrender what appears to be one of the vital interests of the British Empire at large, and one of the chief benefits which the British Empire can at present derive from the dominion which we have acquired over the vast territories of the crown in Australia. I think that by maintaining such a colony as a depot of labour, available to meet the local wants of the older colony, or to find employment for the capital accumulated there, we may rather promote than impede the development of the resources of New South Wales. But even if that hope should be disappointed, I should not, therefore, be able to admit that the United Kingdom was making an unjust or unreasonable exercise of the right of sovereignty over those vast regions of the earth, in thus devoting a part of them to the relief of Van Diemen's Land, and consequently to render that island the receptacle for as many convicts as it may be hereafter necessary to transport there. Having practically relieved New South Wales, at no small inconvenience to ourselves, from the burden (as soon as it became a burden) of receiving convicts from this country, we are acquitted of any obligations in that respect which any colonist, the most jealous for the interests of his native or adopted country, could ascribe to us."

But it never came to this. No antagonism in this instance ever arose between the colonial and imperial governments, for Mr. Gladstone and his colleagues just then went out of power, and the project of the new colony in North Australia was given up by the new ministry which had to deal with the question in two phases: first, the evils actually in existence from the over-crowding of Van Diemen's Land must be mitigated, if they could not be removed; and secondly, some plan must be adopted to obviate their recurrence in the future. The first point was touched by suspending transportation altogether for two years. The stream thus checked, would have to be directed elsewhere; but in the meantime, Van Diemen's Land would be relieved: in the course of two years the probation-gangs would be emptied, and the great labour pressure caused by the crowds of pass-holders would have disappeared. To deal still further with the actual difficulty, new and able men were appointed as administrators: Sir William Denison was to go out as governor, and Mr. Hampton comptroller-general of convicts. So much for the first point.

The second embraced a wider field. The government was bound, not only to provide for the thousands with which it had saddled itself by the cessation of transportation to Van Diemen's Land for a couple of years, but it had to look further ahead and legislate for future years. It was now decided that transportation, as it had hitherto been understood and carried out, should come to an end. Although two years had been the limit of its temporary suspension, any expectation of recurring to the old system at the end of that period was "altogether illusory." The new system, stated briefly, was to consist of a limited period of separate imprisonment at home, succeeded by employment on public works, either abroad at Bermuda or Gibraltar, or in this country; and ultimately followed in ordinary cases by exile or banishment for the remaining term of the original sentence. The following was now to be the ordering of the lives of convicts:

A term of separate confinement, continuing from six to eighteen months, according to sentence and the manner in which prisoners bore the punishment; forced labour at home penal establishments, or at Gibraltar or Bermuda, this term to depend also on sentence, but the time by arrangement of tasks to be shortened by industry; and finally tickets-of-leave in the colonies.

This system remained in force with sanguine hopes of success, until a year or two after the establishment of the system, when Van Diemen's Land, the principal colonial outlet, waxed virtuous, and would have no more convicts, whether whitewashed or not, at any price. The colony would not have them at any price nor in any shape or form. Although pains were taken to explain that these were well-disposed "ticket-of-leave men," not convicts, their reception was violently opposed. A struggle ensued, but in the end the imperial government gave way, and the last convict ship sailed for Van Diemen's Land in 1852. While we cannot withhold approval of the course the colony adopted, there is no doubt that it was almost suicidal. Mr. Trollope, who visited Van Diemen's Land, now known as Tasmania, in 1871, describes in graphic language the consequences to the colony of its conduct. Absolute stagnation and want of enterprise were everywhere apparent, the skeletons of great works in ruins, others half finished and doomed to decay for want of hands, land relapsing into uncultivation, towns deserted, grass growing in the streets—the whole place lifeless and inert. Possibly, if the question had been put at another time the answer might have been different. But in 1850, the discomforts entailed by transportation were so recent and disagreeable, that free colonists could not be brought to believe that by a better system of administration such evils might be altogether avoided.

Nor were the people of Van Diemen's Land singular in their resolve. Even before they had in plain language so declined, other colonies had displayed a similar unmistakable reluctance to become receptacles for convicts. As early as 1848, the British government, in search of new fields for transportation, had addressed a circular to all colonial governors, pointing out in persuasive periods, the advantages to be gained by accepting this valuable labour which, nevertheless, no one cared to have. Strange to say, only one colony—that of Western Australia—replied affirmatively to this appeal. At the Cape of Good Hope, the appearance of the convict ship *Neptune*, from Bermuda, in September, 1849, produced a tumultuous and indignant protest. The moment her arrival was signalled, the church bells began to toll half-minute time, and a public notice was put forth by the anti-convict association, calling on the people to be calm. At the same time the municipal commissioners addressed the governor, Sir Harry Smith, begging that the *Neptune* might be forthwith ordered to leave the shores of the Cape. "The convicts," they said, "must not, cannot, and shall not be landed or kept in any of the ports of the colony." Sir Harry's answer was that he must carry out his orders; upon which the people drew a cordon round the ship and cut off supplies from Government House, so that His Excellency could get no meat, and had to bake his own bread. Finally, he agreed to compromise, and the *Neptune* was allowed to remain in the bay till a vessel could be sent home for instructions. The authorities at home considered the opposition at the Cape too serious to be resisted, and directed the *Neptune* to proceed elsewhere.

At other places the bent of the colonial mind made itself equally unmistakable, so that it was at length openly announced in the House of Commons, that unless the colonies grew more amenable, transportation must cease.

As all these various questions covered a period of several years, it can hardly be said that the crisis which necessitated change came suddenly or all at once. The government was loath to surrender till the very last the idea of maintaining the existing system or something like it, but they were not without fair warning that they were building on hopes delusive and insecure. And it is evident that throughout the period of doubt they gave the question the most anxious care, although the evident disposition was more towards tinkering up what was rickety and useless, than substituting a radically new plan. To this, no doubt, they were in a measure forced. The mere idea of retaining a large mass of convicts at home was hailed by the public with alarm; and it became almost an axiom that offenders sooner or later, but as a rule inevitably, must be banished from the country. This was long the underlying principle of every scheme. The convicts must be removed to a distance, not necessarily as a punishment—it might be as a boon to themselves—but in any case as a benefit to their country. In point of symmetry the method is undoubtedly admirable; theoretically perfect now as it was then. The assisted emigration of discharged prisoners supplies the easiest means of providing them with that honest labour which is theoretically supposed to preserve them from a relapse into crime. But whether as freemen, exiles, or convicts in chains, they were all indelibly branded with the stigma of their guilt, and we cannot even now find a country ready to receive them. At the time indicated, the resolute attitude of all the colonies compelled England to reconsider her position. She was forced, in fact, though sorely against her will, to make the best of a bad bargain and keep nearly all her convicts at home.

CHAPTER IX GIBRALTAR

>Over-sea prisons continued till late date at Bermuda and Gibraltar—Major Griffiths' personal connection with Gibraltar—Called to supreme control by threatened outbreak—His association with convicts—Their demeanour and characteristics—His difficulties in administration—Curious cases—False confessions—Sea-captain who had cast away his ship—Ingenious and daring attempts to escape—A vanishing specimen of prisoner—The gentleman convict—The forbidden weed.

When the British colonies with sturdy, independent spirit refused almost unanimously to be the receptacle for the criminal sewage of the mother country, it became of paramount importance to find other outlets of disposal. The perfected system of penal servitude now in force was of slow growth, and at the beginning many places were utilised that could voice no protest. Two isolated strongholds, Bermuda and Gibraltar, were pressed into service without question; they were both crown possessions at the mercy of the authorities and plausible reasons could be offered for turning them into convict prisons. They were at no great distance, easily accessible by sea, and could very nearly guarantee safe custody. Then the labour of the prisoners would be available there for defensive purposes and colonial development. In both places many monuments to their skill and industry are still preserved; both are decisive points in the national strategy; one at least has a glorious history and the other may any day prove of signal value to the ocean communications of Great Britain.

It was my fortune to be closely associated with the convict prison of the so-called impregnable fortress of Gibraltar, which was for some time under my personal supervision, and I had abundant opportunities for observing the traits and peculiarities of identically the same classes as those who have provided the materials for the historical chapters already compiled.

My call to functions of control came with dramatic suddenness and surprise. I was plunged into the middle of new and strange surroundings without a word of warning. There had been two outbreaks at the prison, where a weak executive had broken down and a collection of turbulent characters was encouraged to oppose and defy authority. An outbreak was imminent at any moment, I was told, as I galloped up to the scene of disturbance and proceeded to take charge. I might indeed have been at Port Arthur or Norfolk Island, but for the comforting reflection that above me the guns of the fortress showed their formidable teeth, tier above tier, and that several thousands of the best troops in the world were within easy reach to check peremptorily any breach of the peace.

The likeness might have been carried further, for there were many among the convicts who had made the dread voyage across to the Southern Hemisphere, who had been in the chain gangs and in assigned service,—veteran survivors of the dark days of transportation and the makeshifts that replaced it. Five hundred paraded for my inspection, and as I slowly walked down the ranks I made my first acquaintance with the physiognomy and demeanour of felons. Many exhibited the peculiar features now commonly assigned to them by the criminologists; the lowering brow, the prognathous jaw, the handle-shaped ear. These were largely the born criminals of the great Italian savant Professor Lombroso, "having projecting ears, thick hair, thin beards, prominent frontal eminences, enormous jaws, square protruding chins, large cheek bones, and frequent gesticulations." I may note the description of another observer. "Their cringing and timid ways," he says, "the mobility and cunning of their looks; a something feline about them, something cowardly humble, suppliant and crushed, makes them a class apart,—one would say dogs who had been whipped; with here and there a few energetic and brutal heads of rebels."

I cannot say that the submissive air was greatly noticeable, when I first saw them. They might have been a pirate's or a slaver's crew; their costume was nautical, a tarpaulin hat, round jacket, wide duck trousers and low shoes. Their faces were mostly unpleasing; their tone and demeanour were arrogant and aggressive. They held their heads high and looked me insolently in the face. I could see plainly that the bonds of discipline had been relaxed, and that there had been no firm hand on them of late; indeed it was the mental failure of my predecessor which had brought me there in his place to try my prentice hand upon a (to me) new and unruly team. No doubt there were many grievances abroad among them. The old comptroller, as the supreme chief was styled, had introduced many irksome regulations and at the same time withdrawn many small privileges and indulgences that had come to be looked upon as a right and were much missed. What would be my attitude toward my charges? It was quite evident that from the moment I appeared I became the cynosure of every eye. Every one was watching me closely, curiously, seeking to make out what kind of man I was.

We soon grew better acquainted. A prominent part of my new duties was to give a personal interview to any convict who applied. I found that afternoon that almost every one had put his name down to see me, and presently I took my seat in the chair of authority, without the smallest previous knowledge, to listen to complaints, grant requests and answer questions of the most intricate kind. I soon found that I was quite unable to deal with matters so entirely new to me. I had hardly a word to say. The only possible course was to acquire knowledge without delay. Laying hands on all the authorities available, books of rules, standing orders, printed circulars, official correspondence—I retired to the comptroller's house, where my servants had made me up a rough and ready home. I studied the voluminous mass of details far into the night, every spare minute the next day and again late into the next night. I worked on, conning my lesson diligently, painfully, but with ultimate success. By the third day, Monday, when the applicants again paraded, their numbers already largely increased, I was in a position to dispose pretty summarily of all but the most complicated affairs.

It was in these interviews, which were accorded in private if so desired, that I first gained an insight into convict character, its guilefulness, its duplicity, its infinite art in seeking to gain the ends in view; to evade or modify the regulations, often harsh enough, to secure a modicum of comfort, an atom more food, lighter and less irksome labour, a little sympathy in listening to a "case" and obtain support for a petition to have a trial revised and secure pardon or mitigation of sentence. As a newcomer and absolute tyro, I was held fair game by every specious impostor, who could "pitch" a harrowing, heart-rending tale. I was victimised very early by the curious craze of the criminal mind for false confession, guilt assumed, without a shadow of proof, for short-lived glorification or a period of idleness while investigation was in progress.

One of the first cases of this kind made an extraordinary impression on me. I was entirely befooled. The play was so well acted by such finished performers that in my inexperienced innocence I was easily carried away. A convict whom I will style X came to me with tears in his eyes, evidently under the influence of the strangest emotion, and asked to speak to me alone. He desired to give himself up as the real perpetrator of a certain atrocious crime, a murder in the city of London which had hitherto baffled detection. He was a tall man with a long yellow face set in coal black, stubby hair, and with baleful black eyes, deep set under bushy black eyebrows. He was in the most agitated state of mind. Remorse most profound and agonising possessed him as he poured forth his piteous tale and enlarged upon the horrible details of the murder. It was impossible not to yield him full credit. If I had any doubt, it would have been removed when his accomplice whom he betrayed was brought in. I will call him Y.

A second scene was now enacted,—a duologue with the parts in strange contrast. X denounced his companion with virtuous indignation. Y altogether repudiated the charge. The first told his story with all the realism of manifest truth. The second denied it as stoutly as he could, but I seemed to see the half-heartedness of conscious guilt. Y was a weaker vessel; a round faced, chubby looking man, smug, self-sufficient, inclined to be off-hand and jaunty as he faced me giving the lie to his accuser. For a long time he fought, but with failing force before the insistence of his opponent. Then, all at once, he threw up the sponge. Yes; it was all quite true. They had killed the poor old woman, the bank caretaker, had brained her with a knuckle-duster, and then stabbed her to the heart.

My course was plain. I was bound to report the strange story to my superiors and ask for instructions. The two convicts were held strictly apart, lodged in separate cells, given writing materials and required to set forth their confessions at length, which were forwarded to England. An answer came in due course. There was not one syllable of truth in the story. Neither X nor Y had been within a hundred miles of the scene of the crime. One of them, indeed, was actually at the time in prison for another offence. They had heard of the crime, had put their heads together while on the works where they laboured in association, and had concocted the whole fraud by which I had been so completely misled. This was the first spurious confession that had come within my purview, but by no means the last. The practice is common enough among criminals, both inside and outside the prison. The reasons are generally the same. The convict, as in this case, hopes to be remanded for a new trial, and to lead an idle life while awaiting it.

The inexperienced prison officer is very apt, and not strangely, to be imposed upon also by eloquent and persistent protestations of innocence. No one is guilty in gaol. A French *aumônier*, "chaplain," once called upon his congregation in the prison chapel to answer him honestly and truthfully, by holding up their hands, whether they acknowledged the justice of their conviction. Only one hand was held up in response. I was as gullible as any other beginner until repeated disappointment hardened my heart. One of the first cases that worked a change was that of the coxswain of my gig. It was a smart little craft, the favourite plaything of my predecessor, who had manned it with a crew of convicts dressed like men-of-war's men, and the coxswain was an ex-master mariner, who had earned a long sentence for casting away his ship. W, the man in question, and I became very good friends. He was a neat, civil spoken, well conducted sailor, and I weakly let him see that I took an interest in him. He came to me on an early occasion praying that his case might be reconsidered. He assured me that he had been wrongfully convicted, the victim of a base plot fabricated and sworn to by some of his crew who hated him for ruling them with too tight a hand. There was not a word of truth in the charges brought against him, and if there were only a criminal court of appeal he would very speedily be released.

I confess I was won over by his specious pleading. I liked the man and was sorry for him, and I promised to make a full inquiry. There was a file of the London *Times* on the shelves of the Gibraltar garrison library and it was easy to turn to the number containing the full proceeding of the trial. All doubt was immediately dispelled, and I saw at the first glance that I had once more been imposed upon. The charge rested upon the clearest evidence, and the facts were proved beyond the shadow of a doubt. Captain W. had deliberately prepared his ship for destruction. It was shown that he had gone himself into the hold and had bored holes in the ship's side with an auger and scuttled her. She was cast away, and sank, but within reach of shore and of diving operations, which proclaimed the criminal ill-treatment of her skipper, to whom the possession and use of the augers were distinctly brought home. The evil intention was further shown by the valueless cargo shipped and the large amount for which it had been insured. After my experience with X, I rather slackened in my excessive sympathy with my unfortunate charges and was prepared to believe that they had had as much fair play as comes to most of us in this crooked world.

The fate which eventually overtook this gig and its convict crew well illustrates the difficulties of management in an oversea prison in near proximity to a foreign country. Spain is within a stone's throw of Gibraltar, and at the time of which I am writing there was no extradition of criminals. The question was complicated by the British reluctance to give up political refugees, and Spain would make no difference between classes. No treaty of extradition was possible which did not extend to all, and the convict at Gibraltar was well aware that he was safe if he set foot on Spanish soil. These facts were known in the prison, for local convicts were also confined there, and they could one and all see the Spanish shore a few miles away. There was always the chance of seizing a boat and escaping to the other side of the bay.

On one occasion a ship's cutter was seized and the fugitives made off. The warning gun was fired, the flag was run up at the yard-arm on the signal station on the top of the rock, and the alarm given at the dockyard. Some one immediately ordered out the convict gig to go in pursuit with an armed escort. The crew bent manfully to their oars and quickly overhauled the chase, but by this time they were half way across the bay. The temptation was too strong for loyalty. The crew of the gig rose upon the warder, disarmed him and consigning him to the bottom of the boat, carried it and him to Algeciras, where all parties landed without let or hindrance. The Spanish authorities were by no means overjoyed at the arrival of these desperadoes, but would not arrest them. They took to the wild hill country around and were a terror to quiet folk until they were gradually taken up for new offences or were shot down by the *quadras civiles*.

Escape was the dazzling lure before the eyes of the Gibraltar convicts and more than one ardent spirit strove to compass it. The patience and ingenuity exhibited by one man was really marvellous. He was employed alone in a remote workshop and had discovered that it communicated with one of the hollows or caves with which the great oolitic rock is honeycombed. In this he had constructed and kept concealed a boat built of the nondescript materials that came to his hand—scraps of canvas, disused cement bags and small pieces of timber. It was not unlike a collapsible boat, in three separate compartments for convenience of carriage, which could be made into one tiny dingy or coracle sufficient to keep one man afloat. He expected to be able to launch this fragile craft unobserved, choosing a favourable opportunity, and to commit himself to the waters of the Straits of Gibraltar, a narrow passage ever crowded with shipping, where he hoped to be picked up by some craft. He had laid by a store of provisions saved from his meagre rations, which he carried out daily from the prison. It was his abstraction of food that betrayed him to a jealous comrade, who treacherously gave him away and led to the detection of his undoubtedly clever scheme. The intensity of his disappointment when discovered was quite pathetic.

A seemingly much more serious affair was a plot set on foot for a combined attempt to break prison after rising upon the guards. When the matter was reported to me, it had all the aspect of a dangerous conspiracy and it imposed upon me, but I have reason now to think it was all a hoax. Convicts have no loyalty to each other and their best laid plans "gang aft agley," for the secret is rarely kept. Some one usually turns traitor. The scheme is at times a pure invention devised by some astute prisoner seeking to curry favour by his revelations to the authorities. If it has any foundation in fact, there is a race between the traitors, each anxious to be the first in betrayal and thus render himself safe.

On this occasion the dread news was broken by picking up an anonymous letter giving the particulars of the coming disturbance. Then came a very confidential message from a patient in the hospital whom I visited and who gave me some startling news. A deep laid conspiracy was afoot to rise while at work in a distant quarry, to overmaster warders and military guards and march straight on board the admiralty brig employed to remove the heavily laden lighters from the quarry. To cast her loose would be the work of a moment, and with steam up she might be taken across the bay before the alarm could be given and pursuit organised. The whole story seemed farfetched but I could not ignore the warning. Upon my requisition to the military authorities, the guards were reinforced. They loaded ostentatiously before marching to the quarry, and on arrival there it was found that the steam tug was absent on some other duty. There was no outbreak, nor the semblance of one. The turbulent spirits were cowed at this exhibition of formidable strength, if indeed there were any who had contemplated mischief.

I must add a few words to the general description of the personnel of the Gibraltar convict prisoners. They were interesting to me, many of them as the survivors of the great tide of criminal exiles that turned for years toward the antipodes. They were to be easily recognised by those who had the key; their swarthy, weather-beaten complexions spoke of long exposure to trying climates. They were hardy in aspect, with muscular, well-knit frames, developed by much manual labour in the open air. They had the bold, self-reliant, reckless demeanour of men who had endured severe discipline and passed through it unbroken. They were hard, bitter men, who had faced the worst and were willing to do it again. Quarrelsome and of hasty temper, they might be cowed into good order, but were ever ready to break out and resist authority, to assault a warder or strike down a fellow convict with pick or shovel, or the first weapon that lay to hand. The type was entirely new to me then, and indeed I have seen little of it since, for they were a fast vanishing species and are to be met with no more in the prison population.

I will pick out one or two for more particular mention. One who was hopelessly "incorrigible," for instance, I will call H. This man happened to be in one of his periodical, almost chronic fits of rage on my first visit to the prison. My way had taken me across a drawbridge leading from the line wall road to the top of a winding staircase that descended to an inner gate which led straight into the main body of the prison. This main prison, by the way, was little better than a shed,—a long, low, two-storied wooden edifice, divided into bunks or cages shut off from each other and a central passage by iron bars. This building was filled with human beings, and, as we approached, the ceaseless hum of voices, angry and even menacing, rose from it into one piercing note, a yell or shriek of wild, or, it might be, maniacal, despair. We were told that it was H, who had broken out again and was now in a separate cell, and were asked if we would like to see him.

They took us through a detached block of strongly built stone cells in their own yard lying close under the line wall, and by this time the noise became almost deafening. Each cell had two doors; an outer door of stout iron bars, protecting an inner one of wood. The bolt of this second door was thrown back and exposed the interior. At that moment a mad figure rushed forward with frightful imprecations, to be checked, fortunately, by the outer iron gate; a wild and terrible beast, human only in form, clad in a hideous particoloured garb, the badge of those who had made a murderous assault on their guardians. He stood raving and raging impotently, threatening us with fluent vituperative tongue to the accompaniment of clanking chains. He was in leg irons and was also manacled with "figure eight" handcuffs on his wrists, and so could do no injury even to himself.

This H was one of a class who presently became a danger to London and complicated the penal question by the alleged inadequacy of the punishment. He was a man of cruel and ungovernable temper, addicted to crimes of violence, who ill-used as well as robbed his victims. There were others like him at Gibraltar, but none that equalled him in his savagery and determined defiance of authority. Nothing seemed to tame him; prolonged doses of dieting, punishment and cellular isolation had no effect. He continued intractable to the last, and was one of those withdrawn and brought home to England three years later when the Gibraltar convict prison was abolished.

"Captain" P.—titular rank is generally preserved among prisoners when speaking of or to each other—was of a different kind, irreconcilable also, but his resistance was rather moral than physical. He was always surly, sulky and impudent; inclined to be disobedient, but keeping within the line of sharp reprimands. I remember him as a smooth-speaking, supple-backed, cringing creature, anxious to show that he had been well-bred and that he had occupied a superior station, but dropping all at once into the other extreme if crossed or offended, when his language was of the foulest and his manner disgusting. I met "Captain" P. again under rather amusing circumstances. One afternoon when standing among my gangs at work upon the foundation of the new Wormwood Scrubs prison, I saw a well-dressed, gentlemanly looking man approach under escort of the gate keeper. He wore a well-cut frock and a shining silk hat, which he lifted courteously as he bowed low, to the manifest delight of some of the convicts around. They knew him well. It was "Captain" P. who had been an old comrade in Portland or Dartmoor, and who, now a free man, had impudently decided to pay me a formal call. He addressed me as an old friend, saying: "You were always so good to me when I served under your orders at Gibraltar" (it might have been in some distinguished cavalry regiment) "that I have ventured to intrude upon you to ask if you can help me to some employment." I am afraid I answered rather curtly and ordered him to be shown out of the enclosure. Had he been a different man, penitent and well-disposed, with a blameless prison character, and determined to turn over a new leaf, I would gladly have given him a helping hand. But there had been a second sentence since the term at Gibraltar, and I soon learned that he was a hardened, habitual criminal. Oddly enough, at the very time of his visit, a friend was standing with me who knew him personally in previous days, when he was a captain in the British army and came to grief over a forged check.

Life in a colonial convict prison was not eventful, and yet not monotonous. Some of the more startling episodes have been recounted. The chase for tobacco constantly kept us busy. Its use is strictly tabooed in British prisons, but the forbidden weed will always find its way inside. Nothing will check its introduction, and its presence is proved by the fact that tobacco has a regular price in articles of food, the only possible circulating medium. The traffic depends upon the dishonesty of officials, who are bribed by prisoners' friends to pass it in, the safe keeping and distribution being the work of the prisoners themselves. At Gibraltar, where "free" people came and went in the quarries almost unquestioned, large transactions were constantly afoot. The new arrivals brought out cash and the "traffickers" were clever in finding hiding places in the rock for the money offered and the weed when bought. We made many searches for both the raw material and its price, and I can call to mind long watches in the night for the agents who brought in the stuff, and elaborate devices to catch the culprits in actual possession of the forbidden weed.

A few months spent in this varied fashion was no bad preparation for the new career on which I was about to embark. I was called to service in the home department, and during many years was closely associated with the entire penal system of Great Britain. From small beginnings, devised under the pressure of great emergency, these experiments have grown into the present system of secondary punishment. Opinions differ as to its value and merits, but these will best be judged by independent critics on learning what measures were adopted upon the cessation of penal exile, and what grew out of them.

CHAPTER X THE BRITISH SYSTEM OF PENAL SERVITUDE

A substitute for transportation—Task entrusted to Colonel Jebb—Initiates Public Works' Prisons in England—Plans to assist in the construction of great breakwater at Portland—Rapid progress—Much useful work executed by the convicts—Old War Prison of Dartmoor prepared for convicts employed in the reclamation of savage moorland—New prison at Chatham for extension of the naval dockyard—Similar undertaking at Portsmouth—New system carried out conscientiously—First results satisfactory—The garroter—Insecurity of London streets—Discipline of penal servitude lax—Royal commission advocates new principles and insists upon greater severity—Strenuous industry enforced under the "mark" system—Favourable results.

Transportation beyond the seas ended when the British colonies positively refused to receive the penal exiles. One of them, Queensland, lately founded in Australia, which was supposed to be favourable, repudiated the idea entirely, and its citizens asked impertinently whether they might be permitted in return to transport their own malefactors to the British Isles. Then the geographers began to search for new lands suitable for penal settlements. One suggested the Falkland Islands, and another New Guinea, while Labrador was felt by many to be exactly the place for convict colonisation. Western Australia, as a matter of fact, did not object; it was a crown colony and could not protest, but it was never very largely utilised.

The excessive costliness of transportation was the principal demerit of this practice. A few figures will show this. As late as 1851, the gross cost for one year was £586,294 for passages out to the antipodes, establishments and staff, including the home depots, Bermuda and Gibraltar. There was a certain set-off in the value of the labour of the convicts, and when this had been credited, the net cost remained at £419,476. To arrive at any general estimate, this annual expenditure must be multiplied by the seventy years the system lasted. It cannot, of course, be denied that the product was Australia, a substantial section, no doubt, for the cash expended, but the evils entailed by the system must be taken into account, and modern feeling revolted from repeating the process even to gain such a large and prosperous dependency, provided additional territory was available. As we have seen, the territory did not exist. Thus the only alternative was to retain the convicts at home, to house and dispose of them as economically as possible, and at the same time utilise them effectively in such works and public undertakings as might reasonably be expected to bring in some adequate return.

The solution of the pressing problem was entrusted to Colonel, afterward Sir Joshua, Jebb, a distinguished officer of the Royal Engineers, who was already well known in connection with prison building and with penal legislation generally. He had for some years past been associated with the two official inspectors of prisons; after that he had assisted in the superintendence of Millbank, when constituting a convict depot, and he had been in reality the moving spirit of the commissioners who built the model prison at Pentonville. In those early years he gave undoubted earnest of his energetic character and great powers, a promise more than fulfilled. His proposal was to construct a great breakwater at Portland, largely assisted by the labour of convicts which was abundant and running to waste. He meant in the first instance to provide accommodation of some sort on the island of Portland wherein the convicts might be securely lodged immediately adjoining their works. He described, in a memorandum dated 1847, the style of place he proposed to build. Naturally, he said, when the works on which the prisoners were to be employed were likely to be completed within a limited time, something less costly than a substantial prison would suffice. Safe custody and the due enforcement of discipline must of course be secured; but these might be obtained without any very extravagant outlay. He suggested, therefore, buildings on wooden frames, with corrugated iron partitions; the whole so constructed as to be easily taken to pieces and removed to another site if required. In these buildings the convicts might be kept safe and separate, at the probable cost of little more than £34 per cell. Similar prisons might be run up anywhere, so that the entire number of convicts for whom accommodation was required might be housed for about two hundred thousand pounds. Colonel Jebb accompanied this proposal with certain figures as an off-set against this outlay. He assumed that the maintenance, including every item, would amount to £158,000, but their earnings would be £180,000. The balance was therefore a gain of £22,000—a sufficient interest on the original cost of the prison buildings. These figures were speculative, of course, nor were they found exactly accurate in practice; the cost of maintenance proved undoubtedly higher than thus estimated, but in return the earnings were also considerably more.

Three years later, in March, 1850, Colonel Jebb reported to the Secretary of State that he had provided room for eight hundred and forty prisoners at Portland. The main buildings consisted of four large open halls, eighty-eight feet long by twenty-one broad, having four tiers of cells on each side. The interiors of the halls were well ventilated and could be warmed; the cells were seven feet by four, and furnished with hammocks, tables and shelves for books. The cells were divided by partitions of corrugated iron, and were sufficient to secure the effectual separation of the men at night, and to admit of their taking their meals in them, and reading or otherwise occupying themselves after working hours, until they went to bed. In addition to the cell accommodation there was, of course, full provision for officers' quarters, chapel, kitchen, laundries and stores. Moreover, ample space was reserved "within the boundary wall for the erection of additional buildings, so as to increase the number of convicts to twelve or fifteen hundred, if it should be found necessary or desirable." Everything was now in fair working order. The foundation stone of the breakwater had been laid in July, 1849, by Prince Albert, who visited the prison and presented a Bible and prayer-book for use in its chapel; but till then, and during the first year of the occupation of a "bleak and barren rock" the convicts were chiefly employed in setting things straight within the prison walls. They had to level parade grounds, make roads and reservoirs, fit gates and doors, paint and clean up the whole establishment. As soon as practicable they were set to work on the breakwater. "The stone," says Colonel Jebb, "is to be removed from the quarries by means of several lines of railways, which are arranged in a series of inclined planes from the summit to the point where the breakwater joins the shore. The wagons will be raised and lowered by wire ropes, working on 'drums,' placed at the head of each 'incline,' the loaded train in its descent drawing up the empty one from the breakwater."

In the general detail of work, the share that fell upon the convicts was the plate-laying, levelling, forming embankments and excavations, getting out and stacking the stone, filling the wagons, sending them down and bringing them back from the incline. Some five hundred men were so employed during the first year, 1849, and their earnings were estimated at about fifteen thousand pounds.

Portland, when thus fairly launched, became the starting point for the new arrangements. Other prisons were needed, and they must be built like Portland. But time pressed, and anything actually available at the moment was eagerly pressed into the service. Down at Dartmoor, on the high lands above Tavistock, was a huge building which had been empty for five-and-thirty years. Its last occupants had been the French and American prisoners of war, who were confined there until the peace of 1814. Ten thousand, some said twelve thousand, had been accommodated within the walls—surely there must be room there for several hundred convicts? Colonel Jebb, hearing that Captain Groves, from Millbank, was staying at Plymouth, begged him to run over to inspect Dartmoor. The place was like a howling wilderness; the buildings in places were without roofs; the walls were full of holes, if not in ruins. But a few repairs would soon make the place habitable, said Captain Groves, and accordingly a gang of convicts, under Mr. Morrish, was sent down to begin operations. In a short time Dartmoor prison was opened. Then other receptacles were prepared. The hulks had been pressed into the service, and were employed at the various dockyards to house the convicts, but only as a temporary measure, until proper buildings on the new plan could be erected. There were ships at Woolwich, and others at Portsmouth. At the first station the old *Warrior*, and the *Defence*, took the able-bodied, while the *Unité* served as a hospital; at Portsmouth there were the *York*, *Briton* and *Stirling Castle*, until 1852, when the new convict prison was occupied. Soon after this, contracts were entered into for the erection of a large prison at Chatham, which was completed in 1858, and to which all those at the Woolwich hulks were in course of time transferred. The intention at both these stations was to devote a goodly portion of the convict labour to further the dockyard extensions. At Chatham the object in view was to construct, high up the tortuous Medway, a chain of artificial basins capable of containing a fleet. Hither beaten ships might retire to refit; while new ironclads, built in the dock close by, might issue thence to retrieve disaster. From the first the work was of an arduous character. The battle was against the tide and the treacherous mud. But all of St. Mary's Island has been reclaimed, and marsh has given place to solid ground. At Portsmouth a feat has been accomplished, not exactly similar, but wonderful also in its way.

So much for the framework—the bones, so to speak, of the new system; let us see, next, something of the living tissues with which it was filled up. Speaking broadly, it may be laid down that the plan of treatment inaugurated by Colonel Jebb and his colleagues, was based on persuasion rather than coercion. This, indeed, they openly admitted. They were not advocates for a "purely coercive and penal discipline." They conceived that there was sufficient punishment without that; the convicts suffered enough in the "long periods during which they remained under penal restraint," and there was further discomfort in "their eventual deportation to a distant colony, and the somewhat severe restrictions to which they are subjected when they gain the boon of a ticket-of-leave," these regulations being drawn up at a time when transportation was still practised, though only to a limited extent. The directors of convict prisons hoped, therefore, to accomplish their object by reward and encouragement rather than by strictness and terror. They desired to put it plainly before every convict that if he would but continue quiet and obedient, he would be sure to benefit in the long run. It was really worth his while to be good, they said, and they encouraged him by the statement: "It will convince us that you are on the high road to reform, and the sooner we are convinced you are reformed, the sooner you will be set at large." Everything was made to depend on conduct—good conduct—in other words, the mere formal observance of rules, a submissive demeanour, and a readiness to echo, even with hypocritical hearts, the lessons the chaplains taught. The word "industry" was tacked on to "conduct," but only in a subordinate sense, and so long as the convict was civil he might be as lazy as he liked.

Precise rules provided the machinery by which a due estimate of each man's conduct was to be obtained. Every governor of a prison kept a character-book, in which he was to enter concisely his observations upon the character and conduct of every prisoner, so as thus to be enabled to reward him by classification and good conduct badges, and more especially "to report with confidence whenever he may be called upon in conjunction with the chaplain to assist the authorities in determining the period of detention of the different prisoners." The same rule went on to say, "He (the governor) shall take every opportunity of impressing on the prisoners that the particulars of their conduct are thus noticed and recorded; and that while no effort at good conduct and industry on the part of a prisoner will be disregarded by the authorities of the prison, every act of wilful misconduct and punishment will be equally noted, and will tend to prolong the period of his detention under penal discipline." The governor's opinion was to be endorsed by that of the chaplain, and even the subordinate officers were called upon to record their views of the demeanour of the prisoners they especially controlled. The whole object of this classification and this supervision was to "produce on the minds of the prisoners a practical and habitual conviction of the effect which their own good conduct and industry will have on their welfare and future prospects."

These extracts from Colonel Jebb's earliest reports will be sufficient to indicate the bias of his mind. He too, like others who had gone before, was hopeful of reformation by purely moral means. As he has himself declared in one of his reports, he thought he might more surely gain the great end he had in view by leading than by driving. Upon this principle the whole system of management was based. There can be no question that those who were its authors took their stand upon the highest ground. They were called upon to inaugurate a new order of things, and they did so to the best of their ability, in the most straightforward, conscientious fashion. The glaring evils of transportation, as it had been administered, were then still staring them in the face. "Speaking humanly," says Colonel Jebb, "the demoralisation of every individual sentenced to transportation was certain. No matter what might have been his previous character, what the amount of his constitution, or what the sincerity of his efforts and resolutions to retrace his steps, he was placed within the influence of a moral pestilence, from which, like death itself, there was no escape." The necessity for great and radical changes was imperative; and these changes were carried out in the manner I have described. Great results were expected to follow from them.

In the first few years everything appeared rosy. The reports continue: "As a body, the men show a spirit of willing and cheerful obedience. The strictest discipline is maintained with a very small proportion of punishment. The industry of the working parties is remarkable." Again, the same report asserts that "any candid and dispassionate inquiry into the condition and prospects of the convicts who have passed through periods of penal and reformatory discipline at Pentonville and Portland, will prove beyond doubt that, to say the least of it, the majority of those now serving are likely on their release to be respectable in their station of life, and useful to those who engage their services; thus realising the anticipations of the Pentonville commissioners, that a large proportion of our convicts would be qualified on their discharge to occupy an honest position in their own or any other country."

This was in 1852 and for the following ten years the new plans were persevered in with very general satisfaction. The public heard with pleasure of the notable results achieved. All indeed were a little weary of the subject of secondary punishment, and were content to leave the problem in the hands of officials whose duty it was to deal with it. How long this indifference might have continued it is impossible to conjecture, but all at once a panic fell upon people that was long remembered. It is only when touched by the sharp sense of personal insecurity that people are universally roused to take an interest in such affairs. The moment came when—in presence of a real or imaginary danger—England awoke to the fact that her penal system was all a mistake.

It was in the winter of 1862 that robberies with violence—garrote robberies, as they were called—suddenly increased to such an alarming extent, and were accompanied with such hideous details of brutality, that general consternation prevailed. The streets of London were less safe, said the leading journal, than a capital in the throes of revolution and under no government at all. No man could walk abroad, even in crowded thoroughfares, without feeling that he carried both his life and his money in his hand. Both might be wrested from him by an insidious malefactor before the victim was even conscious of his danger. On all sides instances of these treacherous assaults multiplied; and though varying somewhat in their method of execution, each and every one of them belonged unmistakably to the same class of crime. One day it was reported that a young lady of fifteen had been attacked in Westbourne Crescent in the afternoon. She was half throttled, and a pistol held to her head, while they rifled her pockets, and tried to tear off her necklace, and the pendants from her ears. Her head was to have been shorn, too, of its magnificent hair, which, as one of the ruffians cried, would certainly fetch a goodish sum; but just then the sound of approaching wheels frightened these human vultures from their helpless quarry. Next, a poor old woman, a feeble tottering creature advanced in years, was knocked down and wantonly maltreated for the half-dozen coppers she carried in her pocket.

These attacks were made at all hours and in all neighbourhoods. Daylight was no protection, nor were the crowds in a thoroughfare. One gentleman was felled to the ground in the afternoon near Paternoster Row, another in Holborn, a third in Cockspur Street. Later on, at night, the dangers, of course, multiplied a hundredfold. Poor musicians, tramping home after performing in some theatrical orchestra, were knocked down and robbed of their instruments as well as their cash. It was a service of danger to take the money at the door of any entertainment. A gang of garroters, for instance, had their eye on Michael Murray in the early part of the night as he stood at the door of the Teetotal Hall in Chelsea, and as soon as he left for home, they followed with stealthy step till they overtook him in Sloane Square, and knocked him down, having first throttled and rifled him. If you stood still in the street, and refused to give a drink to any man who accosted you, he would probably then and there give you a hug. Those who took a delight in attending public executions did so at their own peril. A Mr. Bush, who was standing in front of the Old Bailey when Cooper was hanged, was hustled by several men, who first forced his hands up over his head, then unbuttoned his coat and stole his watch.

In every case, whether the victim resisted or surrendered, he was nearly certain to be shamefully ill-used. Now and then the biter was bitten, as when three men fell upon a certain foreign gentleman who carried a sword, and was a master of the art of self-defence; or when another, who knew how to hit out, was attacked by two ruffians, both of whom he knocked down. But as a general rule the victim suffered tortures. When down on the ground, as often as not he was kicked about the face and head, usually with savage violence; his teeth were knocked down his throat, his eyes closed, and he was left insensible, streaming with blood.

In most cases, there was every appearance that the outrage was deliberately planned beforehand. There were accomplices—women sometimes; and all were banded together like Hindoos sworn to the practice of "Thuggee." For months these crimes continued to be prevalent. Every morning's news chronicled "more outrages in the streets;" until, as the fogs of November settled down on the devoted heads of the honest inhabitants of London, men's hearts failed them for fear, and life in sequestered streets or retired suburban villas seemed hardly worth an hour's purchase. Every journal teemed with complaints; *Punch* took up the question with grim humour; at the theatres audiences roared at some amusing actor, then shuddered to think they had still to get home after the play was over.

At length the horrors of garroting culminated in the arraignment of a crowd of such offenders in one batch at the central criminal court. There were twenty-seven of them. The cases of all bore a certain family likeness: though differing somewhat in detail, there was in each the same insidious method of attack, followed by the same brutality and wanton violence. Speaking to the most hardened, the judge, Baron Bramwell, said, as he passed sentence, that it was his belief that they were "utterly destitute of morality, shame, religion, or pity, and that if they were let loose they would do what any savage animal would do, namely, prey upon their fellows." Therefore he was resolved to keep them out of mischief as long as he possibly could. All got heavy sentences, ranging from "life" downward, and all were consigned to prison, where they are still well remembered—strong, able-bodied, determined looking scoundrels; top-sawyers in the trade of thieving, ready for any kind of daring work, treating their incarceration with the utmost contempt, as indeed they might, for it was nothing new to them. One or two had graduated in crime during the days of the Penitentiary; but neither Mr. Nihil, then the chaplain-governor, nor any one else had succeeded in reforming them. One of them, Leats, had actually at one time been a prison officer, a warder. Formerly a soldier in the marines, his career had been checkered. He had been present at the siege of St. Jean d'Acre, and was at that time servant to the admiral, through whom he obtained a situation at Millbank, from which he was soon dismissed for drunkenness. After this he went rapidly to the bad; was caught, and sentenced for obtaining goods under false pretences, next for robbing a lady at Richmond Park, and now for the third time he entered prison as a garroter. Although they maintained throughout, from the moment of their capture, in the dock and after sentence, an insolent and defiant demeanour, yet in the prison these murderous rogues conducted themselves fairly well; only two of them got into serious trouble. These were Dixon and another, Needham, who together made a vigorous attempt to escape. Dixon cut out, by means of a sharpened nail, the panel in his cell door, unbolted it, got out, and then set Needham also free. Their idea was to surprise the night patrol, and seize his keys. With this object they concealed themselves behind a passage door, and as he appeared struck him behind the ear. Fortunately the blow fell light, and the officer turned to grapple with the prisoners.

Such were the men, and such the work they did. Was it strange that the public should complain of a system of penal repression which left them to the tender mercies of ruffians like these? Transportation had been abandoned and what had been given them in exchange? A system which, as administered, had completely failed. It may have been a necessity, but it clearly had not been a success. They might perhaps be compelled to retain, or even to extend it; but its administration must be altered. As it was it had no terrors whatever for the evil-doer, while it gave but little protection to society. So said the *Times*; and it spared no pains to support its views with tangible evidence. Its columns teemed with letters on the subject, and special correspondents visited the chief convict establishments to spy out their nakedness and report their inefficacy as places for the punishment of criminals. Convicts, it was agreed on all sides, quite scoffed at the terrors of penal servitude. Barring the loss of actual liberty, which is doubtless the dearer to a man the closer he approaches to a lower species of animal, the convict prison was made so comfortable to the convict that he was loth to leave it, and hardly dreaded to return. Well-housed, well-fed, with labour just sufficient to insure good digestion and a healthy circulation; debarred only by a fiction of the luxuries he chiefly loved; let free from prison as soon as he chose to evince signs of amendment, a convict was altogether master of the situation. So said the critics. Penal servitude was like going down into the country after "the season." A little slow, perhaps; but very healthy and re-invigorating after a racket in town—just the discipline, in fact, to which men careful of themselves are ready to submit for a time, so as to issue forth afterwards braced and strengthened for a fresh campaign of pleasure. In these retired residences there was rest for the tired thief, for the burglar whose nerves had suffered, and for the playful miscreant who had been able only to half kill his victim, and who wished to recruit his strength. Here they found congenial society, such as a man meets at his club: others of his own set, with whom he could chat about the past, or concoct new plans for the future. His creature comforts were well looked after; he never worked as free labourers did, in the rain; and if, by mischance, he wet his feet, there were dry stockings for him on his return to his cosy well-warmed cell. If he had any special "whims" which called for gratification, an attentive official almost forestalled his wish. The leading feature of the whole system was to keep the convict comfortable and contented.

All this, and more, the panic-stricken public, speaking through the press, found fault with. Reform was called for, and immediate reform. The usual panacea was prescribed, a royal commission, which was that of 1863, long famous in British records as paving the way for the system of secondary punishment which, with various modifications, has existed to the present day. It was admitted on undoubted evidence that the régime established by Sir Joshua Jebb erred on the side of overmuch tenderness to the criminal. Far-seeing and able as was Sir Joshua Jebb, however skilful and capable as an administrator, on one point he was weak. It was an amiable weakness, but it did both himself and his system incalculable harm. He had formed too high an opinion of the criminal class; he was too hopeful, too ready to accept the shadow for the substance, to be satisfied with promise rather than performance, and to view the outward whitewashed semblance of purity for the radical transformation of the inner man. This was the key-note of his system, and this, as time passed, grew and gained strength, till at least there was some semblance of truth in the allegations so freely made by his opponents. It became known, beyond contradiction, that the diet in those days was far too generous; that the care taken of the convicts was tender to the extent of ridiculous coddling; that the labour exacted was far below the amount that each might be expected reasonably to perform. These facts are fully borne out by the traditions of the department itself. Old officers have told me that in all the prisons discipline was almost a dead letter. The convicts themselves ruled the roost. They did not break away, because there were troops at hand who would shoot them down; but otherwise they did just what they pleased. Their warders, taking their cue from the supreme power, sought to humour them into obedience by civil speeches rather than by firmness and resolution. The officers were afraid to enforce their orders, and the convicts saw that they were afraid. Men who are over-fed, if they are also idle, are sure to prove untamable and run riot. Some of the scenes at the convict prisons were disgraceful, almost rivalling, at times, the anarchy and disorder of Norfolk Island. That the convicts were thus insolent and insubordinate was undoubtedly due to the petting and pampering they received. But another cause was the unsettled, dissatisfied spirit evoked by several successive alterations in the law—alterations which it was absolutely necessary to make, but which none the less produced unevenness of treatment between various classes of prisoners.

The net result was stated in the report, to the effect that the system was clearly not sufficiently dreaded by those who had undergone it, or by the criminal classes in general. The number of re-convictions, they thought, proved this; moreover, the report continues, "the accounts given of penal servitude by discharged convicts, and the fact that they generally come back so soon to their original haunts, tends to prevent its being regarded with fear by their associates. Indeed, in some (though doubtless exceptional) cases, crimes have been committed for the sole purpose of obtaining the advantages which the offenders have supposed a sentence of penal servitude to confer." The system therefore stood condemned, and the commissioners attributed its shortcomings in a minor degree to defects in the discipline maintained, but thought the blame lay really in the shortness of the terms of imprisonment awarded in the courts of law.

To speak first of the latter point: the commissioners reported that there had been a notable reduction for some years previous in the length of sentences, and to make them still lighter a remission of time was granted under the new rules. It was a curious fact that the recent increase of crime had corresponded in point of date with the discharge of prisoners who were first sentenced for short terms under the Act of 1857, and was probably mainly attributable to their release from custody. They had come out unchastened. "The discipline to which convicts are subjected," declared the commission, "does not produce its proper effect in short periods of punishment."

Next as to the discipline. It was clearly a mistake to lay so much stress on conduct only. It was wrong, too, that the convicts should be allowed to earn enormous "gratuities," the cash presents handed over to them upon discharge. Many left prison with £30, £40, sometimes £80, in their pockets. The effect of this was to make a sentence of penal servitude an object of desire, rather than of apprehension. Besides, the longer a man's sentence—presumably, therefore, the greater his crime—the larger the sum he was entitled to take away with him. Again, the measures to keep the prisoners in submission were far too mild. Punishment did not follow fast enough on acts of violence and aggravated misconduct. The infliction of corporal punishment was too restricted, and the "cat" used was too light. There should be more power to use it and greater promptitude in its infliction. Then came the question of work and diet; but on these points the committee spoke with less confidence. Last of all, there was an entire absence of supervision of those who were at large on ticket-of-leave.

Having enunciated these propositions, the commissioners recommended certain important changes in the manner of carrying out penal servitude, chief among which were:

That in future no sentence should be passed of less than seven years.

That re-convicted criminals should be treated more severely than others.

That convicts, after enduring separate imprisonment for nine months, should pass on to public works, where they might be permitted to earn by industry and good conduct an abridgment of a part of their imprisonment.

That all males, if possible, should be sent to Western Australia during the latter part of their sentences, "it being highly desirable to send convicts, under proper regulations and without disguise, to a thinly peopled colony, where they may be removed from their former temptations, where they will be sure of having the means of maintaining themselves by their industry if inclined to do so, and where facilities exist for keeping them under more effective control than is practicable in this country with its great cities and large population."

That all who were unfit to go, and, gaining a remission of sentence, were discharged at home, should while on license be subjected to close supervision by the police.

Such was the substance of the report. But it is right to mention here that the commissioners were not quite unanimous in the conclusions arrived at. Two of them, Mr. Henley and the Lord Chief Justice, would not sign the report. Mr. Childers put his name to it, but under protest. He could not agree to the proposals as to transportation. His view was that of Australia, and he was of opinion that "the measures recommended—while costly to the country and odious to her colonies—would at best afford only a brief delay in the solution of a question daily becoming more difficult."

By far the most important of the dissentient voices was that of Sir Alexander Cockburn, the Lord Chief Justice, who appended to the report a long memorandum giving his reasons for not concurring in it. After a careful perusal of this memorandum any one would, I think, be ready to concede that the Lord Chief Justice was nearer the mark than his colleagues. They hesitated to admit that the penal system was entirely defective. Sir Alexander Cockburn had no doubt of it, and maintained that the same impression was pretty generally abroad. But if there were faults in it, said the commissioners, then the administration of the law was to blame; it was too lenient. To this the Lord Chief Justice would by no means agree. The leniency of the judges, as it had shown itself of late, was nothing. "The spirit in which the law is administered," he observed, "is not the growth of yesterday. It has arisen gradually out of the more humane and merciful disposition of men's minds in modern times, whereby punishments inflicted without scruple in former days would now be regarded as cruel and inhuman." No; the inefficacy of penal servitude did not lie in the shortness or inequality of sentences, but in the manner in which the punishment was inflicted. "Moderate labour, ample diet, substantial gratuities," he maintained, "are hardly calculated to produce on the mind of the criminal that salutary dread of the recurrence of the punishment which may be the means of deterring him, and, through his example, others from the commission of crime."

And then the Lord Chief Justice proceeded to put forth the following pregnant sentences, which I quote in full. In taking up the question of punishment, he says, "It is necessary to bear in mind what are the purposes for which the punishment of offenders takes place. These purposes are twofold: the first, that of deterring others exposed to similar temptations from the commission of crime; the second, the reformation of the criminal himself. The first is the primary and more important object: for though society has, doubtless, a strong interest in the reformation of the criminal, and his consequent indisposition to crime, yet the result is here confined to the individual offender; while the effect of punishment as deterring from crime, extends, not only to the party suffering the punishment, but to all who may be in the habit of committing crime, or who may be tempted to fall into it. Moreover, the reformation of the offender is in the highest degree speculative and uncertain, and its permanency in the face of renewed temptation exceedingly precarious. On the other hand, the impression produced by suffering inflicted as the punishment of crime, and the fear of its repetition, are far more likely to be lasting, and much more likely to counteract the tendency to the renewal of criminal habits. It is on the assumption that punishment will have the effect of deterring from crime, that its infliction can alone be justified; its proper and legitimate purpose being not to avenge crime but to prevent it.

"The experience of mankind has shown that though crime will always exist to a certain extent, it may be kept within given bounds by the example of punishment. This result it is the business of the lawgiver to accomplish by annexing to each offence the degree of punishment calculated to repress it. More than this would be a waste of so much human suffering; but to apply less, out of consideration for the criminal, is to sacrifice the interests of society to a misplaced tenderness towards those who offend against its laws. Wisdom and humanity no doubt alike suggest that, if, consistently with this primary purpose, the reformation of the criminal can be brought about, no means should be omitted by which so desirable an end can be achieved. But this, the subsidiary purpose of penal discipline, should be kept in due subordination to its primary and principal one. And it may well be doubted whether, in recent times, the humane and praiseworthy desire to reform and restore the fallen criminal may not have produced too great a tendency to forget that the protection of society should be the first consideration of the lawgiver."

By far the most important improvement that followed this report was the adoption of the "mark system;" in other words, of a method by which remission was to be regulated, not by conduct as heretofore, but solely by labour actually performed. For it must be understood that the commissioners unhesitatingly accepted the principle of remissions. In this they were at issue with the Lord Chief Justice, who thought that no prisoner should escape one particle of the whole sentence laid upon him by the judge. "It was most material," he said, "to the full efficiency of punishment that its infliction should be certain." The door was opened to doubt and uncertainty the moment the precise term of the sentence was interfered with.

The objection was cogent if the remissions were to be granted in a haphazard, capricious fashion and not by regular rule. But surely, if the scale were drawn up on a regular plan and worked without deviation, a sentence with remission might be just as certain as one without. The former might, perhaps, be shorter than the latter—the judges, being perfectly aware of the possible remission, would regulate their sentences in proportion to this abridgment. And, on the other hand, there was a clear and distinct gain to be expected from the practice of remitting sentences. This was fully recognised by the commissioners, who considered the hope of earning some remission the most powerful incentive to industry and good conduct which could be brought to act upon the minds of prisoners.

The commissioners perhaps laid more stress on good conduct than was absolutely imperative, although they pointed out, very pertinently, that "good conduct in a prison (apart from industry) can consist only in abstaining from misconduct, which gives no just claim for reward." But this harping upon good conduct was a weak point in their armour which the Lord Chief Justice quickly discovered. He would not admit the necessity for thus coaxing convicts into obedience by promising them an earlier release if they behaved well. That was no argument, he said, for remissions. Discipline ought to be strong enough to be independent of such questionable support. "I can see no reason to think," he continues,—"considering the powers of coercion, discipline, and reduction of diet, possessed by the prison authorities—that, by the application of firmness and determination with a sufficient force of officers, convicts, especially if not massed in too great numbers, but judiciously distributed, may not be kept under perfect control and discipline."

No doubt the commissioners over-estimated the necessity of remission as a means of insuring good conduct; but they were clearly in the right in recommending the principle as a certain incentive to industry. The experience, both of this and of other countries, has demonstrated that it is impossible to compel convicts to work hard by mere coercion, the attempt to do so having invariably failed, while it has produced a brutalising effect on their minds and increased their previous aversion to labour. On this ground the late Captain Maconochie many years ago recommended that the punishment to be inflicted on criminals should be measured, not by time, but by the amount of labour they should be compelled to perform before regaining their freedom; and he devised an ingenious mode of recording their daily industry by marks, for the purpose of determining when they should have a right to their discharge.

Captain Maconochie himself experimented on his own suggestions in Norfolk Island, but not with any great success. The state of Norfolk Island, indeed, was never such as to encourage experiments of any kind. It was really reserved for the officials who superintended the working of transportation in Western Australia to give the system its first practically successful trial. There a convict was allowed to earn by each day's labour a number of marks, and as soon as they amounted to a total previously calculated according to his sentence, he was granted a ticket-of-leave. Industry became the test, and not good conduct; the latter was only recognised by making misconduct carry with it a forfeiture of some of the marks already earned by industry.

The convict's early release was no longer a matter of certainty provided only that he avoided certain acts of rebellion, but it was made contingent on something he had to earn. His fate rested in his own hands; it was not to depend upon an opinion of his character formed by others. The success which was shown to have attended the adoption of this principle in Western Australia has been equally apparent in Great Britain. The mark system is the keystone, the mainspring of the latest British method of dealing with convicts, and the valuable results which have grown out of it, as now clearly apparent, will be set forth presently in the final chapter of this volume.

CHAPTER XI FRENCH PENAL COLONIES

Penal exile in favour with other nations—Systems of France, Italy, Spain and Portugal—Earliest French ventures—Guiana a fiasco—High sounding names—Renewed attempt—Settlement made in New Caledonia in 1864—Capital at Noumea—Convict population increases—Noumea in 1888—Results of convict labour meagre—Loose discipline and low moral tone—Agricultural settlements—Life at the smaller stations—Arab convicts—Enforced labour unremunerative—Delay in development—The emancipists—Same warfare with free settlers as in Australia—A later view—Visited by Mr. George Griffith in 1900—Free immigrants refuse to remain—Present condition proof of failure of penal exile.

The vast and costly efforts of Great Britain to make use of exile as the penalty for crime, and the strange, unlooked for results achieved, have been set forth. These efforts were undoubtedly successful, although not in the manner expected. To add a great colony to the British Empire was no small feat, even though the sources were impure and the foundations laid by the dregs of society. But the gain was some compensation for the means adopted. In any case, the convict stigma has long since been washed out by honest industry and reputable development. A vast territory, richly endowed, offered special advantages to an enterprising people with the genius of colonisation. Other nations, who overlooked the difficulties faced and overcome by England, have endeavoured to follow in her footsteps, and have made but little progress. France, as we shall see, has gone to great lengths in the practice of deportation, but to no purpose. Portugal still transports her criminals to the African colony of Angola, where the system is established on a small scale and has exhibited no glaring defects. Italy has long favoured the formation of criminal colonies on the many islands that surround her coast, and has removed numbers of prisoners to agricultural stations at Sardinia, to Pianosa and Gorgona in the Tuscan Archipelago, as well as to Monte Cristo and Capraja. Spain had a penal settlement at Ceuta on the north African shore as far back as the fifteenth century, and has more recently added large stations at Melilla and Alhucemas. Spanish experience in convict colonies is said to be satisfactory, but the conditions are much the same as in Australia,—no better, if no worse.

The efforts of France to found penal colonies range far back into history. They date from a period long antecedent to the latest craze for colonial aggrandisement. The very first attempt to sow the seeds of a prosperous community with the failures of society was in 1763, when the colonisation of French Guiana, already often attempted without success, was again tried on an ambitious scale. The project failed miserably. An expedition fourteen thousand strong, recruited mainly from the scum and sweepings of the streets of Paris, melted away within a year, and starvation carried off all whom the deadly climate spared. A second similar experiment was tried in 1766, with a like disastrous result. No serious importance could be attached to the colonising efforts of the victims exiled to Guiana by the revolutionary tribunals. Barely half the number survived the voyage, and the balance were in no condition to act as pioneers. The records of French Guiana are full of such fiascos, the most unsuccessful of which was the philanthropic attempt of the Baron Milius, in 1823, to establish a penal colony on the banks of the Mana, by the marriage and expatriation of habitual criminals, *recidivistes*, and degraded women,—a most ill-judged undertaking, speedily productive of ghastly horrors.

After this, penal colonisation seems to have fallen into disfavour with France. Not only was it not renewed, but the principle of criminal deportation, of exile as a penalty, was formally condemned in 1847, both by such eminent publicists as MM. Lucas, De Beaumont and De Tocqueville, and by the government of the hour. Yet within a few years the practice was suddenly restored. To the new men in power there was probably something attractive in the theory of transportation, as may be seen from the high-sounding phrases that accompanied their decrees. The idea was not merely to banish the dangerous social elements to a distant soil: the young republic wished to prove that "humanity presided over all its actions." Deportation, with the disciplinary processes that surrounded it, was expected to bring about the moral regeneration of those subjected to it; the criminal would be transformed into a useful citizen; no longer a terror in his old home, he would aid the development of and become a positive benefactor to the new. The government was, indeed, so fascinated by the prospective advantages of transportation to the convicts themselves, that it expected them to accept it as a boon. Registers were opened at all the *bagnes*, or seaport convict-stations, on which prisoners might inscribe their names as volunteers for the high favour of removal to the promised land beyond the seas. The philanthropic wish to benefit the exile was not, however, the sole object of the government, as may be seen in various articles in the decrees. The hope of founding substantial colonial possessions was not disguised. The convict might benefit by expatriation, but so would his new country, and to a greater degree. He went out, in a measure, for his own good; he remained, perforce, for that of the community. It was ruled that even when emancipated he was to be kept in the colony; those sentenced for eight years and less must spend there a second period as long as the original sentence; those sentenced for more than eight years must remain in the colony for life. Their labour and their best energies were thus impounded for the general good, in the sanguine expectation that they were being utilised in the progress and development of French colonisation.

The revival of transportation was formally promulgated by the law of May, 1854, which declared that thereafter the punishment of *travaux forcés* should be undergone in establishments created in a French colonial possession other than Algeria. As the only available outlet at this time was French Guiana, this tropical colony alone was adopted as a convict receptacle. In doing so, the very first principles of penal legislation were ignored. To consign even convicts to a pestilential climate, and expand the lesser penalty into capital punishment, was a monstrous and illegal misuse of power. Exile to French Guiana meant nearly certain death. For three years every attempt to colonise the country had ended in disaster. Yet the government of Napoleon III accepted deportation with a light heart and on the most extended scale.

The French government, slow to accept the evidence of facts, has never abandoned deportation to Guiana. But it is no longer sanguine of success, and the attempt to colonise is continued with other than native-born Frenchmen. The total convict population of Guiana, as shown in recent French official returns, had dwindled down to 3,441, and of these barely a thousand were Europeans; the rest were Arabs from Algeria, and Annamites, Asiatic blacks from the new French possessions in Cochin-China and Tonquin. The Europeans were made up, in nearly equal proportions, of convicts still undergoing sentence, and emancipists compelled to reside in the colony. Large numbers of both classes are now retained in the penitentiaries on the seacoast, where they can be constantly employed at industrial labour under cover; as at Cayenne, the capital, where vast administrative establishments exist, built at great outlay in more prosperous times.

The French government has sought by every means to encourage the young settlement of Saint Laurent, but its progress has always been disappointing. It has been dependent for some years past upon the Arab recruits, and the French officials already sorrowfully confess that members of the Arab race transplanted to French Guiana are not of the stuff to make good colonists. They are idle, discontented, and a prey to unceasing homesickness. A great effort has been made by the administration to attach the Arab emigrant to the land of exile by transporting thither—I use the words of a late report—"the image of the Arab family, its customs, habits and religion." Marriages are encouraged with Arab women according to the Mussulman law. But little success has attended these well-meant efforts. The Arab soon develops nomadic instincts; he will not stick to one spot, but wanders abroad in search of work which will give him the means of a speedy return to Algeria. Not seldom he shows a clean pair of heels. Escapes in French Guiana have been a source of trouble and annoyance to the authorities. The total number of convicts who had escaped or disappeared from French Guiana between 1852 and 1883 was 3,146; and since Arabs have been sent there, they have supplied the largest proportion of fugitives. They went off in bands; nothing could check them; no surveillance was effective. The Government cutters cruising along the mouth of the river were easily evaded, and the country boats once gained, they were soon out of the colony. A report from the governor-general of Algeria in 1890 states that a great cause of the insecurity of Algeria is the presence in the colony of large numbers of Arab convicts who have escaped from Guiana and returned home. Hence transportation has little terrors for the Arab population, knowing how easily exile may be avoided.

A more remarkable case of escape was that of a French convict sent to Guiana, who was anxious to see the Paris Exposition of 1889. He became possessed of some eight hundred francs through successful gambling, and spent six hundred in taking passage to Amsterdam; he embarked without let or hindrance and went direct to Paris on arrival. He was present at the opening of the exposition, where he stood not far from the president of the republic. Later on he was captured for a fresh offence, and taken to one of the large Paris prisons, where he was at once recognised as a convict exiled not long before to Cayenne. He admitted the charge; he had gratified his wish, had enjoyed *quelques bons moments*, and was satisfied to go back to Guiana, as he would not have to pay his own passage out. It was, in fact, established beyond question that it was easier to escape from Cayenne, and even New Caledonia, than from a *maison centrale* in the department of the Seine.

It must be sufficiently plain from the foregoing facts that the attempts to colonise French Guiana with convicts have ended in more or less disheartening failure. Even in sections where the climate was not fatal to Europeans, the conditions of life were opposed to the growth of a prosperous community. There was little increase of population possible. The ill-assorted marriages of convicts with degraded women of their own class proved generally unproductive. Infant mortality was excessive; children born in the colony could never be reared. The substitution of Arabs for Europeans has been accompanied, as I have shown, with little more success. Now, according to a late report of the French Colonial Office, Annamite convicts, hitherto retained in their own country for the completion of various important colonial works, are sent to French Guiana. "The Annamite," says the report hopefully, "is a good agriculturist; he can face the climate of Guiana without danger, and the convicts of this race will doubtless largely contribute to the development and cultivation of the colony."

The melancholy miscarriage of deportation to French Guiana did not suffice to condemn it. The locality was only at fault, it was thought; the system deserved a fuller and fairer trial. France now possessed a better site for experiment, a territory in those same southern seas where English transportation had so greatly prospered. New Caledonia was annexed to France in 1853, but its colonisation had proceeded slowly, and there was only a handful of white population when the first shipload of convicts disembarked in 1864. A town, at this time little better than a standing camp, was planted at Noumea, a spot chosen for its capabilities for defence rather than its physical advantages. It had no natural water supply, and the land around was barren. Exactly opposite lay the little island of Nou, a natural breakwater to the Bay of Noumea, well-watered, fertile, and commanded by the guns of the mainland, and here the first convict depot was established. The earliest work of these convict pioneers was to build a prison-house and to prepare for the reception of new drafts. The labour was not severe, the discipline by no means irksome, and some progress was made. Prison buildings rose upon the island of Nou; a portion of the surrounding land was brought under cultivation, and outwardly all went well. As years passed, the prison population gradually increased. In 1867 the average total was six hundred; in the following year it had increased to 1,554, after which the yearly gain was continuous. Various causes contributed to this, among them the gradual abolition of the *bagnes* or convict stations at the French arsenals, and the wholesale condemnation of Communists, many of whom were deported to New Caledonia. In 1874 the convict population exceeded five thousand. In 1880 it had risen to eight thousand; and according to recent published official returns, the effective population, taking convicts and emancipists together, numbered nearly ten thousand. From May, 1864, to December 31, 1883, a total of 15,209 convicts had been transported to New Caledonia.

The development of the young colony was slow. Efforts were chiefly concentrated upon the penitentiary island, and the convict labour was but little utilised on the mainland. Those public works so indispensable to the growth and prosperity of the settlement were neglected. The construction of highroads was never attempted on any comprehensive scale, and, notwithstanding the force of workmen available, Noumea, the capital, was not enriched with useful buildings or rendered independent of its physical defects. Henri Rochefort, who saw it in 1872, ridicules its pretensions to be called a town. It might have been built of old biscuit-boxes, he said; imposing streets named from some book of battles—the Rue Magenta and the Rue Sebastopol, the Rue Inkerman and the Avenue de l'Alma—were mere tracks sparsely dotted with huts, single-storied and unpretending. The town lay at the bottom of a basin surrounded by small hills. "It was like a cistern in wet weather, and in the hot season it might be the crater of a volcano." A great mound, the Butte Conneau, blocked up the mouth of the port and inconveniently impeded traffic. Water was still scarce, and, according to Rochefort, a barrel of it would be the most acceptable present to any inhabitant of "Elephantiasopolis," as he christened Noumea from the endemic skin affections. It took ten or a dozen years to improve Noumea. But by 1877 the Butte Conneau had been removed and levelled. About the same time an aqueduct 8000 metres long was completed, which brought water to the capital from Port de France and Yahoué. A number of more or less ambitious residences had also been erected: a governor's house, bishop's palace, administrative offices, hospitals, and barracks for the troops.

A later account of Noumea is given by M. Verschuur, who visited the Antipodes in 1888-9, and spent some time in New Caledonia. On arrival he was at first much struck by the appearance of Noumea. He was agreeably impressed by the brightness and gaiety of its aspect as compared with "the monotonous appearance of the little English towns" of Australia. Cafés and taverns were numerous; crowds of lively folk filled the streets through which he drove; and the well-built Government House, surrounded by pretty grounds, looked homelike. A closer inspection much modified his opinion. He remembered the large cities of the neighbouring island continent with their imposing architecture, their fine public gardens, and the prosperous home-like atmosphere pervading every part. "But now I found myself in a small town somewhat resembling those of the Antilles; the houses, which were all alike, were low and roughly built, often of wood. Some of them were no better than the huts of the backwoodsmen I had seen in the Australian bush. The shops were small, and the wares displayed were inferior in quality and of a mixed description. Toys hung side by side with saucepans and boots; calicoes and hats were framed by jams and spirit-bottles. The streets were badly kept and filthy; the roads outside the town had not been properly levelled and the numerous bogs made travelling after dark very dangerous. The only promenade was a public square planted with cocoanut palms, which gave little shade. The harbour was meagre, the quays small and inconvenient; but few ships can load or unload at the same time. If there is one colony more than another where public building might be carried on at the least expense, it is certainly New Caledonia, with its hosts of convicts sentenced to 'hard labour.' In many of the places I had visited, the numerous fine public works had been executed at great cost; but here was a colony where labour would cost nothing and yet it is never utilised. It is a strange anomaly, and a singular waste of means, which might well be used for the advantage and progress of the colony."

According to M. Verschuur, the amount of work gotten out of the convicts was not very great. In his opinion France is maintaining in New Caledonia an "army of drones who find means of evading the labour to which they have been condemned. Many an honest, hard-working French peasant might envy the fate which the government reserves for that part of the population which is steeped in vice and crime. The law passed in 1854 prescribes that the convicts shall be kept to the most laborious works of the colony." As soon as he landed, M. Verschuur heard an excellent band playing in the public square. The bandsmen were all convicts, who played three times a week and practised the rest of the time. Men whose crimes had been the talk of all Paris were employed as gardeners, or in the easiest kind of work, smoking and chatting with their companions. The convicts work, nominally, eight hours a day; they sleep another eight; and then there still remains another eight in which they are absolutely idle. They do less than a quarter of the daily work of an ordinary labourer. In the stone yard they simply work when they see the warder is observing them. "I noticed a gang one day just outside Noumea; out of the sixteen men, twelve were calmly seated on the heap of stones they were supposed to be breaking, rolling cigarettes, and talking; the remaining four made a stroke now and then, when the warder chanced to glance that way. Several times, when travelling in the interior of the country, I have come upon well-known murderers, living in service with the unsuspecting inhabitants." A certain number were regularly employed within the prison of Nou, where M. Verschuur saw them engaged as shoemakers, carpenters, and at the blacksmith's forge. All were busily at work, yet he was certain that before he entered with the prison director, not a soul was doing anything. Great laxity, however, prevailed in these shops. A convict carpenter was permitted to have access to the stores of turpentine and spirits in the workshop, with which abominable mixture he managed to get horribly drunk. Extraordinary license was allowed in another direction. A convict quarrelled with and murdered a comrade; they had been partners in a store kept inside the prison for the sale of coffee, tobacco and spirits. The deeds of partnership had been legally drawn up, and were actually engrossed upon the official paper of the prison. It may be mentioned that this murderer had been twice guilty of murder before and was yet allowed to keep a knife in his possession, which he was seen to sharpen quite unrestrained on the very morning of the last crime.

The influx of convicts produced many projects for their employment over and above the development of Noumea. Following the practice that had prevailed in Guiana, agricultural settlements, half farm, half prison, were established at various points on the mainland. One of the first of these was at Bourail, about a hundred miles from the capital. Another was founded nearer home at Ourail, on the mouth of the Foa. A third was at Canala, on the opposite and northern shore of the island. A fourth was at its eastern end, in the Bay of Prony. Besides these a number of smaller stations were distributed at various points through the colony. The works undertaken were everywhere much of the same kind. At Bourail the sugar cane was cultivated, and various vegetables; at Canala, rice, maize and coffee; at Ourail the land was poor, and the settlement was moved further up the river to Fonway, where the raising of tobacco, and the cultivation of fruit trees and the quinine bush were attempted; at the Bay of Prony the convicts became woodcutters to supply fuel for the rest of the colony.

The inner life of one of the smaller stations, the labour camp of Saint Louis, has been graphically described by M. Mayer, a political transport, who published the "Souvenirs d'un Deporté," relating his personal experiences, on his return to France. This camp consisted of 124 convicts, a heterogeneous collection, herded together indiscriminately in the wretched *cases*, or straw-thatched huts, the prevailing prison architecture of New Caledonia. Among these, of whom forty were political and non-criminal convicts, there were twenty-six Arabs, four Chinamen and two negroes. Several notorious desperadoes, Frenchmen born, were associated with the rest. One had been at the head of a band of poisoners of Marseilles; another, who had murdered a girl in Paris, had been arrested and sentenced during the Commune by a Communist commissary, who, by a strange fate, was now his comrade convict in this same camp of Saint Louis. Except for the scantiness of diet and the enforced association with the worst criminals, M. Mayer did not find the work hard. The hours of labour varied; the daily minimum was eight, the maximum from ten to twelve. But the work performed was desultory and generally unproductive. The principal aim was to clear the land by removing the rocks, which were afterward broken up for road-making material. The supervision was lax and ineffective; the few warders were most active in misappropriating rations. The chief warder himself, who had a fine garden and poultry yard, stole the wine and soft bread issued for the sick. Many convicts eked out their meagre fare by cooking roots and wild fruits, *pommes de lianes* and Caledonian saffron.

The lot of the Arabs was most enviable; they monopolised all situations of trust. One was the quartermaster, another the chief cook, and others worked as carpenters, bootmakers, and blacksmiths. The baleful practice of putting one convict in authority over another, long condemned by enlightened prison legislators, was always in full force in New Caledonia. Strange to say, too, the French authorities preferred to choose their felon overseers from an alien race. The Arabs seem to have found most favour with their masters, although, if Mayer is to be believed, these Arab officials were all fierce, untamed ruffians. Yet they were entrusted with great authority over their less fortunate comrades, and were especially esteemed for the vigour with which they administered corporal punishment. Mayer has preserved the picture of one Algerian savage, six feet high, who went about seeking quarrels and striking his fellow convicts on the smallest excuse. This man was considered an artist with the *martinet*, or French cat-o'-nine-tails, and was said to be able to draw blood at the first stroke.

It is an admitted axiom in penal science that enforced labour is not easily made productive. Unless peculiar incentives to work, such as provided by the English mark system, are employed under a strict yet enlightened discipline, the results have always been meagre and disappointing. As these conditions were absent from New Caledonia, the consequences are what might have been foreseen. Notwithstanding the very considerable efforts made and the vast quantity of convict labour always available, the colony still owns no great public works; while large and sustained efforts to develop its agricultural resources by the same means have also failed. No doubt the nature of the soil has been unfavourable.

New Caledonia, while not without its natural advantages, such as a nearly perfect climate, freedom from reptiles and animal life inimical to man, is not very richly endowed except in unprospected and undeveloped mineral wealth. The island consists of a rugged backbone of mountains clothed with dense forests and grooved with rushing torrents, along whose banks lie the only cultivable ground. A thin and sandy soil covers a substratum of hard rock, which makes but scanty return for the labour bestowed and serves best for pasturage. Hence the convict farms already referred to have never been profitably worked. Those especially of Bourail and Koe, the largest and most ambitious, show a positive loss. At the former only three and a half tons of sugar were turned out in one year by four hundred men, and ten years of toil had brought only fifty hectares of land into cultivation. At Koe, five years' receipts were valued at 50,000 francs, and the expenses for the same period just trebled that sum. In 1883 the minister of marine approved the suppression of the penitentiary farms on the island of Nou and at Canala, and the limitation of the sugar cane cultivation at Bourail, on the ground that the returns were altogether inadequate to the outlay.

It was only too evident, as the outcome of early years, that efforts had been misdirected, and that the labour had been wasted and frittered away instead of being more usefully employed for the benefit of the whole colony. One signal instance of the shortcomings of the colonial administrators is shown by their neglect to develop the means of internal communication. It was not until 1883, that is to say, after nearly twenty years of colonial life, that road-making, that indispensable preliminary to development, was undertaken on any extensive scale. New Caledonia, an island 230 miles long and 50 miles broad, owned only 57 kilometres of road before the year 1882.

It was Captain Pallu de la Barriere, a governor whose administration was severely criticised on account of his excessive humanitarianism, but whose views as regards the utilisation of convict labour were far-seeing, who removed this reproach. His idea was to substitute what he called movable camps for the *bagnes sedentaires* or permanent penitentiaries. He thought that the severest toil should be the lot of all convicts, at least at first; and this, he conceived, could be best compassed by employing them in road-making, thus benefiting the colony while effectively punishing the convict. His whole scheme of organisation reads like a page from the despatches of British colonial governors some thirty years previous. The measures he proposed, his plans for housing the convicts and providing for their safe custody, were almost identical with those in force with the road-gangs of New South Wales and Van Diemen's Land. He was very hopeful; he had no fear of escapes or of aggravated misconduct scattered over the wide area which he now proposed to people with convict gangs. His intentions were no doubt excellent, but in the twenty years following the initiation of his scheme they have borne no very substantial fruit.

The colonial administration has found even less satisfaction in the emancipists than in the convicts still under restraint. The former are a great and increasing body, for whom work cannot easily be found. The hope that the labour markets of the colony would absorb a great proportion soon proved illusory. For some time past the free colonists, by no means a numerous class, have declined to employ emancipists, declaring that while they claimed the free man's wages they would not give the free man's work. The settlers preferred to import native labour from the neighbouring islands, especially the New Hebrides, thus coming into direct conflict with the authorities, who soon put their veto on such importation. The settlers were told that if they wanted hands they must seek them among the emancipists, and all protests were silenced by reminding the colonists that New Caledonia was a penal settlement and that if they lived there they must abide by its constitution. At this time there were some four or five thousand emancipists living as free charges, lodged, fed and clothed at the cost of the state, yet making absolutely no return. The greater number of these were kept in a military camp under some semblance of discipline, but undergoing little restraint beyond the prohibition to wander abroad, and within the limits of the camp the occupants could do as they pleased.

Later and more specific information is now at hand in the accounts brought back by an enterprising traveller, Mr. George Griffith, who visited New Caledonia in 1900. The penal colonisation undertaken by France with such philanthropic motives, and so sedulously carried out, has resulted in failure. The experience is the same as that of New South Wales and Tasmania; the penalty of banishment and penal exile inflicted upon the majority of convicts has been accomplished, but not the regeneration, to any appreciable extent, of the criminal classes. Their conversion into a prosperous community, self-reliant, self-supporting and able to stand alone, is still a vague, unrealised dream. All the conditions that favoured the growth of its great neighbour have been absent in New Caledonia, and it was hampered also by special disadvantages. There has been none of the steady influx of free settlers such as immigrated to Australia when first difficulties were removed, nor yet the amazing stimulus of the discovery of gold as on the near-by continent. Peculiar racial disadvantages have further impeded development.

The present state of New Caledonia affords abundant proof of the truth of this position. It will doubtless never advance to the rank of a first-class colony. It is still and must always be a prison house beyond sea peopled mainly by convicts past or present, by those in various stages of ameliorating change, but who cannot shake off the original taint, and the general low level is maintained by constant reinforcement of those who have it full upon them. To-day the larger part of the population of the colony is based upon the criminal element, which is divided into three principal classes: First, the *forçats*, or convicted prisoners still in a state of servitude; second, the *libérés* or emancipists in semi-freedom, who emerge in due course from the first class, and, third, the *relégues* or those sent from France to serve a sentence of perpetual exile. There is hope in the future for the first, partially attained freedom and approaching comfortable assurance for the second, but for the last named there is nothing but black despair. Life alone remains theirs, but with not the faintest prospect of remission or release.

It is obvious that under such conditions healthy colonisation is about as impossible as healthy physical being in a colony of lepers. Free emigrants may declare it their intention, but they will not persevere in the attempt to build up new homes under such false conditions; they will not leave the mother country, or if they do, will take the earliest opportunity to return to the hard, clean, industrious life of agricultural France. We have seen that, with the larger influx of the vigorous Anglo-Saxon, the same difficulties were faced and overcome; but at what risks, what degradation and how great a waste of men and means!

New Caledonia is nevertheless an interesting study, and its present condition an object lesson in penal legislation. It is a prison planted in the tropics, to a large extent worked and governed on the same lines as the prisons in the heart of a mother country. Wrong-doers are transported to the other end of the globe to endure a penalty that might be better inflicted, more cheaply and under better supervision and control, by the strong arm of an omnipresent public opinion at home. Some remote advantages are no doubt obtained in the later stages of the terms of imprisonment, and at least society is rinsed effectively of its lees and leavings.

The principal home for the *forçats* in the penal stage of exile is still on the island of Nou, already mentioned and immediately opposite Noumea, the capital of the colony, which is now, after fifty years of life, a pretty white town of villas and squares, and streets of shops brightened by a luxuriant tropical vegetation. On the island of Nou a pleasant looking settlement of white houses and shady streets has been formed at the foot of a hill crowned with the imposing and extensive prison buildings. On this commanding site and at this remote point, so-called penitentiary science has planted the same sort of machine for the coercion of erring humanity as may be seen nearly everywhere else on the civilised globe. The latest experiment is being made with the oldest methods. Here are separate cells, dark cells and condemned cells, bolts and bars, iron doors and loaded revolvers. France desires to emancipate her criminals and set them on the high road to regenerated life, but they must tread the old thorny paths and suffer the same trials by the way as their predecessors elsewhere. Discipline must be maintained, and it is enforced at times by terrible means. The lash and the "cat-o'-nine-tails" are not permitted, but a most ingenious deceptive method of torture has been invented, mild enough at first sight, yet more cruel than the rack, thumb-saw or boot.

Mr. George Griffith's description of the punishment as it existed when he saw it—happily much modified soon afterward—is horrifying in the extreme. The "black cell" was absolutely isolated. Not a sound reached it, not a ray of light penetrated it, and in his day the doors were only opened once in thirty days, when the hapless inmate was extracted for an hour's exercise and the doctor's inspection. The effect of this treatment may be best realised by Mr. Griffith's own words when he was permitted to extend relief to one of the inmates.

"Out of the corner (of the cell) came something in human shape, crouching forward, rubbing its eyes and blinking at the unaccustomed light. It had been three years and a half in that horrible hole about three yards long and half as wide. I gave him a feast of sunshine and outer air by taking his place for a few minutes. After the first two or three, the minutes lengthened into hours. I had absolutely no sense of light. I was as blind as though I had been born without eyes. The blackness seemed to come down on me like some solid thing and drive my straining eyes back into my head. It was darkness that could be felt, for I felt it, and the silence was like the silence of upper space. When the double doors opened again, the rays of light seemed to strike my eyes like daggers. The criminal whose place I had taken had a record of infamy which no printable words could express, and yet I confess I pitied him as he went back into that living death of darkness and silence."

The extreme penalty of death is by no means rare in New Caledonia, and the condemned cells in the prison of the island of Nou, six in number, are sometimes simultaneously full. An execution in that far-off place of penitence reproduces the scene in Paris; the preliminaries are the same and the ceremony is identical. The same cruel uncertainty hangs over the fate of the condemned, who hears his doom only an hour or two before he is guillotined. The commandant of the island, the chaplain and the chief warden, visit him at three o'clock in the morning and convey the dread summons, *c'est pour aujourdhui*, the final, fatal decision he has been awaiting day after day for weeks. Then follows *la toilette de la mort*, the dressing for death, when the headsman "*Monsieur de l'Ile Nou*," pinions him and cuts away the collar of his shirt lest it should break the fall of the swiftly descending knife.

The actual performance takes place in the great courtyard, where the scaffold has been erected and the audience is ready. All the great officials of the colony are there, and a sufficient number of troops to overawe the body of convicts arranged row behind row within full view of the stage to which the principal performer ascends. He is allowed to make a short address to his comrades, kneeling and bareheaded before him. Then he is put into position upon a sloping plank, which slides into place so that his neck is pushed out through an opening and is ready for the swift-falling blade.

The *forçats* are distributed all over the colony where there is work in progress, on farms and agricultural stations, clearing forest primeval and in mining operations of a very arduous character. The idle and ill-conducted, the incorrigible who will not labour and are in a chronic state of insubordination, are committed to disciplinary camps partly for punishment, partly for seclusion. Nowhere is the régime more severe, the daily rations less, the daily task harder. There are none of the small luxuries of wine and tobacco, and they sleep on guard beds with a leg in iron chained to a bar at the end. The penalty of solitary confinement on bread and water is promptly inflicted for any breach of discipline, and those who prove perfectly intractable are sent as hopeless to the cells of the central prison at the island of Nou. Henceforth there is no further change—they are deemed hopeless and incurable.

One form of punishment is peculiar to these camps. It might be called perpetual motion. A number of convicts, twenty or thirty, are ranged in single rank in a large shed, some sixty feet in length and forty in breadth, and set to march round and round incessantly, pausing only for a couple of minutes every half hour. Stone seats, each a kind of flat topped pyramid, are fixed at intervals around the shed and afford a brief rest from time to time, but the march is speedily resumed and continues from dawn to sunset of the nearly interminable day.

The tardy development of the colony has been shown as it was at an earlier date. Twenty years more and it still lags behind. After forty years of occupation, with an average total of from eight to ten thousand able-bodied criminals available, but little progress has been made. The colony is still but sparsely provided with roads. The internal communications are barely fifty miles in length; one road, fit only for two-wheeled traffic and thirty miles in length, connects Noumea with Bailoupari, and there are some short roads in the agricultural settlement of Bourail. There are as yet no railways and no network of telegraphic wires. All of the transit from point to point is performed by small coastwise steamers.

Bourail is the show place where the *forçats* blossom into the emancipists, and where penal labour is replaced by individual effort of the state-aided freedmen, the criminal who has expiated his offence and is now to make himself a new life. Liberal assistance is given to those who intend to do well. After fair assurance of amendment, the forger or assassin, the unfortunate felon who got into the clutches of the law, gets a new start, a concession of land with capital advanced to stock it, materials to build his home, tools and agricultural implements, six months' food, and seed to sow the first harvest. Some of them thrive and prosper exceedingly; it is much the same as in early Australian days, but no doubt to a lesser degree, for not a few fail and must return to servitude with more successful comrades or free settlers. There are those who champion the system as the best solution of the disposal of the worst offenders who cannot be rehabilitated under the conditions existing in a country long settled. The logic is a little weak perhaps, and it is difficult to concede that crime should be the official avenue to state assistance.

A good story is told of one reformed criminal who prospered exceedingly and was congratulated by the governor of the colony when he came up to receive the prize awarded for raising first-class stock. He was reminded how by the fostering care of a paternal government he had been transformed from the degraded *forçat* into an honest owner of property. The ex-convict was moved to tears, but his emotion was caused by his regretting the time he had lost before he came to benefit by the change. "Had I had any idea of the good fortune awaiting me," he whined, "I would have arrived here ten years sooner." In other words, he would have qualified ten years earlier by committing the deed which resulted in his transportation—cutting his wife's throat.

The boons extended to the reformed one are not limited to a life of ease and comfort in the colony. Rehabilitation may be earned, and with it permission to return to the mother country with the restoration of civil rights. Several have sold their farms and effects to the colony, and have gone home to France as *rentiers*. Their reappearance hardly tends to emphasise the deterrent effect of penal exile.

That the conditions in New Caledonia were until within the last few years in many respects more encouraging, and that the labour of the colonists was increasingly productive, may be gathered from the following extract from the London *Times* in 1890:

"The governor states that agriculture, which has hitherto been of only secondary importance, seems to be entering upon a period of rapid development under the influence of the fresh means of action afforded it by the immigration from the New Hebrides, and New Caledonia will produce this year 400 tons of coffee, while it is expected that in four years' time the production will exceed 1,000 tons. The cultivation of the sugar cane and of wheat is also making good progress.... The governor reports that what New Caledonia is most deficient in is labour, but he adds that the work done by the convicts, and especially at the Thio penitentiary, is much more satisfactory than that of the convicts in Guiana, while the men who have served their time and who choose can always find employment at wages from 4*s*. to 5*s*. a day, and at piece work they in many cases earn 10*s*. a day."

Some ten years later reports continued to be favourable as to the prosperity of New Caledonia. According to the governor, the population was steadily increasing and the demand for the minerals mined on the island was so great that it could not be satisfied. In 1903, however, the *Times* published a news item stating that "emigration from France has practically ceased and numbers of colonists have left," the cause of the exodus being the high taxation and great cost of living. In the same year, the agent-general for South Australia wrote to the French government pointing out how anxious Australia was to see the use of New Caledonia as a penal settlement abandoned, and a date fixed after which prisoners should not be sent to the Pacific.

CHAPTER XII PENAL METHODS IN THE UNITED STATES

No common system—Each state takes care of prisoners in its own way—Prisons under the control of the general government—Lack of system not altogether without advantage—The "Pennsylvania System" *versus* the "Auburn System"—Other prisons—Convict *versus* free labour—Prison newspapers—The Elmira Reformatory—Similar experiments in other states—Obstacles to prison improvement—Institutions for juvenile offenders—Children's courts—Advantages and disadvantages of juvenile institutions—Interesting experiments.

There is no prison system common to the whole United States. Each of the forty-six states and the territories as well deals with its prisoners in its own way. The United States has two great prisons, one at Fort Leavenworth, Kansas, and the other at Atlanta, Georgia, besides a small one in the state of Washington, in which some of the offenders against the general government are confined, but the greater number of Federal prisoners are confined in state prisons by special arrangement with the state authorities. The general government, however, prescribes rules and regulations for the treatment of Federal prisoners, but has no authority whatever over the state prisoners confined, perhaps, in the same building.

Naturally conditions vary in different states and often in different prisons in the same state. Few states have a Department of Correction, and usually each prison is in the charge of a separate board, appointed either by the governor or the state legislature. The county jails in which short term prisoners or offenders awaiting trial are confined are almost invariably under the management of the local authorities and the condition of many is deplorable. Some state prisons are models in construction, sanitation, and government, and challenge comparison with the best in Europe. Others are poorly constructed, overcrowded, badly kept and worse governed. Conditions depend entirely upon the state of the public conscience and the sense of responsibility prevailing in the jurisdiction. Manifestly it is difficult to make general statements of American policy in penology.

Yet this very diversity has its advantages. While because of the lack of a uniform system, the prisons in some states are worse than they would be under general laws, still the various states are constantly experimenting. A new idea in prison construction, or a new method of government, will be tried in some state, by an officer who has been able to convince his board of governors of its practicability. A general board or commissioner would be less likely to interfere with the existing order. This very fact of independent jurisdictions is responsible for much of the American progress exhibited particularly in reformatory institutions.

A rough classification as to methods shows four different systems of dealing with felons. These are first, the cellular or separate; second, the congregate; third, the reformatory; fourth, the convict lease system. In addition there is a multitude of institutions organised to deal with the youthful offender, variously known as juvenile asylums, protectories, training schools, etc. Among them all there is much variation.

The only prison of the cellular type now existing in the United States is the Eastern Penitentiary of Pennsylvania in Philadelphia which was opened in 1829, though Walnut Street jail had in 1790 cells designed for solitary confinement. This prison is built in the form of a star with galleries radiating from a central hall. Most of the galleries are only one story, though a few are two. The architecture was probably borrowed from the prison of Ghent designed by Vilian, and begun in 1771.

Each prisoner is assigned to a large cell averaging in size perhaps sixteen by eight feet and twelve to fifteen feet in height. A yard about the same size open to the sky adjoins the cell and prisoners are allowed to take exercise for a specified time daily. Each cell contains the necessary furniture for a bedroom, including an electric light, a water tap and sanitary conveniences.

In theory the prisoner is confined in this cell without intercourse with any other prisoners, from his entrance until the sentence has expired. He sees and speaks only with prison officers or instructors, including the chaplain. He lives, works, eats, and sleeps in his cell. No machinery or at least none that can not be introduced into the cells is allowed in the prison. The prisoners make shoes, clothes, shirts, cigars, stockings, etc. A specified amount is expected from each prisoner and any greater production is credited to him. One half of the surplus goes to the county from which he was sentenced, and the other half may be spent for tobacco or other permitted luxuries, or may be sent to his family.

The results, according to Michael J. Cassidy, warden for many years, are exceedingly satisfactory. The first offenders are not corrupted by older prisoners and there is almost no question of discipline. There are few punishments. If a prisoner is not dressed when his breakfast is brought he may lose his meal, or if the utensils presented to be filled are not clean, the officer may in his discretion refuse to place the food in them. In rare cases the prisoner is deprived of work which has been found to be the most serious punishment of all. There are no dark cells, and corporal punishment is not employed.

Mr. Cassidy emphatically denies that the system causes insanity or that serious physical injury follows, and on the other hand declares that the reformatory results obtained are greater than in other prisons. About seventy-five per cent. of the first offenders do not appear again and four per cent. of the habitual criminals reform. The results in his judgment justify the greater cost of the system compared with the Auburn or congregate system of which more will be said.

Though the idea put into execution at Philadelphia was not new the prison has been often visited and the "Pennsylvania system" as it is called, (though the Western Penitentiary at Allegheny is organised on the congregate system) has been widely copied, chiefly in Europe. In the United States it has been tried and abandoned in New Jersey, Rhode Island, Virginia, Maryland, and to a limited extent in New York, partly on account of the expense and partly because of doubts as to its humanity. On the other hand the system was adopted in Belgium in 1838, in Sweden in 1840, in Denmark in 1846, and to a limited extent by other countries. Pentonville in England is modelled after this prison, as are also Mountjoy in Dublin, and the Antrim jail in Belfast in Ireland.

The great majority of the prisons of the United States are organised according to the "Auburn" or congregate system. Here the prisoners are confined in separate cells at night, but work during the day in large workshops, supposedly in silence. The New York state prison at Auburn was organised in 1816. For a considerable time it was under the charge of Elam Lynds, formerly a captain in the army, and a strict disciplinarian. He was able to preserve almost absolute silence in the workshops, using corporal punishment if necessary. His success while preserving at the same time the general good will of his charges is another striking illustration of the fact that a good man can make any system work.

Though the system was not original with Auburn, the plan of organisation has passed into prison history by that name, and violent controversies have raged between the partisans of the opposing ideas. To it has been added since the organisation, the system of classification of prisoners, of good conduct marks, and of shortening sentences by good behaviour, which is in force in many states. In some states the indeterminate sentence which first was applied only in the reformatories has been extended to certain classes of offenders confined in state prisons.

The general regulations applying to the prisons in New York state, including Auburn, Sing Sing, at Ossining, Clinton, etc., are practically the same. The prisoner is assigned on entering to certain work depending upon his physique, intelligence and previous training. The efficient prison book-keeper at Sing Sing a few years ago was a convict, and the chief clerk for the superintendent of industries was also a convict.

The regulations provide for lights in the cells until ten o'clock, and for the use of the prison library. A letter may be written once a month and all proper letters received at the prison will be delivered after examination. The prisoner may also receive a visit of a half hour's duration in presence of a keeper once in two months and at the same intervals a box of proper eatables may be received from friends, or purchased from private funds. For breach of the prison regulations, a prisoner may lose a part of the time which would otherwise be gained by good behaviour, and may lose his privilege of receiving visitors. Serious infractions are punished by confinement in a dark cell, and in spite of the regulations, by physical punishment in many cases.

Formerly the labour of the convicts was contracted to outside parties at a fixed price for each individual. While the contractors were not supposed to inflict punishment, by bribing prison officials the reluctant were forced to do the amount of work required. Undoubtedly there were grave abuses. Some convicts were worked beyond their strength to satisfy the greed of the contractor. During this period there was a stone shed, a foundry, a hat shop, a file shop and a laundry, all of which paid good profits to the contractors, and from a financial standpoint were advantageous to the state.

The prejudice against this form of convict labour was sufficient in 1887 to cause the passage of a law absolutely forbidding contract labour. At the same time an appropriation was made to purchase the plants then existing and continue them on the state account. The results were not satisfactory, especially as another law later required all goods manufactured to be stamped "prison made." The labour unions continued to object to the competition of convicts with free labour and by a constitutional amendment adopted in 1896, it was finally forbidden. For a time the prisoners were idle, but shortly they were ordered to manufacture so far as possible goods required by other public institutions, and these institutions on the other hand were ordered to submit all lists of supplies desired to the prisons, in order that they might have the opportunity of furnishing them.

Since that time, the prisoners have been partially employed in manufacturing stone, knit goods, clothing, furniture, window sash, shoes, etc., but the demand is not sufficient to require full work, and the system is wasteful and uneconomic. The management is not stimulated to do its best and little or no attempt is made to keep the men from loafing. The system furnishes sufficient physical exercise but no training in systematic work which will be of value when the prisoner is released.

At Sing Sing prison the prisoners publish a paper, the *Star of Hope* written and printed entirely by themselves, and a few other prisons also issue papers. The founder of the paper has since his release published an interesting book giving his experiences and his views upon matters of prison discipline and government.[2] Speaking of the contributors to the paper he says: "Nor was the literary tone of the paper at all despicable. It would have been quite possible to make it more elaborate and dignified, for there was no end of talent available, but the aim held in view was to make it representative.... Poetry was the favourite medium employed by the contributors, and I suppose the *Star of Hope* printed and still prints more and worse verse than any other publication in the world."

The question of prison labour has been a serious one in many states. All agree that the convict must work for his own sake, and yet the objections to placing his products in competition with free labour have been loud and strong. In some states the labour unions have also objected to the policy of teaching trades at the expense of the state, claiming that in this way the offender is given a decided advantage over the youth who has kept within the law.

Prison managers have been at their wits' end to find work to which objections would not be made. In San Quentin prison, California, the convicts work in a jute mill and at crushing stone for roads. The alleged monopoly price for sacks demanded by the few jute mills in the country has been lowered by prison competition, and the farmers approve. On the other hand, the labour performed while in prison has little relation to outside employment. In the Minnesota state prison, the manufacture of binding twine for cereal crops was begun to break down an alleged monopoly. North Carolina, and perhaps other states, use the labour of a large number of their convicts in agriculture. Here the product of convict labour is so small a proportion of the total product that the price received by free labour is hardly affected at all, and no objection has been made.

The larger number of the prisons which still engage in manufacturing are organised on the "piece-price" system, *i. e.* materials are furnished and a price as nearly as possible what must be paid to free labour is charged for each unit of product. By this method the abuses of contract labour, and the wastefulness of the state account system are avoided.

There are in the United States few great prisons which are known to all. The best known are of course those of states which contain large cities; first, because a larger number of the more notorious criminals come from the cities, and second, because the city newspapers give a larger proportion of their space to criminal news than do the journals of the smaller municipalities. Besides those already mentioned, other well known prisons are at Joliet, Illinois; Trenton, New Jersey; Columbus, Ohio; Baltimore, Maryland, and on Blackwell's Island in New York City.

The reformatory system of the United States strictly speaking began with the organisation of the Elmira Reformatory at Elmira, New York, in 1876, which was largely due to the efforts of Rev. E. C. Wines, who gave his life to the improvement of prison conditions, and to Dr. Theodore W. Dwight. They were much interested in the success of Colonel Montesinos, Captain Maconochie and Sir Walter Crofton abroad, and drew up a plan which was adopted by the legislature in 1869. The institution was to be distinctly reformatory, and sentences were to be indeterminate.

It was opened for reception of offenders between sixteen and thirty years of age in 1876 under the superintendency of Z. R. Brockway who has given to the institution its peculiar character. The statistics kept for a number of years show that sixty-seven per cent. of those entering are illiterate, that eighty-nine per cent. have no trade, and that more than sixty-eight per cent. do not have what could be classed as good physiques, and a considerable number may be classed as degenerates. Further ninety-eight per cent. are committed from the cities.

Effort is made to develop the inmates on all sides. Athletic training, gymnastic work and military drill are required. Attention is given to baths, massage, and diet. Instruction in the common branches is given, and there are frequent lectures, and entertainments. Debating societies are organised and every effort is made to turn the misdirected energy into saner channels. At the same time a part of every day is spent in the shops and the rudiments of trades are taught.

The inmates are divided into four grades with different privileges. Conduct marks based upon performance of duty, cleanliness, progress, etc., are given, and promotion to a higher or removal to a lower grade depend upon the prisoner's record. When a boy or young man has been in the upper first grade for six months he becomes a candidate for release on parole. If his record is good for six months after leaving the Reformatory he is usually discharged.

The officers claim that the institution has been an unqualified success, that out of five thousand discharged only three hundred and sixty-five were returned, and that about eighty-two per cent. of those committed are permanently reformed. On the other hand the officers of the regular prisons declare that their prisons are full of "Elmira graduates," and the state has built another institution at Napanoch which is to receive the more incorrigible material from Elmira, and with sterner measures again attempt reformation.

A number of states have adopted the system wholly or in part, including Massachusetts, Pennsylvania, Ohio, Michigan, Illinois, Minnesota, Kansas and South Dakota. The degree of success has varied with the superintendent. The most interesting experiment is perhaps the Massachusetts Reformatory for women at Sherborn.

This institution for several years seemed on the point of failure, owing partly to the management and partly to the fact that sentences were too short. Finally a woman of strong character, and broad sympathies, Mrs. Ellen C. Johnson, was induced to take charge and success appears to have followed her efforts. The general plan is the same as at Elmira, except that restraint is not so prominent. The large majority of the commitments are the result of intemperance and unchastity, and undoubtedly mother love plays a part in drawing back the inmates from improper or immoral lives. Inmates released on parole are in demand as domestics, and in many cases give entire satisfaction.

The fourth plan mentioned in the classification, the convict lease system, now exists in only a few states, chiefly in the South. Under this system convicts are leased to work in gangs outside the prison walls at mining, railroad and turnpike building, canal cutting and similar employments. The contractor pays the state a fixed sum per head for the convicts, feeds, clothes and guards them. Their management is in his hands, restrained in some degree by the continuous or intermittent presence of a state inspector. The work is generally laborious, the intelligence of the labourers is low and they are disposed to shirk. The contractor desires to make a profit and generally works the unfortunates to the limit of their endurance, clothing and feeding them as poorly as he dares. Almost unbelievable brutality has occurred in these convict camps, ending in many cases in the death of stubborn or rebellious individuals. A partially awakened public conscience no longer permits former abuses but disgraceful conditions are still periodically brought to light.

The authorities responsible for the leases excuse or defend them on the following grounds. They say that a large majority of the leased convicts are negroes of an order of intelligence so low that they can be utilised only to a limited extent in any work performed in the prison; that confinement without labour is regarded as rather pleasant than otherwise, as imprisonment in itself means to them little or no disgrace; that the labour is of the same kind at which they would be employed, if free. Therefore the state must support in idleness without punitive effect a large number of offenders, or else lease their labour outside the prison walls. While all these statements are in a measure true, it may well be doubted whether any state is ever justifiable in surrendering the guardianship of its own delinquents.

The two great obstacles in the way of prison improvement in the United States are parsimony and politics. Though the cost of some prisons is excessive the money is not always wisely spent. The salaries paid are seldom high enough to secure men of a high type of intelligence and character, for the subordinate positions at least. There are few men who are fitted for the work who are willing to take the places with the low salaries and uncertain tenure of office. In many cases attendants and keepers are ignorant and brutal and by their defects neutralise any reformatory effect.

This brings us to the second great evil; politics. Usually the higher positions at least in the prisons are regarded as a part of the patronage of the party in power. Appointments of superintendents, wardens and other officers are too often made with more regard to political expediency than to fitness. The rule is not universal. As mentioned above Mr. Cassidy of Philadelphia and Mr. Brockway of Elmira held their places regardless of political changes, but many men have been removed, just when they were beginning to become really efficient. Where civil service rules are applied to the lower positions it has been charged that the result has been rather to protect the inefficient, than to secure satisfactory service.

Institutions for the control and discipline of delinquents under sixteen years of age exist by the score. Some are under the control of the different religious denominations, as for example the Catholic Protectory in New York, while others are supported by private contributions or by the city or state. Street waifs without parents or with drunken or immoral parents may be committed by the courts, rather than to regular orphan asylums if they have shown vicious traits or are considered incorrigible. A parent who is unable to control a son or daughter, by making an affidavit to that effect before the proper officer, may secure admission for the child to some institutions.

The larger number of children committed however have broken the law. If sent to prison to associate with hardened criminals they are almost certain to become habitual criminals themselves, while discharge with a reprimand may be regarded by the boys themselves as weak leniency, and may cause contempt for the law. In some American cities, special children's courts are organised to take charge of complaints against children. Where the judges have that indescribable combination of qualities which gives influence over boys, they have been successful without resorting to confinement. A striking example is Judge Ben. B. Lindsay of Denver, Colorado, whose court has been widely described. Attempts by others to copy his methods have failed. When ordinary judges without particular sympathy or qualifications are assigned in turn to the courts, there seems to be little advantage in the organisation. Conditions however are so chaotic, that it is impossible to pass a judgment worth while.

The purposes of such institutions may be stated as the following: to inculcate respect for authority and create the habit of obedience; to impart the rudiments of education, to form habits of industry, to impart moral instruction. Some in addition teach or begin to teach trades. In the execution of these aims, we have very diverse organisations. Some of the institutions are in effect prisons, with walls, bars and guards. Others apparently exercise no more restraint than is seen in an ordinary boarding school. It is true that it is not entirely easy to leave the dormitory without detection, and that generally while at work or at play the inmates are under some sort of supervision, but the idea of restraint is not made prominent.

Another interesting experience is the George Junior Republic at Freeville, New York. Here a miniature state is organised with legislative, executive and judicial departments. So far as practicable, all offices are filled by inmates, with the idea that responsibility will bring out the better qualities. The plan has not been widely adopted, however, and the institutions are generally organised as schools.

Some of the more successful of this sort are the school at Glen Mills, Pennsylvania, at Golden, Colorado, at Lancaster, Ohio, and at Dobbs Ferry, New York. The Jackson Training School at Concord, North Carolina, organised on the plan of the Glen Mills school, has seemed to show that the same methods successful in an urban commonwealth are equally successful in a semi-rural state.

A large proportion of the children are orphans or half-orphans, and a larger proportion have been habitual truants. The average of energy and intellect is higher than will be found in an ordinary school. Sometimes it is their excess of energy that has caused their transgression. When subjected to discipline and compelled to attend school, many make rapid progress and also acquire a sense of order and self-respect. On the other hand in very large institutions an unexpected danger has arisen. The manifold disciplinary influences have taught them obedience and industry but have at the same time deprived them of initiative. They have become "institutionalised" and find difficulty in adjusting themselves to life outside. They require constant direction.

For the purpose of avoiding this danger, the newer institutions are organised upon the "cottage plan." Instead of large dormitories, small houses, each under the charge of an officer and his wife, are built to accommodate twenty to forty boys. These are grouped around the administration building and the workshops. The results seem to show a great gain over the old methods but no one is yet ready to say that the ideal has been attained. Nevertheless, it can be said without fear of contradiction that the institutions for the training of juvenile offenders are more successful than any other part of the disciplinary and penal systems of the United States.

The combat of crime may be adjudged to have entered upon its latest stage by the acceptance of the more enlightened principles daily gaining attention in the most civilised countries. The treatment most in favour is preventative rather than punitive, which is considered at once the humane and efficacious method of dealing with crime. It is now being attacked in the youth when still impressionable and susceptible of cure. All criminality may be roughly separated into two principal divisions; first, those who should never be committed to prison; and secondly, those who should never be released from it. The widespread adoption of this axiom must go far to diminish the volume of crime. There is less and less recourse to imprisonment; sentences are inflicted for shorter terms, and it is avoided whenever possible by sparing first offenders from incarceration and postponing sentence on all who give promise of future amendment. The effect of this very commendable leniency is to be seen in the diminishing numbers of the actually imprisoned and the increased economy of gaol administration.

FOOTNOTE:

[2] Life in Sing Sing by Number 1500.

CHAPTER XIII BRITISH PRISONS OF TO-DAY

> Steady progress toward improved methods—Legislation to secure uniformity and proper principles of management—First effort to bring all local jurisdiction into line—Decision that all prisons must be under state control—Unification of system—Burden borne by the public exchequer—Remarkable results—Marked diminution in number of jail inmates—How convict labour has enriched the nations—Results at Portland, Chatham, Dartmoor—Extension of output—Chattenden and Borstal.

Forty years have elapsed since England was forced to revise her methods of penal treatment, and to replace the system of transportation beyond the seas with home establishments, rather hastily improvised to meet a sudden demand. Reference has already been made to the institution of "penal servitude," so-called, the process of expiation to which condemned felons were subjected in the newly devised state prisons. The flaws and failures that became prominent in the earlier phases of the system have also been touched upon, as well as the salutary changes introduced from time to time by the legislature. Year after year steadfast and consistent efforts have been made to improve and develop, to remove blots in administration, to remedy shortcomings; to reform offenders, while obliging them to labour to recoup expenditure and to secure thereby some restitution from them. A brief survey will show the existing conditions of the British penal system of to-day.

The chief reason of the merit of the British system is, that it is the growth of time, the product of experience. In the many changes introduced in this century, the great aim and object has been progressive improvement. The movement has all been forward. There has been no slackness in correcting errors and remedying abuses since John Howard struck the key-note of indignant protest. Reform may not always have gone hand in hand with suggestion, but that has been because of the quasi-independence of the prison jurisdictions. British prisons in the eighteenth and nineteenth centuries were largely controlled by local authorities upon no very uniform or effective principles, although act after act of Parliament was passed for the purpose of betterment. In 1823 and 1824 two acts first laid down the rule that health, moral improvement and regular labour were as important objects in prison maintenance as safe custody. At the same time, some attempt at classification was made, and it was ordered, for the first time, that female prisoners should be controlled only by female officers. In 1835 a fresh act insisted that all prison rules should be subjected to the approval of the Secretary of State; a proper dietary was made essential, without the "stimulating luxury" of tobacco. Classification, too, was again tried, but without good results, and the rule of separation at all times except during divine service, labour or instruction, was gradually adopted in theory and practice. Inspectors of prisons were appointed to exact obedience to the new laws. In 1839, an act permitted, but did not actually order, the confinement of each prisoner in a separate cell. The dimensions of these cells were stipulated, and it was insisted that they should be certified as fit for occupation. A surveyor-general of prisons was also appointed to assist and advise the Secretary of State as to prison construction.

The first substantial progress was made in the building of Pentonville, a prison which has served as a model for all prisons. Although copied in a measure from the old Roman monastery prison of San Michele, and following in design the famous Cherry Hill Penitentiary of Philadelphia, Pentonville was really a type in itself, and embraced so many excellences that it has never yet been greatly improved upon. In the six years following the establishment of Pentonville, fifty-four new prisons were built in England, providing cells for eleven thousand prisoners; but in 1850 a select committee of the House of Commons reported that several prisons were still in a very unsatisfactory condition, and that proper punishment, separation, or reformation in them was impossible. Parliament even then was strongly urged to entrust the supreme control of all prisons to one central authority, wholesome advice which was not accepted for nearly thirty years. But, although convicts sentenced to longer terms, which were usually carried out beyond the seas in the manner described in the earlier chapters, obtained much attention, the successive recommendations to improve the small outlying gaols, for short terms, were very imperfectly adopted.

The next great step was the Prison Act of 1865, which grew out of the report from a committee of the House of Lords, and which strongly condemned the lack of uniformity in the prison buildings, and in the punishments inflicted. Many of the practices which still prevailed even at that late date (1865) were really a disgrace to our civilisation. In some of the prisons the inmates lay two in a bed in dormitories without light, ventilation or control. Warders were afraid to enter them after dark. There was no uniformity in labour, or in the hours in which it was performed. In one prison the inmates lay in bed for fifteen hours daily. One of these gaols, which existed until the passing of the Act of 1865, and which was situated in the heart of a densely populated seaport town, has been described by its last governor. It was an ancient edifice, consisting of four parallel two-storied blocks. The lower story opened on a corridor, the windows of which were unglazed and communicated with the outer air. Above each cell door was a barred opening without glass, which served as a ventilator. In wet weather the rain poured into the passage; in a snow storm the snow flakes drifted through the cell-ventilators upon the bed which was just beneath, and which was often covered in the morning with snow an inch or two deep. There was no heating apparatus, and the place was desperately cold in winter. On the first floor there were a number of larger cells in which as many as seven prisoners were associated together, day and night, so crowded that the beds were stowed upon the floor, while hammocks were also stretched across them above. Sunday was the worst day of the week in this horrible old prison. After morning service, the prisoners took their dinners with them to their cells and were then and there locked up till the following morning. No one could get out, even if he were dying; there was no communication with officers or others outside. Here, in an atmosphere laden with fetid exhalations, amid filth of all kinds, the wretched prisoners were imprisoned for eighteen consecutive hours. These modern "black holes" were far worse than that of Calcutta in that their unfortunate inmates had daylight in which to observe with loathing and disgust the indecencies which surrounded them. Nor was it only in the accommodation provided that these poor creatures suffered. They were continually ill-used by their warders, who harassed and harried them at every turn. Each officer had a prisoner to wait upon him as a personal attendant, called his "lackey," who was always at his heels serving him hand and foot, and performing every menial office except that of carrying his keys. The outgoing governor who escorted his successor (my informant) around the gaol was imbued with the same brutal, reckless spirit, which he displayed by rushing into a cell, seizing a youthful prisoner by the shoulders, and shaking him violently, after which he threw him roughly upon the ground with the brief explanation, "You've got to show them you're master sometimes." The boy had not been guilty of any misconduct whatever.

In this gaol, all kinds of work was performed for the private benefit of the officers, a practice very generally prevalent in the gaols until a much later date. It was of the governor's perquisites to employ prisoners for his own behoof. There was jubilation in his family when a clever tailor or seamstress "came in;" new suits were at once cut out and made for the governor, his wife or his children. His house was fitted and half furnished by prisoners; they made arm-chairs, picture-frames, boot-racks. In one prison I heard of an excellent carriage constructed by a clever coach-builder who had gotten into trouble, and whose forfeited hours were thus utilised for the governor and not for the taxpayers. In another gaol an unexpected inspection revealed the mouth of a mysterious pipe leading from the kitchen, which when followed to its outlet was found to convey the grease and scourings straight to a flower bed in the governor's garden.

This deplorable state of affairs continued without change long after 1865. Twelve years later the uniformity sought by the act of that year had not been secured. Justices had not in every case realised their duties and responsibilities. Many prisons remained defective. All differed in their treatment of prisoners, and the criminal classes were themselves aware of the differences. It was a common practice for intending offenders to avoid a locality where the gaol discipline was severe. To secure the same measure of punishment in each institution was all the more important since criminals had learned to avail themselves of the many modern facilities for travelling from place to place, and crime was no longer localised. The same reason added another argument in favour of making the support of prisons an imperial rather than a local charge. It was a little unfair, too, that a district which had already suffered by the depredations of an evil-doer should bear the heaviest part of the expense of his correction. With these, there was a still stronger reason for concentration. Some relief of local taxation was earnestly desired, and the assumption by the public exchequer of prison expenditure seemed to promise this in an easy and substantial way, more particularly as the transfer of control would be accompanied by a revision of the means, and followed by a diminution in the number of prisons required. Such arguments fully justified Mr. (afterward Viscount) Cross in introducing the measure known as the Prison Act of 1877, which was passed that year, and contemplated great changes in the system as it then was; the first and chief being the transfer and control of all local prisons to a board of commissioners acting for the state.

All these have now taken effect, and after a test of twenty years may fairly be judged by the results achieved. Certainly the uniformity desired has at last been attained. Every prisoner now finds exactly the same treatment, according to his class and sentence, from Land's End to the Orkney Isles. Whether only an accused person, a debtor, misdemeanant, or condemned felon, he is kept strictly apart, occupying a cell to himself, the dimensions of which assure him a minimum air-content of 800 cubic feet, and which has been duly certified by one of the government prison inspectors as fit for his occupation, being lighted, heated, ventilated, and provided with bell communications, which are electric in some of the new prisons. From the moment he passes into the prison until he again finds himself on the right side of the gate, he is under exactly the same discipline, whether he is in the gaol of Bodmin, Newcastle, Norwich, Liverpool or Carlisle. Everywhere his bath awaits him; his prison clothing, if he is convicted, is furnished him; his first and every succeeding meal is based upon a dietary framed by medical experts after the most mature deliberation. His day's task is fixed. If he is able-bodied, he must do six hours at more or less severe labour, breaking stones, making cocoa mats with a heavy beater, making sacks, digging, pumping, and so forth. This, the most irksome phase of his prison life, continues for one month, or more exactly, until he has earned 224 marks in the first series of the progressive stages which have been ingeniously adopted to secure industry and good conduct. Every prisoner holds in his own hands the ability to modify the penal character of his imprisonment, and by the exercise of these two qualities may gradually earn privileges and improve his position.

Whatever the cause—and it is easier to state the effect than apportion it among the causes that have produced it, there has been a steady diminution in the numbers sentenced to imprisonment, as compared with increased population in the years succeeding 1878, when the new system came into force. In that year the population of England and Wales stood at twenty-five millions and 10,218 was the number imprisoned of both sexes. In 1904 the general population was 33,763,468, while no more than seventy-nine hundred were imprisoned. And during the intervening years there has been a continuous falling off in the number of imprisonments.

"It certainly seems justifiable to infer from these figures that our penal reformatory system has been made effective," says Du Cane, in his "Punishment and Prevention of Crime;" "and the remarkably steady and sustained decrease ... must be considered to show that recent legislation, with which it so remarkably coincides in point of time, has in principle and execution not only completely succeeded in promoting uniformity, economy, and improved administration, but also in that which is the main purpose of all—the repression of crime." The decrease is even more remarkable in the convict prisons, those which receive the more serious offenders, sentenced to penal servitude.

The convict population of Great Britain is now just about half what it was some five and twenty years ago. Going back to 1828, when the population of the country was barely fifteen millions, there were in all,—in the penal colonies at the Antipodes, at Gibraltar and Bermuda, the Hulks at home and the Millbank Penitentiary, just fifty thousand convicts, or ten times what the total is to-day with a population of nearly thirty millions. Carrying the comparison a little further, there were 3,611 sentenced to transportation in 1836; in 1846, 3,157; in 1856, 2,715; in 1866, 2,016 (combined with penal servitude); in 1876, 1,753 to penal servitude alone; in 1886, 910. In 1891 only 751 imprisonments are recorded. This progressive decrease is doubtless largely due to the growth of that more humane spirit which has in recent years mitigated the severity of punishment, and which prompts the judges to avoid the heavier penalties, as is shown, for instance, by the fact that in 1836 there were 740 life sentences, while in 1891 there were only four. It may be attributed also to the admitted punitive efficacy of penal servitude. That it is sufficient to visit even serious offences with shorter terms, a practice much facilitated by the recent reduction of the minimum period from five to three years, is amply shown by the record.

A few words must be devoted to the work of the convicts in the great British prisons. At Portland, during the years from 1848 to 1871 the convicts quarried no fewer than 5,803,623 tons of stone, all of which was utilised in the now famous breakwater, a stone dam in the sea nearly two miles in length and running into water fifty or sixty feet deep. The now presumably impregnable defences of the island, Portland Bill, the great works on the Verne, the barracks, batteries and casemates, were executed by convicts, who, as these works progressed, performed all the subsidiary services of carpentering, plate-laying, forging, and casting the ironwork. The enlargement of Chatham dockyard, a great feat of engineering skill, begun in 1856, was accomplished by convict labour. The site of St. Mary's Island, a waste of treacherous shore so nearly submerged by the tide that the few sheep that inhabited it were to be seen daily huddled together at the topmost point at high water, is now occupied by three magnificent basins capable of floating almost the entire British fleet. In fourteen years the convicts made one hundred and two million bricks for the retaining walls of these basins and excavated all of their muddy contents. The first, or repairing basin, has a surface of twenty-one acres; the second, or factory basin, twenty acres; the third, or fitting-out basin, twenty-eight acres. These basins were skilfully contrived to utilise the old watercourses which intersected the island. The bottom of the basins is twelve feet below the old river bed, and thirty-two feet below St. Mary's Island, which has been raised about eight feet by dumping on it the earth excavated from the basins. The whole island has been surrounded by a sea-wall and embankment nearly two miles in length, principally executed by convict labour. Work of a very similar nature and extent has been carried out at Portsmouth, and the enlarged dockyard there was given over to the admiralty a few years ago.

Dartmoor was an ideal penal settlement: a wild, almost barbarous place when the labour of the convicts was first applied to its development—to fencing, draining, making roads and parade-grounds, and to converting the old buildings into suitable receptacles for themselves and their kind. But the eventual employment of the prisoners was to be the farming of the surrounding moorland as soon as it was reclaimed; and this work has in effect occupied the Dartmoor convicts for more than forty years. What they have accomplished is best told by experts. The following is extracted from a report in a recent number of the Royal Agricultural Society's journal.

"The management of the prison farm, Princetown," reads the report, "has converted a large tract of poor waste land into some of the most productive enclosures in the kingdom. The farm, which lies in the wilds of Dartmoor, at an elevation of some fourteen hundred to sixteen hundred feet above the sea, ... comprises in all two thousand acres, the whole of which was mere common or unenclosed waste land prior to 1850.... The land is divided into square fields of from fifteen to twenty acres by high stone walls, built of granite boulders raised in the prison quarries or from the land as the work of reclamation proceeds. An excellent system of reclamation, with scientific rotation of crops, has been devised. If the herbage fails, or becomes unsatisfactory, the land is again dug up ... but so good has been the management ... that the greater portions of the pasture laid within the last fifteen or twenty years are now in far too good a condition to require rebreaking. One field which twenty years ago was mostly rushes is now able to carry a bullock per acre through the summer. No purer or cleaner pastures are to be found anywhere.... Sixty-seven acres of meadow land have been laid out for irrigation and utilisation of the sewage from the prison establishment, which at times numbers upwards of one thousand persons. A dairy herd of forty-five cows is kept, and all the cows are reared.... A flock of four hundred sheep, 'Improved Dartmoors,' is kept and has frequently been successful in the local show-yards. The wool, for so high a district, is remarkably good and of long staple. Pony mares and their produce are run on the fields. One of the ponies bred on Dartmoor won first prize in its class at the Royal Show at Plymouth. Thirty acres of garden are devoted to the growth of garden vegetables, of which all kinds are grown, and much success has been obtained with celery and cucumbers. The whole of the work is done by convicts, without the aid of horses except for carting."

A great extension of convict labour has been seen in recent years. It has been employed in novel ways which would have been impossible but for the excellence of the present prison organisation and of the discipline now enforced. In 1876 a small prison for one hundred inmates was erected at Chattenden, near Upnor, on the north bank of the Medway. It was intended to house convicts to be engaged in constructing new magazines at Chattenden for the war department. The prison was built by a detachment of prisoners sent across the river from Chatham convict prison, and then by tramway to the site of the proposed work. The tramway passed through dense woods, and the site of the prison was surrounded by thick undergrowth. These seemingly hazardous operations were carried out without a casualty of any kind; no gang chains were used; no escapes, successful or frustrated, were recorded. The work was continued for nearly ten years, when the magazines were finished, and the prison, which throughout had been treated as a branch of the great headquarters prison at Chatham, was closed. During these ten years, besides the prison buildings, this small party had put up five large bomb-proof magazines, in addition to the formation and drainage of the roads, traverses and slopes adjoining. The experiment at Chattenden afforded an example of the use to which convict labour can be put, and of the circumstances under which comparatively small works can be undertaken by a small body of convicts in a separate prison erected for the purpose. A number of the buildings, being easily removable, have since been taken down to be otherwise made use of.

It is only fair to observe here that the same experiment had been made under the Austro-Hungarian government by M. Tauffer. This eminent prison official had recommended the adoption of the "progressive system" as far back as 1866, and had carried it out under his own direction at Leopoldstadt and Lepoglava, where his prisoners were employed on outside labour at the rate of thirty or even forty to each overseer, and yet no escapes occurred. These prisoners built another prison at a distance from Lepoglava, and were lodged for the purpose in sheds and outhouses beyond the prison walls. The doors were not even locked at night; there were no bolts or bars, the only barrier to escape being the rule that no one should leave the building after the hour for retiring at night.

The work at Chattenden had, however, been preceded by other similar and more extensive undertakings in England. The first was the preparation of a new and very simple prison edifice at Borstal, near Rochester; the second, the erection of the great separate prison at Wormwood Scrubs, with which I was myself closely identified from the beginning. The prison at Borstal was to house convicts who were to be employed under the war department in building fortifications for the defence of Chatham arsenal, and indirectly of London. As a preliminary measure, a boundary fence was erected at Borstal around the site of the new prison, and this work—but this alone—was performed by free labour, the very timber for the fence having been prepared in the prison at Chatham, four miles distant, which served as general centre and headquarters for the Borstal as well as the Chattenden prison. Parties of selected convicts were despatched daily to Borstal, under escort, of course, but without chains, and travelled back and forth in open vans. Temporary huts were put up for cooking, storage and the accommodation of the guard, and within sixteen weeks the prison buildings were so far advanced that forty cells were ready for occupation by prisoners, and the establishment was then regularly opened as a prison. During this sixteen weeks there had been no accidents, no escapes, no misconduct. The convicts employed in this really "intermediate stage," having a larger amount of license and liberty than Sir Walter Crofton had ever dreamed of giving a prisoner, had behaved in the most exemplary manner. Within a year afterward, when the number of convicts had gradually increased to more than two hundred, all necessary buildings had been put up to accommodate a total population of five hundred prisoners.

The completion of the prison left the convicts free to carry out the works for which they had been brought to Borstal. But the very nature of these works was such as to startle prison administration of the old school, and to forbid, at first thought, the employment of convicts upon them. The site of the proposed forts was quite in the open country, and the first of them, Luton, at least two miles from Borstal prison. How were the convicts to be conveyed to and fro, without loss of time, without unnecessary fatigue, and above all, without risk of losing half the number by the way? A novel plan was boldly but happily conceived, and its absolutely successful adoption constitutes an epoch in prison history. It was decided to lay down a narrow gauge railway, along the line the forts were intended to cover, and send the prisoners to their work by train. Part of this plan was the invention of a special kind of railway-carriage, constructed with a view to safe custody, and this very unique and ingenious contrivance has since been constantly employed. These carriages are small, open, third-class carriages, with a sliding gate of iron bars. When the train is made up, a chain passes along the exterior of these gates, and it is padlocked at each end. The warders on duty occupy raised seats at each end of the train, and have the convicts under supervision continually. The compartments hold from eight to ten men each, and a train-load is made up of from eighty to a hundred convicts. The engines used are the once famous little locomotives that were sent out to the Sudan for service on the Suakim-Berber railway. Extreme simplicity characterises all these arrangements, yet they are perfectly suitable and quite sufficient. The same device was tried with success at Portsmouth convict prison, for the conveyance of convicts to Whale Island, distant a mile or more from the prison.

The effectual guarding of the convicts when at work was, however, a matter of equal importance. This, with the experience of many years gained in all varieties of outdoor employment, has been reduced almost to a science at Borstal. The works are enclosed by a wall ten feet high. There is a ditch on the inner side, and there are wire entanglements on the inner side of the ditch. The convict-laden train runs within the palisading and its passengers are marched to the various points on which they are employed. Some of these are in the open beyond the palisading; but outside all, on a wide outer circumference, are sentries of the civil guard, on high platforms at regular intervals, commanding the ground between them. No fugitive could pass them unobserved, as they are on such a radius that they would have the fleeing convict a long time under their eyes while he was approaching. In addition to this, an elaborate system of signaling has been devised by means of semaphores at the highest points. These are worked by good-service convicts, men in the last year of their sentence, who can be trusted to use field-glasses and to communicate promptly any news that has to be sent on. In this way escapes are signaled, or a call for help made, if help be required, in event of disturbance among the parties at work. Escapes have no doubt occurred at Borstal, but they have been few and far between, always resulting in recapture, except in one or two instances.

Thus we have traced, in this and the preceding volume, the course of the beginning and the development of the prison system of Great Britain. Much that we now rightly consider inhuman marked its early history, in common with the conduct of all prisons of that early day. The period of deportation is certainly gloomy enough, until we stop to consider the splendid secondary results that have grown out of it in the building up of an Anglo-Saxon commonwealth in the southern hemisphere. The prison system of Great Britain, as it is to-day established, is perhaps as advanced as any in the world, while the future promises advance and improvement wherever the one is called for and the other is possible.

Milton Keynes UK
Ingram Content Group UK Ltd.
UKHW030624061024
449204UK00004B/348